UPPER CLYDESDALE

UPPER CLYDESDALE

A History and a Guide

Daniel Martin

TUCKWELL PRESS

First published in 1999 by
Tuckwell Press Ltd
The Mill House
Phantassie
East Linton
East Lothian
EH40 3DG
Scotland

Reprinted 2003

ISBN 1 86232 057 8

A catalogue record for this book is available on request from the
British Library

Typeset by Carnegie Publishing, Carnegie House, Lancaster
Printed and bound by Bell & Bain Ltd., Glasgow

Contents

Illustrations

Preface

In writing this book as a labour of love in my old age, I have tried to provide a readable and informative account of the rural part of Lanarkshire for both visitors to the district and residents who wish to learn more about their own particular localities. Since the area, one of great natural beauty, is steeped in history, is rich in archaeological remains and is both interesting and delectable in so many ways, a great deal more could be written about it than has been included here. The bibliography refers to a substantial body of material dealing with the geology, archaeology and history (ecclesiastical, local and natural) of the area in greater detail than it is possible to give in a book of reasonable size. I have tried hard to maintain a high standard of accuracy throughout the book but, with surprisingly many inconsistencies in the available literature, doing this has been rather a painstaking task. The book should be used in conjunction with the Landranger Series of Ordnance Survey maps on a scale of 1 in 50,000. Map 72 includes almost all of the places mentioned in the text, but 78 is needed for the Elvanfoot-Leadhills district and 64 for a small area including Garrion Bridge. The Pathfinder Series on a scale of 1 in 25,000 is also very helpful, but eight maps are required if this series is used.

I could not possibly have written the book without the generous assistance of many friends and acquaintances. Those who vetted the particular chapters on which they are knowledgeable and/or provided useful information include Mr Paul Archibald, Mr James Arnold, Dr Teresa Cranstoun of Corehouse, Mr John Darbyshire, Mrs Lorna Davidson, Mr Stewart Forrest, Dr Rosmairi Galloway, Dr Jacqueline Goldberg, Mr Alan Grant, Mrs Margaret Harvie, Mr Julian Hodgson, Mrs Grizel Howatson, Mr William Jackson, Mr Brian Lambie, Dr John McCaffrey, Mr Iain MacIver, Mr John Munro, Mr William Murray, Dr Gillian Rodger, Mr Russell Rodger, Mr George Russell, the Rev. Ian

Sandilands, Mr Kenneth Scott, Mrs Kirsteen Scott, Professor David M. Walker and Mrs Christine Warren. If I have unconciously used information derived from others, either verbally or through their writings, then I can only express my regret at not having acknowledged their help. I am particularly indebted to Miss Irene M. Bryson, Mr Thomas Dick and the late Dr Elizabeth A. McHarg, each of whom scrutinised the whole manuscript with meticulous care, pointed out not a few inaccuracies and made many valuable suggestions for the improvement of the text. Finally, I owe a special debt of gratitude to Mrs Kay McWhirter for her unfailing care and skill in typing the various drafts of the manuscript.

The generous help of the following in making available photographs and slides in their possession is greatly appreciated: Biggar Museum Trust 7.2, 7.3, 7.4, 8.2, 8.4, 11.5; Carluke Parish Historical Society 5.1, 5.2, 5.3; M. Ludovic de Bert 3.1, 3.5; Greater Glasgow and Clyde Valley Tourist Board 6.1, 6.4, 7.1, 11.3, 12.1, 12.5; Lanark Museum Trust 2.1, 2.2, 2.3, 2.4, 2.6, 2.7, 2.8; Mr J. Muncie 4.4, 5.5, 5.6, 5.7; the National Galleries of Scotland 12.3; New Lanark Conservation Trust 3.2, 3.3; Mrs G. Paul 10.2; South Lanarkshire Council 2.5, 3.4, 3.6, 4.1, 4.3, 4.5, 5.4, 6.2, 6.3, 8.1, 8.3, 9.1, 9.2, 9.3, 9.4, 10.1, 10.3, 10.4, 11.1, 11.2, 11.4, 11.6, 12.2, 12.4, 13.1, 13.2, 13.3, 14.1, 14.2; the Master and Fellows of Balliol College, Oxford 14.3. Grateful thanks are also due to the Ordnance Survey for permission to make a map based on one of its own, to Mr Neil Smith for help with this matter and to Mr Robert Copeland for general advice on photographic matters.

Daniel Martin

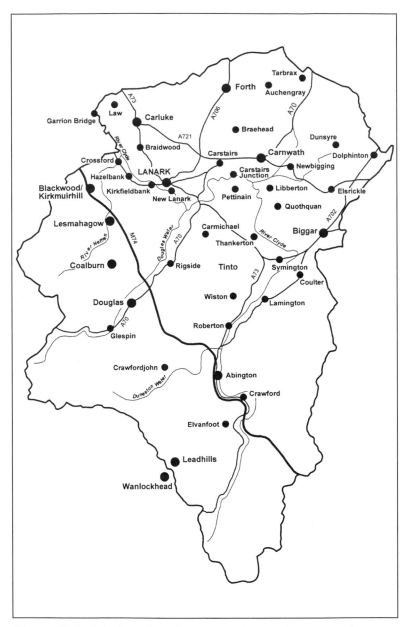

Upper Clydesdale. Based on the 1996 Ordanace Survey map by permission of Ordnance Survey on behalf of The Controller of Her Majesty's Stationery Office ©Crown copiright. MC88784M0001

1
Introduction

The district, which I shall call Upper Clydesdale, covered by this book is the pre-1996 Clydesdale District, now the southern part of South Lanarkshire District, together with a few places such as Wanlockhead, just outside the District, which it would be unnatural not to include. Upper Clydesdale has an area of over 500 square miles (1280 square km.) with a population of around 58,000 and, with about 85% of the land devoted to agriculture, is mainly rural in character. The main centres of population are, in descending order of size: Carluke, with a population of almost 13,000 in 1991, Lanark, Kirkmuirhill/Blackwood, Lesmahagow, Law, Forth and Biggar, the last with a 1991 population of just under 2,000. Prior to regionalisation in 1975 Lanark was a royal burgh.

Upper Clydesdale is divided geologically into two parts by the Southern Uplands Fault which, going from St. Abbs Head to Ballantrae and forming the southern boundary of the Central Lowlands, runs in a south-westerly direction across the District from Coulter to beyond Crawfordjohn. South of the fault the land is hilly, the highest hills being Green Lowther (732 m., 2402 ft) about 3 km. (2 miles) south-east of Leadhills, Lowther Hill (725 m., 2379 ft) a similar distance south-east of Wanlockhead and on the former county boundary between Lanarkshire and Dumfriesshire, and Culter Fell (745 m., 2454 ft) about 7 km. (4⅓ miles) south-east of Coulter and on the former boundary between Lanarkshire and Peeblesshire. The rocks are Ordovician, i.e. about 430–500 million years old. North of the fault the landscape is open and rolling except that Tinto (703 m., 2320 ft) rises just north of the fault. Tinto is part of a large sheet of igneous rock that runs parallel to the fault from Douglas to Dolphinton. Old Red Sandstone and coal of the Carboniferous period, and therefore about 345–395 million years old and 280–345 million years old, respectively, are much in evidence north of the fault. South of the fault, where the altitude is high and the weather often severe, the farming of Blackface sheep with their coarse fleeces, used for making carpets rather than cloth, is extensive. North of the fault mixed farming, including the breeding of beef and dairy cattle and a few Cheviot and Border Leicester sheep, prevails.

For long, the source of the Clyde was taken to be Clydes Burn, which rises near Beattock Summit, where the M74 road and the railway reach heights of a little over 1000 ft above sea-level not far from the former county boundary between Lanarkshire and Dumfriesshire. However, since this minute stream joins the very much more substantial stream formed by the confluence further south of the Daer and Potrail (Powtrail) Waters, many geographers now regard the Daer Water as the source of the Clyde. This stream rises in the extreme south of the District in the range of hills of which Queensberry Hill (697 m., 2,286 ft), outwith the District, is the highest. The old couplet

> Annan, Tweed and Clyde
> Rise a' oot o' ae hillside

is simply not true.

After passing Elvanfooot, where it receives the Elvan Water on the left, the Clyde is augmented on the right at Crawford by the Midlock Water and the Camps Water, and then on the left just south of Abington by the Glengonnar Water. Three miles (5 km.) or so further on the more substantial Duneaton Water, which rises on the eastern slope of Cairntable on the former boundary between Lanarkshire and Ayrshire, enters on the left. Near Roberton, where the burn of that name joins on the left, the Clyde crosses the Southern Uplands Boundary Fault and passes into a more arable and gentler countryside. After passing Lamington, the river begins to swerve eastwards round the foot of Tinto Hill and, flowing towards Biggar, is close to the watershed between the Tweed and the Clyde. Indeed, at times of severe flooding at Wolfclyde, some water from the Clyde can enter the nearby Biggar Water which flows along the valley known as the Biggar Gap to enter the Tweed at Dreva near Broughton. In the opinion of Sir Archibald Geikie there were originally two Clydes, the Upper Clyde, which flowed through the Biggar Gap to enter the Tweed, and the Lower Clyde, which rose somewhere near the present Falls of Clyde and flowed northwards. The Lower Clyde gradually extended backwards and in due course captured the Upper Clyde which then abandoned the Biggar Gap. Meandering on, the Clyde receives the Medwin, formed by the confluence of the North and South Medwins at a point fully a mile (1.6 km.) south of Carnwath. Then, after a most tortuous course through an extensive flood plain, it passes under Hyndford Bridge and, after receiving the Douglas Water on the left, turns north-west to reach the gorge containing Bonnington and Corra Linn Falls. At Kirkfieldbank the Mouse, after dropping 800 ft (244 m.) from its source 2 miles (3 km.) north- north-east of Wilsontown and passing the tremendous crags at Cartland, enters the Clyde on the right. Except for the falls at Stonebyres the river then flows gently through beautiful orchard country, receives the Nethan on the left at Crossford and reaches Garrion Bridge, where the interest of this book in it ceases.

Extensive deposits of glacial sand and gravel, found around Lanark, Carstairs and Carnwath, make Clydesdale a main producer of sand and gravel in Strathclyde. The material is of good quality and is lignite-free; indeed, the sand is sufficiently good for it to be used in the making of asphalt. Much sand and gravel from here was used in the recent work on the M74. It is reckoned that the present quarries can meet all requirements until at least the end of the present century.

Upper Clydesdale is rich in bird life and is an exciting area for bird-watchers. South of Lanark, where open fields and moorland prevail, moorland species of bird such as the curlew and lapwing are evident. The higher moorlands are the habitat of red grouse, golden plovers, hen harriers and buzzards, although in cold weather the birds come down to a lower altitude. Close to the river, waders such as the common sandpiper can be seen, and oyster catchers, which have been breeding on the upper reaches of the Clyde for several years now, are recognizable by their black and white plumage, their bright orange beaks and pinkish legs. The Falls of Clyde Nature Reserve, where at least 100 species of bird can be seen at some time or other during the year, is specially interesting. The Visitor Centre is a mine of interesting information with a full-time ranger in attendance. In the Valley, downstream from Kirkfieldbank, swallows, swifts, sand martins and house martins can be seen in summer flying along the river and swallowing insects from the surface of the water or from the air just above it. Dippers can also be seen feeding under the surface of the water, while on the banks grey, yellow and pied wagtails can be observed. In winter, flocks of geese, having migrated from a colder climate, can be seen, as well as both whooper and mute swans.

Upper Clydesdale is rich in archaeological remains. Remains dating from the Mesolithic Period (c. 6500 to 4000 B.C.), the age of the primitive hunters, are scarce except for primitive stone implements found on sites along the Clyde between Symington and Pettinain and about 2000 flints found on the exposed shore of the Daer reservoir during the exceptional drought in the summer of 1995. These remains are the earliest evidence of a human presence in this part of Lanarkshire.

The Neolithic Period (c. 4000 to 2000 B.C.), the age of the earliest farmers, is better represented. A marked concentration of stone axes east of the Clyde between Carnwath and Lamington suggests that the Carnwath – Biggar – Dolphinton area was well populated in Neolithic times. This is being confirmed by local archaeologists who, in carrying out a major excavation of a hillside near Melbourne crossroads, are making very significant finds of pottery and flint tools.

The Bronze Age (c. 2500 to 600 B.C.), at the beginning of which immigrants arrived from the Rhineland, is well represented in Upper Clydesdale. The new settlers introduced the practice of individual burial whereby the Neolithic tradition of collective burial was abandoned and replaced by cremation or by inhumation in a grave or cist, sometimes surmounted by a cairn or barrow, i.e. an earthen burial mound. Hundreds of cairns have been recorded in the area but many more were removed during agricultural operations in the eighteenth and nineteenth centuries. For example, in the parish (that was) of Lesmahagow about 40 have been recorded but only four now remain. The cairn on the top of Tinto Hill is thought to be the largest cairn in Scotland. It is continually being enlarged by climbers adding stones to it. The new settlers brought with them the type of pottery now known as Beaker ware and also the technology for working with copper; copper was replaced by bronze around 2000 B.C.

The evidence available for the periods considered so far is almost exclusively derived from burial sites, but, when we come to the Iron Age (*c.* 600 B.C. to A.D. 400), the information comes from hill-forts. The ones in Upper Clydesdale are relatively small in size when compared with other hill-forts of similar date in Scotland. The two largest are on Black Hill between Kirkfieldbank and Auchenheath and on Quothquan Law.

The Roman occupation in Lanarkshire, which lasted from A.D. 80, when Agricola began his campaign in Scotland, to about A.D. 170, when the fort at Crawford was abandoned, belongs to the Iron Age. The native Celtic tribes with whom the Romans had to contend in Upper Clydesdale were the Damnonii, whose territory included Clydesdale and possibly extended over the Campsies into Southern Perthshire, and the Selgovae in Peeblesshire and further to the east with their headquarters, according to Ptolemy, at Trimontium, undoubtedly the Eildon Hills at Melrose. The importance of the large fort at Castledykes between Lanark and Carstairs was due partly to its situation on the borderland between the domains of these two tribes.

The Roman road system was obviously determined by the natural features of the countryside. The main arterial highway from Carlisle to the Forth came up through Annandale and, after passing Beattock Summit, followed the right bank of the Clyde to the fort at Crawford and then went over Raggengill Pass to Lamington, Coulter and Biggar. The road then went by Candy Mill to Melbourne crossroads and Dolphinton before striking along the southern slopes of the Pentland Hills towards Inveresk. The parts of the road that are still visible are indicated on the Ordnance Survey maps. The road linking Newstead near Melrose with Loudoun Hill in Ayrshire entered Clydesdale at NT 099444 and, after passing Lammerlaw near Elsrickle and crossing the North Medwin near Carnwath Mill, reached Castledykes Fort. From there it made for the summit of Silvermuir Ridge (NS 913449) and then, having crossed the Clyde near Kirkfieldbank, it probably went over the north shoulder of Black Hill before crossing the Nethan and heading for Loudoun Hill. At Silvermuir Ridge a branch road broke off from this east-west road and

headed for Barmuildy Fort on the Antonine Wall between Bears-
den and Kirkintilloch. After crossing the Mouse at Cleghorn Mill,
it climbed to Kilncadzow from where it descended by Calagreen
Farm and Yieldshields to Belstane Farm. After crossing the Garrion Burn and passing Gillhead Farm (NS 814536), it followed
the line of the present A 721 to Wishaw, whence it headed for
the fort at Bothwellhaugh and the Antonine Wall.

It should be noted that the claim that there was a branch road
leaving the Crawford to Inveresk road somewhere near Roberton,
and crossing over the south shoulder of the Tinto Hills to Castledykes, is no longer regarded as valid and that some ancient
monuments in Upper Clydesdale have been mistakenly identified
as Roman. Examples are the denuded remains of the medieval
castle at Carstairs and the seventeenth century bridge across
the Mouse near where the river enters the Clyde opposite
Kirkfieldbank.

Since the settlements in the district with which this book is
concerned are of feudal origin and since so much of the countryside is steeped in Covenanting lore, brief general accounts of
feudalism and of the religious wars of the seventeenth century
are now given.

Feudalism

The essential idea of the Anglo-Norman feudal system of government, developed in Scotland especially in the reign of David I
in the twelfth century, was that authority was delegated by the
King to certain lords by granting them lands in return for services
rendered. The lord could then subdivide his land to tenants who
were responsible to him, and each tenant could subdivide his
share to subtenants and so on. The tenants rendered certain
services to their lord in return for the land and for his protection,
and were subject to the jurisdiction of the lord's court. The lord
was responsible to the King, who came to be regarded as the
lord of all land and the source of all justice. To make sure that
every part of the realm was properly governed, the King built
castles in many places and into these he put his own administrative officers, known as sheriffs. In each locality, or sheriffdom,
the sheriff acted for the King in all judicial, financial, military

and administrative matters. To keep in touch with his subjects the King moved about frequently from castle to castle.

When land was given to a lord in the manner described, a charter was granted defining the powers of the lord and the services to be rendered by him to the King. During the reign of Robert the Bruce these charters became more specific than formerly and stated that certain lands were held of the King 'in free barony' (*in liberam baroniam*). A lord whose land was designated in this way enjoyed greater power and privileges than he would otherwise have possessed. His court could deal with criminal matters of all kinds and could even pronounce sentence of death by hanging or drowning. In due course the more powerful barons obtained even more extensive powers and privileges. In such a case the barony became a regality, the land being held *in liberam regalitatem*, and even the sheriff had no authority to enter it. The lord was more or less king in his own land and treason was the only crime with which he could not deal.

The powers given to the lord of a free barony usually included those of 'sock, sack, thane, bluidewite, infangthieff, outfangthieff, pit and gallows'. 'Sock' was the power to hold courts and 'sack' was the right to impose and appropriate fines; 'thane' was the right to possess and dispose of slaves; 'bluidewite' gave authority to deal with any case involving bloodshed, while 'infangthieff' and 'outfangthieff' referred respectively to the punishment of thieves who committed their thefts in the barony in which they resided and of those who belonged to another barony and were brought back for trial to the barony in which they had committed their robberies; the 'pit' was for drowning women convicted of theft and the 'gallows' for hanging men guilty of a similar offence. Actually, the officers of the baron courts were not keen on hanging criminals, preferring to banish them. They clearly thought that they had done their duty if they had rid their own district of some nuisance and sent him away to rob the next. The dislike of hanging sprang not from humanitarian grounds but from consideration of expense. The higher the status of the culprit, the higher the gallows had to be and the cost entailed evidently varied from about seven shillings to about £4. For the same reason prison sentences were rarely imposed; there were few prisons in existence and, in any case, the prisoner had to be fed while confined. However, there were plenty of alternative punishments available. There were, for instance, the pillory and the jougs or iron collars, which were attached to the walls of the kirk and into which the culprit's neck was fastened for 'ye terror of ye others'.

On acquiring his new possession from the King, the baron built not only a castle in which to live but also a church for himself and his retainers, who paid him tithes for the upkeep of the church. The baron, of course, appointed the priest and so began the system of *patronage*. The district served by a church was known as a *parish*.

After the rebellion of 1745 the Government, determined to subjugate the Highlands and to break down feudal power in Scottish society, abolished heritable jurisdiction by an Act of Parliament in 1747. Although baronies (unlike regalities) and baron courts continued to exist legally, the baron could try only criminal cases where the fine could not exceed 20s. and civil cases in which the sum involved did not exceed 40s. All other cases were dealt with by the sheriff. Eventually, baron courts were mainly concerned with disputes among the baron's tenants. In recent years baronies have been much sought after as prestige symbols, and large sums of money have been paid for them.

In the twelfth century, trading between Scotland and other European countries started on a considerable scale and the economy of Scotland gradually changed from being largely agricultural and self-supporting to one in which organised trading played a prominent part. Arrangements had to be made for the buying and selling of goods, and it was to this end that burghs were created by the King. These were known originally as king's burghs and later as royal burghs; there were ultimately 66 of them. Each burgh was allowed by its charter to hold a weekly market and a specified number of fairs each year. The main purpose of a fair being to enable people to stock up with food and other things not usually available on a daily basis, the ordinary commercial business of the burgh was suspended during the fair. It was in this way that Fair Holidays arose. After the Industrial Revolution arrived and mass-produced goods became readily available, burgh fairs eventually died out. Merchants and craftsmen in a burgh could become burgesses by paying a certain rental to the King and on undertaking to perform certain communal duties. The burgesses held exclusive rights to trade in foreign goods and, being very jealous of their privileges, kept a careful watch to see that no illicit trading was carried on elsewhere. This restriction of trading to royal burghs having been found to be very awkward, since many townships were 20 miles (32 km.) or more from the nearest royal burgh, a large number of burghs of barony were created. As the name suggests, these were usually created in favour of the local baron. Burghs of barony had much less power than royal burghs (and were somewhat frowned upon by the latter), but were empowered to trade in both local and foreign goods provided that these foreign goods had been procured from a royal burgh. In a burgh of barony justice for its inhabitants was administered by its baron court, presided over by the baron bailie. However, the importance of these courts eventually declined and, after the passing of a 'police' statute in 1833, they ceased to exist in practice. The latter statute enabled householders with £10 rentals to decide (at a meeting convened for the purpose) to introduce a 'police system' and appoint 'commissioners of police'. These officers had power to assess the inhabitants for watching, lighting, water, scavenging, drainage etc., 'watching' meaning much the same as the modern word 'policing'. In this way a new local authority was established by the *inhabitants* and, since the baronial officers were left with virtually no power, they in due course ceased to be appointed.

The Covenanters

The period of religious strife in the seventeenth century in which the people in Upper Clydesdale were deeply involved was that known as the 'Killing Times', which lasted from 1662 to 1688. A brief account of the main events leading up to this terrible period is as follows.

James VI of Scotland, after he became James I of England in 1603 and had gone to live in England, greatly enjoyed his new way of life with its pomp and luxury and the magnificence of the English Court. He admired the elaborate ritual of the Church of England and, being already predisposed to Episcopacy – he believed in the Divine Right of Kings and distrusted any

democratically elected assembly – was determined to impose it
on the Church of Scotland. By working patiently and quietly he
was able to establish a mild and generally acceptable form of
Episcopacy in Scotland by 1610 but, when he tried to alter the
form of worship, as distinct from the type of Church government,
by pushing through the Five Articles of Perth at the General
Assembly of 1618, he ran into trouble. The Articles ordained that
the festivals of the Christian year such as Christmas and Easter
should be observed, that confirmation should be carried out by
bishops and not by ministers, that private communion and
private baptism should be allowed in case of illness and that
Holy Communion should be received in a kneeling position.
Finding the articles unpopular because they were regarded as
savouring of Popery, James was wise enough not to enforce them
rigidly.

After the death of James in 1625, Charles I continued to
implement his father's ecclesiastical policies but with much less
tact and diplomacy. In 1625 he distanced himself from the nobles
by passing the Act of Revocation under which the Church lands
and tithes, distributed among the nobles at the time of Reformation, were restored to the Church to pay for the clergy. Then,
when Charles, accompanied by Laud, soon to become the Archbishop of Canterbury, came to Edinburgh in 1633 for his
coronation, the service was held in the abbey church of Holyrood
with full Anglican rites. Next, in 1637 Charles imposed a new
prayer book, Laud's Liturgy, on the Church of Scotland, the
reading of which in St. Giles' Kirk led to the riot with which the
name of Jenny Geddes is traditionally associated. The consequent
discontent throughout the country led some prominent church-
men and nobles to devise in 1638 the National Covenant, which
was later to play such a prominent part in the history of Scotland.
Anti-Roman in character but loyal to the King, it was signed by
noblemen, ministers, lairds, burgesses and others throughout the
country. The Covenanters pledged themselves to maintain 'the
true religion'. Later, in 1638, the famous General Assembly of
that year met in Glasgow. The atmosphere being very hostile to
Charles, the King's Commissioner dissolved the Assembly at an
early stage in the proceedings but, taking the view that it had
been properly constituted, the Assembly carried on and deposed

or excommunicated all the bishops. It also condemned the new Prayer Book as being 'heathenish, Popish, Jewish and Arminian'. Things were now at crisis level. The ensuing Bishops' Wars of 1639–1641 ended with Charles coming to Edinburgh to try to win favour with the Scots by distributing a number of peerages and accepting all of the decisions of the General Assembly of 1638. He failed in his attempt for, when the English Civil War broke out in 1642 between the Royalists and the Parliamentarians, the Scots presbyterians allied themselves with the latter group. The Royalists having initially won one victory after another, the Parliamentary leaders turned to Scotland for help and in 1643 signed the Solemn League and Covenant with representatives of the Covenanters. The Scots agreed to this not for political reasons but with the object of guaranteeing Presbyterianism in Scotland and of promoting it in England and Ireland as well. The terms of the agreement were that the Covenanters would attack the Royalist forces from the north with an army to be paid for by the English Parliamentarians, and a promise was given that there would be 'a reformation of religion in the Kingdoms of England and Ireland in doctrine, worship, discipline and government, according to the Word of God and the examples of the best reformed churches, and that popery and prelacy should be extirpated'. With the help of Scottish troops under the command of Alexander Leslie, Cromwell heavily defeated the Royalists at Marston Moor in Yorkshire in 1644.

Meanwhile, the English had set up the Westminster Assembly with the task of establishing uniformity of worship in Scotland, England and Ireland. From this Assembly, which sat from 1643 until 1648, little emerged that affected England, but Scotland acquired the Westminster Confession of Faith, which is still the subordinate standard of faith in the Church of Scotland, in 1647 and the metrical version of the Psalms, based on the work of Francis Rous, Provost of Eton at the time, in 1650.

Just after the defeat of the Royalists at Marston Moor, James Graham, 5th Earl of Montrose, who was becoming more and more out of sympathy with the Covenanters, especially with one of their leaders, Archibald Campbell, 8th Earl of Argyll, and who was not in favour of the Solemn League and Covenant, changed sides and supported the King. Having gathered together a force consisting mainly of Highlanders, but including some Irishmen and some Lowland lairds of Royalist persuasion, he set out to win over the Scots for the King, who, in recompense, made him a marquis. Initially, he had great successes. He defeated the Covenanters at Perth and occupied the city; a few weeks later he entered Aberdeen, where the Highlanders and the Irishmen showed no quarter; and then with help from the MacLeans and the MacDonalds he burned down the town of Inveraray, Argyll's stronghold. After routing the Campbells and their Covenanter allies at Inverlochy in February, 1645, he had further successes at Dundee, Auldearn (near Nairn), Alford in Strathdon and Kilsyth. However, the glory did not last for long. In September of the same year, Montrose was surprised and heavily defeated at Philiphaugh near Selkirk by David Leslie, the nephew of Alexander, who had returned to Scotland with his army of Coven-anters after the disastrous defeat of the Royalist forces at Naseby. After the battle the Covenanters showed absolutely no mercy to the vanquished. In the following year, 1646, King Charles sur-rendered to the Scots at Newark and, in accordance with the terms of the surrender, Montrose disarmed his forces and fled to Norway.

By this time the Covenanters were becoming disillusioned with their English allies who, it was now apparent, were not interested in making England a Presbyterian country and who had not made the monthly payments agreed to in the Solemn League. The Covenanters then handed over the King to the Parliamentary Commissioners for £400,000 and returned to Scotland. In 1649 the King was executed and a Commonwealth under Oliver Crom-well proclaimed. This was not to the liking of the Scots, who were annoyed that they had lost their King through a purely English action. Under Argyll they lost no time in proclaiming the King's eighteen-year-old son as King Charles II. It was clear that, if the young man wanted to come to Scotland as King, he would have to accept the Covenants. This he did in 1649 although he hated Presbyterianism, regarding it as 'not a religion for gentlemen'. War between England under Cromwell and Scotland under Argyll was now inevitable. Cromwell immediately invaded Scotland whose army he routed at Dunbar in 1650. David Leslie tried to undo this defeat by crossing the Border into England in

1651, but his troops were annihilated at Worcester. However, in various ways that need not be gone into here, Scotland fared not at all badly during the Cromwellian occupation, which lasted until Cromwell died in 1658. The régime was efficient, with good civil justice complementing the good order established by military force.

In 1660, after the death of Cromwell and the collapse of the Protectorate in England, Charles II, at the request of General Monck, returned from exile and began his active kingship. With his dislike of Presbyterianism he had by 1662 brought back bishops to Scotland and restored patronage, which had been abolished by Parliament in 1649. Calvinistic theology, Knox's Book of Common Order, the metrical psalms, presbyteries and kirk sessions were retained, but ministers appointed after 1649 had to resign from their charges and seek reappointment by their bishops and patrons. About 270 ministers, mainly in south-west Scotland (i.e. about a quarter or a third of the whole), refused to do this and therefore were forced to leave their churches and manses. This created much bitterness at a time when the need of the restored monarchy was conciliation. As a consequence, services known as conventicles at which these 'outed' ministers preached the Word and administered the Sacraments were held on the hills and moors. An Act passed in 1665, which banned coventicles under pain of fine, imprisonment or corporal punishment on those who attended them, provoked the Pentland Rising of 1666 in which the Covenanters were defeated at Rullion Green. Making an attempt at conciliation in the next few years the Government offered an Indulgence to the 'outed' ministers in 1669 on condition, of course, that they promised obedience in the future. Forty-two ministers accepted and returned to their parishes. By another Indulgence in 1672 a further ninety ministers returned. Harsh measures against those who refused this Indulgence only added to growing popular support for the Covenanters so that by 1678 the Government had lost control, at least in the south-west. The Highland Host, a body of 6000 Highlanders and 3000 Lowlanders, was then sent to maintain order in the area. The land was looted, many fines were imposed and some estates forfeited. Revolt was clearly in the air.

In June 1679 a small Government force led by John Graham

of Claverhouse was repulsed when it attacked an armed conventicle at Drumclog. However, three weeks later the Covenanters were routed at Bothwell Brig by an army led by the Duke of Monmouth, an illegitimate son of the King. The Covenanters' army numbered about 4000, of whom 400–500 were killed and about 1400 taken prisoner. Some of the prisoners escaped but most of the others were offered their liberty in return for a pledge of future good behaviour. Most of 260, who were shipped off to Barbados, were drowned when their ship sank off Orkney. Fewer prisoners were executed than after Rullion Green when about 40 were hanged. Monmouth who, it should be said, favoured some clemency being shown, succeeded in getting a third Indulgence offered. The 'indulged' ministers returned to their parishes but the resistance of the remaining Covenanters continued to be as stubborn as ever despite the increasingly repressive measures being taken against them. With Richard Cameron and Donald Cargill as their leaders, they became known as the Cameronians. Some of them in June 1680 denounced their allegiance to the King by affixing a Declaration to this effect on the Mercat Cross in Sanquhar. A month later the Cameronians were defeated and Cameron killed at Airds Moss in Kyle. Donald Cargill was hanged in 1681.

On the death of Charles II in 1685 his brother James VII succeeded to the throne. Being an ardent Roman Catholic and wishing to help his co-religionists, he used the royal prerogative in 1687 to allow Catholics, Presbyterians and Quakers to worship in their own particular ways provided that they did not encourage disloyalty in any way. This Indulgence did not apply, of course, to the Cameronians, of whose ministers James Renwick was the last to be executed (in 1688). Opposition to James, because of his Catholicism, was strong both in the Lowlands of Scotland and in England and was encouraged from Holland by William of Orange, a Dutch Calvinist, who was married to James's daughter Mary. In November 1688, William of Orange, at the invitation of certain English magnates, came over from Holland with an army, and in December James fled to France. William and Mary were proclaimed King and Queen of England and Ireland in February, 1689 and of Scotland in April of the same year. There was, however, opposition to William and Mary in the Highlands from those who wished to see James VII on the throne. John Graham of Claverhouse, now Viscount Dundee ('Bonny Dundee'), rallied some of the clans and defeated William's forces at Killiecrankie in July, 1689; 'Bonny Dundee' was killed in the battle. Shortly afterwards, however, the position was reversed at Dunkeld, where the Cameronians, who had by now made themselves into a regiment, remembering the atrocious behaviour of the Highland Host during the 'Killing Times', inflicted heavy losses on the Highlanders and scattered them. Jacobite opposition to William and Mary was thus ended.

On 7th June, 1690 the Presbyterian form of Church government was restored in Scotland, Parliament approved of the Westminster Confession of Faith and patronage was again abolished. The Covenants were disregarded much to the disappointment and annoyance of the Cameronians.

In conclusion it should be said that opinions on the Covenanters have varied over the years from excessive adulation to absolute denigration. Although the Covenanters can be regarded as martyrs, who died for freedom of worship and for the Presbyterian form of Church government, they can also be thought of as enemies of the state, who incited rebellion and who therefore had to be subjugated by military action. It is probably true to say that the rank and file of Presbyterians, though very unhappy about the way they and their sincere religious beliefs had been treated, neither approved of nor countenanced the Covenanting extremists of the post-Cromwellian years with their self-righteous exclusiveness and their readiness to kill anyone thought to favour the ungodly.

2
Lanark

The market town of Lanark, with a population of 8877 in 1991, stands at a height of 500–800 ft (150–240 m.) above sea level on sloping ground overlooking a gorge of the river Clyde, and was a royal burgh until the reorganisation of local government in 1975 abolished all counties and burghs despite the fact that Article XXI of the Act of Union of 1707 guaranteed their continuance 'in all time coming'. The name *Lanark*, which occurs as *Lannerc* in 1187–1189, is by the general consent of Celtic scholars derived from the Cumbric word *lanerc* meaning a *glade* or *clear space*. (Cumbric was the *p*-Celtic language spoken in much of southern Scotland during the Dark and Early Middle Ages.) The word, which is *llanerch* in modern Welsh, is also seen in the place names *Lanrick* found twice in Perthshire and *Lendrick* found in Angus and in Kinross-shire.

The earliest known charter erecting Lanark into a royal burgh was granted by Alexander II in 1227. It seems certain, however, that there was a charter of earlier date, for William I (the Lion), who frequently made the Castle of Lanark his headquarters during his reign (1165–1214), in granting lands to the Abbey of Dryburgh refers to a toft, i.e. a homestead, as being *in meo burgo*. Since the foundation of royal burghs is usually assigned to the latter part of the reign of David I (1124–1153), the year 1140 has been decided upon as the nominal date on which Lanark was made a royal burgh. The prestige of Lanark was greatly enhanced in 1369 when the town was included in the Court of the Four Burghs. These burghs were originally Edinburgh, Berwick, Stirling and Roxburgh but, when Berwick and Roxburgh fell into the hands of the English, they were replaced by Lanark and Linlithgow. The Court, legislating with sovereign power, formed a code of burgh laws (*leges burgorum*) containing 119 articles relating to all aspects of burgh life ranging from trading practice to the election of magistrates. It also adjudicated on cases brought to it by other burghs. By its decision, too, standards of the ell (for length), the firlot (for grain), the pint and the stone were entrusted to the keeping of Edinburgh, Linlithgow, Stirling and Lanark, respectively. The 'stane wecht' and all other weights derived from it were originally made of stone but latterly of brass or lead. Any burgh requiring a set of weights had to get it from Lanark. This monopoly was lost after the Union of the Parliaments in 1707. Several sets of weights are at the time of writing (late 1998) still possessed by South Lanarkshire Council. The Court of the Four Burghs was eventually enlarged to become the Convention of Royal Burghs, which carried on until 1975, when it was effectively replaced by the Council of Scottish Local Authorities (COSLA). Lanark itself was granted a warrant by the Convention of Royal Burghs on 9th June, 1715, 'to pursue unfree traders within the parishes of Carnwath, Carstaires, Pittinain, Carmichall, Biggar, Douglas, Lesmahagow and Carlook'. Royal burghs were very jealous of those of their trading rights that were not possessed by burghs of barony.

Apart from the old St Kentigern's Church on Hyndford Road, the part of Lanark of greatest historical interest is that part around the foot of what is now High Street and including the North and South Vennels, the Wellgate, the Castlegate, the Broomgate, the Bloomgate, Friar's Lane and Westport. The word *vennel*, meaning a lane, is derived from medieval French and is thought to have been introduced into Scotland in the fourteenth century. The Scots word *gate* or *gait* means a way; it occurs in the old saying 'gang y'r gait' meaning 'go your way' or 'get ye gone'. The two vennels are joined to the High Street by ten closes, such as the Wide Close, Duncan's Close and so on, in which the poorer element of the population resided in medieval times. The closer a house was to the High Street, the higher was the status of its occupier. Prior to 1730 the High Street was known as Hietoun and, with houses scattered here and there, was a small district rather than a street. It was only in the nineteenth century that an alignment of the houses on both sides of the street was gradually achieved. Some of the seventeenth century houses with crow-stepped gables remain to this day. Until 1834, when it was converted into a sewer, a stream known as the Puddin' Burn ran down the High Street into the Castlegate. The width of the High

2.1. High Street, Lanark.

Street has been sufficient to enable it in modern times to be made into a dual carriageway with a central flower bed studded with chain-linked pillars along its entire length.

The most prominent landmark at the foot of the High Street is St Nicholas' Parish Church, erected in 1774 at a cost of £600 to replace the *burgh* church, then in poor condition and known as the 'In Kirk' or 'Town Kirk' or 'Laigh Kirk' to distinguish it from the old Church of St Kentigern, which was the *parish* church and, being outside the burgh, was known as the 'Out Kirk' or 'High Kirk'. The 'In Kirk' was the successor after the Reformation of the Chapel of St Nicholas, the earliest reference to which is dated 1214. In 1668, by which time the 'Out Kirk' had fallen into such a state of disrepair that it had to be abandoned, the worshippers joined the burghers in the 'In Kirk'. However, it was not until 1708 that the 'In Kirk' was officially designated as the Parish Church of Lanark. The architecture of the present building, which has just recently been restored at a cost of about £450,000, is not noteworthy in any way. During the restoration in 1994 the skeletons of ten adults and two children were unearthed from what is thought to have been a pre-Reformation burial ground.

The steeple of St Nicholas' Church has an interesting history. It was built by the Town Council to accommodate the bell of the abandoned 'Out Kirk' and is therefore the property of South Lanarkshire Council. The bell, dating from the year 1110 and still functioning, must be one of the oldest in Europe; it has been recast four times. A plaque on the north side of the tower bears the inscription

1. DATE ... ANNO 1110.
I did for twice three cent-ries ring
And unto Lanark city ring.
Three times I Phenix – like have past
Thro' fiery furnace till at last ...
2 ... ANNO 1659.
Refounded at Edinburgh
By Ormiston and Cunningham
ANNO 1740.

In a niche in the steeple there is a statue of Sir William Wallace, 8 ft (2.45 m.) in height and executed by the sculptor Robert Forrest from what he described as 'an ancient drawing in possession of the Society of Antiquaries'. Forrest offered the statue to the Town Council in 1820 'to commemorate the great achievements of the noble hero in the town where his most early and notable exploits took place' on the condition that the statue be set on a suitable sandstone pedestal and that it be given three coats of oil paint the last of which was to be in a bronze or dark stone colour. When the statue was placed in its niche in 1822 the Town Council disregarded the condition that it be on a pedestal on the grounds that a pedestal would partially obscure the view of the church as seen from the High Street. The statue, which had fallen into a state of disrepair, has been restored along with the church. Forrest was born at Orchard, Carluke, in 1789 and, after working there and at Crossford, a short distance away, he moved to Edinburgh, where his work was greatly appreciated. Most of the 30 or so statues that he made are massive, one of John Knox 12 ft (3.65 m.) high and standing on a tall Greek column in the Necropolis in Glasgow, and one of Viscount Melville 14 ft (4.28 m.) high and standing on a column 136 ft (41.45 m.) high in the centre of St Andrew

2.2. Statue of William Wallace, Lanark.

Square, Edinburgh, being among the better known ones. Forrest died in 1852.

The Mercat Cross, which stood at the foot of Hietoun and which is referred to in a record dated 1488, was where the burgesses met to make decisions. From a platform reached by an interior staircase public announcements of importance were made. For example, the Old Pretender was proclaimed there as James VIII by a band of Jacobites on their retreat from Derby on Christmas Day, 1745. On 12th January, 1682 a well-armed body of Covenanters fixed to the Cross a copy of the Declaration of Sanquhar (1680) and burned a copy of the Test Act (1681). The Declaration was an incitement to rebellion while the burning of the copy of the Test Act meant the renunciation of allegiance to the King (Charles II). For allowing the Covenanters to escape unpunished, the Privy Council fined the town 6000 merks, i.e. £4000 Scots or £3332 English. One of these Covenanters was the famous James Renwick who was executed in Edinburgh on 16th February, 1688. On a King's birthday, his health was drunk at the Cross, the bells were rung and the town lit up by 'luminaries', i.e. candles in the windows of the houses. The Mercat Cross was demolished in 1775 and the stones used to build a small wall (no longer existing) at the front of the church. It should be realised that, before the advent of railways and canals, stone for building purposes had to be obtained locally and was in many places very scarce. The foot of the High Street is now known as the Cross.

At the foot of the High Street on the south side there still stands the property dating from 1779 known previously as the Council House or Tolbooth; it replaced an older building. The building, protruding from the line of shops on the High Street, narrows the street considerably and is very conspicuous. It included a Court room, a Council room, public offices, a room for the Gentlemen of the County (the J.P.s) and a jail. Until the earlier years of the nineteenth century the laws against transgressors were savage in character and were administered relentlessly. For example, a man who stole an article worth five shillings was liable to suffer the death penalty. For lesser crimes he could be subjected to punishments such as whipping, the stocks, the jougs, branding, a fine, imprisonment and banishment. Thus, on one occasion, some tinkers were 'whipped through the town' at the West Port, at the Steeple, at the Tron and at the East Port, being given 39 lashes each (as in the Old Testament), the punishment being repeated at intervals of four or five days for about a fortnight. The stocks were made of heavy bars of wood by which the culprit's feet were enclosed. The jougs was a kind of collar formed by two semicircles of iron, joined at one place by a hinge and fastened at the other by a padlock, into which the neck of the culprit was placed. The instrument was fixed to some building at such a height from the ground that the offender could neither stand nor sit and must therefore have been very uncomfortable indeed. After the Reformation punishment by the jougs was transferred to the Church, which applied it mainly to persons who had shown contempt for ecclesiastical authority. The instrument in these times was attached by a chain to the wall of a church and was usually placed near the main door. When the English soldiers in Cromwell's army occupied Scotland, they were so horrified at the Church using such a form of punishment that they removed the jougs from the walls of most churches and destroyed them. Jougs can still be seen at Dunsyre Church and part of a set at Biggar Kirk. Branding was done by an iron rod about 2ft in length with a square piece of iron attached at one end and on which the letter L (for Lanark) was raised. The square end of the instrument was heated and then thrust against the offender, usually on the forehead or palm of the right hand in the case of a man and on the cheek in the case of a woman. Banishment was a frequent punishment. The offender was taken to the boundary of the parish and warned that if he returned he would be whipped or branded.

In 1836, the Tolbooth building of 1779 was abandoned when more extensive premises including a Council room, a Court room, a hall for County meetings, public offices and a jail were opened on the east side of the then new street called Hope Street. The jail was discontinued in 1882 when the prison of Glasgow began to receive prisoners from Lanark. After the move to Hope Street the Tolbooth was let for commercial use and then sold. Then, in 1992, part of the property was bought by Clydesdale District Council and Lanark Community Council with help from the Common Good Fund to serve as a meeting place and for development as a heritage centre. The refurbishment has now been completed.

Near to the Tolbooth stood the Tron, where all goods coming to market were weighed by an officer called the Customer, who charged customs dues as prescribed by the Council. A high beam on the Tron was frequently used as a means of humiliating offenders, who were tied to it for a prescribed period of time. Thus on 23rd October, 1718 a certain Margaret Watson was taken from prison, set upon the Tron for an hour with a paper narrating her crime put on her forehead, and then taken back to prison.

The pre-eminent historical figure associated with Lanark is the patriot William Wallace (c. 1270–1305) whose house in the town stood, according to tradition, on a site in the Castlegate next to where the present Clydesdale Bank stands. For details of Wallace's association with Lanark and its neighbourhood we are largely dependent on *The Actes and Deides of the Illustre and Vallyeant Campion Schir Willaim Wallace*, twelve books of verse written by Blind Harry (or Henry the Minstrel)(1440–1493). There is very little information available about the poet, but there is evidence that he appeared at the court of James IV on various occasions and was given money by James. Judging by his descriptions of the weather and the countryside, it would seem that he was not blind from birth. The traditional heroic figure of Wallace stems from Blind Harry's poem which, although claimed by its author to be based on a Latin account (now lost) by John Blair, a Benedictine monk who became Chaplain to Wallace, was probably made up to a considerable extent from surviving oral tradition and the poet's own imagination. It was written about 180 years or so after the events it describes and cannot be regarded as a reliable source of information. The poem, it may be remarked, influenced the poet Robert Burns, who wrote in a letter: 'the story of Wallace poured a Scottish prejudice into my veins which will boil along there till the floodgates of life shut in eternal rest'. Blind Harry's account of Wallace in Lanark now follows for what it is worth.

Wallace visited an uncle, who resided near Lesmahagow, during the winter of 1295–1296 and paid frequent visits to Lanark. Here in the old church of St Kentigern he met Marion Braidfute, heiress to the estate of Lamington and of great personal charm, and fell in love with her. He married her in 1296 and lived with her in the house, whose site has already been referred to, until 1297. By this time Edward I was in control of Scotland (after his victory at Dunbar) with Sir William Heselrig as his sheriff in Lanark where, as in many other places, there was a strong feeling of resentment towards the English troops because of their arrogance and oppression. This feeling was shared by Wallace who, after a skirmish on the street in which several Englishmen fell, had to flee from his home by the back door while his pursuers hammered on the front door; he fled to a cave in the western precipice of the Cartland Crags near where the present bridge on the A73 crosses the chasm. Enraged by the failure to capture Wallace, Heselrig ordered his house to be burnt down and everyone in it to be put to the sword. When Wallace heard of the murder of his wife, he vowed an undying vengeance against the English. Without delay he gathered together some faithful followers and at night surprised the English garrison, which had no watch arranged and which was unprepared for any attack. Wallace not only killed the sheriff but also hewed his body into small pieces with his own sword and set fire to a building in which most of the garrison perished. From then onwards Wallace was an outlaw.

The Castle of Lanark, of which no trace remains, was situated on a mound at the foot of the Castlegate. William I (the Lion), who reigned from 1165 to 1214, often resided in it and it was there at some time between 1200 and 1210 that he granted a charter erecting the town of Ayr into a royal burgh. This charter is the oldest surviving Scottish burgh charter. Alexander II (1214–1249) is known to have resided in the Castle, as did Robert I (the Bruce) who, early in the fourteenth century, granted a manor and orchard to a small group of Franciscan monks for the setting up of a friary. It stood where the Clydesdale Hotel, built in 1791, now stands in the Bloomgate. The friary was in a ruinous state by 1566, its stones having been removed by builders.

The origin of the orders of Friars is interesting. A failing of monasticism with its stress on withdrawal from the world was that it did little or nothing for the spiritual needs of ordinary people. As a result a reaction against it set in, and early in the thirteenth century the new orders of Friars were created with papal blessing. Although friars took the same vows as monks, namely, chastity, obedience and poverty, they were not cloistered like monks – whose duties did not include preaching – but worked in the outside world, where they preached in the vernacular on the streets and markets of towns, tended the sick and heard confessions; the whole world was their parish. By 1286 the *Dominicans* (or *Black Friars*) had at least twelve houses in Scotland, the *Franciscans* (or *Grey Friars*) had six and the *Carmelites* (or *White Friars*) had three. Since the friars had no endowments except in some cases a small income from burghal rents, they had to depend on alms and were therefore often known as *mendicants.*

Two further remarks about the Castle must be made. Firstly, the mound on which the castle stood has been the site of a bowling green since 1758. Secondly, the castle was almost certainly a motte. There are also mottes at Carnwath, Wolfclyde, Biggar and Abington.

After the feudal system of land tenure had been introduced into Scotland in the twelfth and thirteenth centuries, fortifications known as *mottes* began to be erected. Essentially, a motte consisted of a mound, which could be either an outcrop of rock or an artificially raised erection, with the laird's wooden house built within a palisade, i.e. a fence made of wooden stakes, on top of it. The mound was surrounded by a wide, deep ditch often filled with water. The mound, in fact, was frequently made from the upcast of the ditch in the way that a child makes a sandcastle on the beach. The house was reached by a ladder-like bridge that stretched from the outer edge of the ditch to the top of the mound. A motte was often surrounded by a *bailey* which was a piece of land on which ancillary properties such as stables and storehouses were erected. The bailey, also protected by a palisade, often had its own ditch. To prevent damage by enemy fire in the form of arrows carrying burning tar, the wooden buildings sometimes had their roofs covered with turf and their walls faced with clay. The whole of the motte and bailey was known as the *castle*, whose ground area could be anything up to three acres (fully 1 ha.). All the features of a motte are shown in the depiction of the Castle of Dinan on the Bayeux Tapestry, perhaps the most famous piece of embroidery in the world; it is a strip of linen about 23 ft long and 19 inches broad portraying in coloured wools the story of the Norman Conquest.

A short distance to the west of Lanark Castle and not far from the junction of Friar's Lane and St Patrick's Road stands Castlebank House. This house, built with a beautiful terraced garden in front of it in 1780, or slightly earlier, by John Bannatyne, is a magnificent example of a country house of its time. A woodland garden, with many fine rhododendrons and trees such as the Paperback Maple, was laid out by Mr J. Hamilton Houldsworth, Chairman of the Coltness Iron Company from 1933 until 1941. In the 1950s the house was divided into flats which, having fallen into disrepair, were refurbished towards the end of 1996 at a cost of about three quarters of a million pounds.

In 1995 a stretch of the Clyde Walkway – a projected footpath running from the centre of Glasgow to the Falls of Clyde – from Castlebank to New Lanark and about 1 mile (1.6 km.) in length, was opened. After climbing to a viewpoint giving a magnificent view over New Lanark of the river upstream from there, it opens out on to New Lanark Road at the hairpin bend above the village. The cost of about £200,000 was paid for by Clydesdale District Council, the Clyde and Avon Valley Project, Lanarkshire Development Agency, Scottish Natural Heritage and Strathclyde European Partnership. In 1998 a further stretch of walkway, from Castlebank to Crossford, was completed.

Lanark, being a royal burgh, had its grammar school. A fee-paying school for boys with two teachers is known to have existed in 1183. In a marginal note on a papal bull given in that year by Lucius III confirming the gift by David I of the parish of Lanark to the Abbey of Dryburgh, there are the words '*nec magistris in parochia vestra de Lanark scholarium studia sine prava exactione regere temere quisquam audeat inhibere*'. The Latin may be translated: 'in your parish of Lanark let no one lightly take it upon himself to put difficulties in the way of schoolmasters in the direction of their pupils' studies so long as there is no unfair treatment'. The teachers were clergymen appointed by the Abbot of Dryburgh. Latin, being both the spoken and the written language of the Church and of the learned world in the Middle Ages, was the main subject of study; indeed it was the prominence given to the teaching of Latin grammar in many medieval schools that led to their being designated grammar schools. There is no known break in continuity between this small school, probably run first of all in St Nicholas' Chapel, and the present large Lanark Grammar School in Albany Drive and Hyndford Road with, in 1998, 1059 pupils. The school remained a two-teacher school until the middle of the nineteenth century. For hundreds of years the boys either boarded with the Rector or had lodgings in the town. Girls were admitted for the first time in 1884 and fees were abolished in 1893. The school celebrated its octocentenary in 1983 when it was honoured by a visit from Princess Anne on 25th June of that year. The school can list many distinguished persons amongst its former pupils, of whom William Lithgow ('Lugless Willie')(1582–1645), a famous traveller, William Smellie (1697–1763), the famous obstetrician, the 3rd Earl of Hyndford (1701–1767), an outstanding diplomat, Lord Braxfield (1722–1799), the notorious High Court judge, Major-General William Roy (1726–1790) of Ordnance Survey fame, and John Glaister (1856–1932), forensic scientist, may be regarded as pre-eminent. Lithgow, Smellie, Braxfield and Glaister were all Lanarkians.

William Lithgow ('Lugless Willie') was the son of a leather merchant in Lanark and proprietor of Boathaugh, later a part of the Bonnington estate. Educated at the Grammar School, he was well acquainted with the ancient classical authors. He acquired his pseudonym after his ears had been barbarously cut off by the brother of a young lady whom he had hoped to marry. Some have been of the opinion that the girl was a Lockhart of Lee but others have thought that she belonged to a family of Wilkies (or Wilkins) who were great social climbers at the time. Anyway, disgusted with his nickname, William left Lanark and after making two trips to Orkney and Shetland and 'in the stripling days of his adolescence' visiting Germany, Switzerland, the Low Countries, the Near East and North Africa, he returned to Lanark in 1623 and published his principal work, *The Totall Discourse of the Rare Adventures and Painful Peregrinations of long Nineteen Years' Travels from Scotland to the Most Famous Kingdoms in Europe, Asia and Africa* (London, 1632). This book, of unusual interest because of its description of people and their manners, must have been popular for a long time, for the 12th edition of it was printed in Leith in 1814. Lithgow is thought to have been the first Scotsman to write about his travels. The peregrinations were certainly painful because in Malaga in Spain he was thought to have been a spy and as a consequence was subjected to terrible suffering by the Inquisition. A rigid Calvinist, his attitude to the Roman Church was now more bitter than ever. The book dealt not only with his adventures abroad but also with such things as Turkish baths, coffee drinking, the pigeon post from Aleppo to Baghdad and the author's disapproval of tobacco-smoking.

Lithgow's other publications included six poems printed between 1618 and 1640, the most interesting of which was *Scotland's Welcome to King Charles* (1633). The poem gives a curious picture of Scotland at the time with its expostulations on the decay of education and football, runaway marriages to England, the taking of snuff by ladies to relieve headaches and the immorality of the plaid. Lithgow died in Lanark in 1645 and was buried in St Kentigern's Churchyard.

William Smellie, renowned as an obstetrician and as one of

2.3. William Smellie.

the greatest writers on midwifery, was born the son of a burgess of Lanark in 1697. He practised in Lanark from 1719 until 1739 when he moved to London where he set up a practice and where in 1741 he started teaching midwifery in his own home. He was awarded the degree of M.D. by the University of Glasgow in 1745. Smellie's *magnum opus* was his book *A Treatise on the Theory and Practice of Midwifery*, published in 1752 with a supplementary volume added in 1764. His description of the mechanism of parturition was more complete than any given previously. In 1759 he retired from his London practice to live in Lanark, where he built a house in which he resided until he died in 1763. He called his house Smellum, but the name was later changed to Smillum and then to Smyllum. Eventually the house was bought in 1792 by Sir William Honeyman, a son-in-law of Lord Braxfield who joined the Court of Session as Lord Armadale in 1797. He altered the house sometime around 1800 to form the 'B' listed house now standing. In 1864 this house was bought by the Roman Catholic Church authorities, with considerable financial help from Mr Robert Monteith of Carstairs, for use as an orphanage, which continued until 1980. The house, which stands at NS 893 436, is now derelict.

Because of his high regard for Lanark Grammar School, Smellie bequeathed to the school his library of 496 volumes, nine English flutes, a thick quarto-size music book, three pictures, 'my father's, my mother's and my own drawn by myself in 1719', a reading desk and a few other items together with a sum of £200 to add a storey to the school, then in Broomgate, to house the bequests and provide an extra classroom. The addition to the building was made in 1770 after the money became available on the death of Smellie's widow in 1769. In 1934 the library was moved to the Lindsay Institute in Hope Street, where a brass plaque erroneously states that the library was bequeathed to the Town. In 1882 the Faculty of Physicians and Surgeons in Glasgow tried unsuccessfully to have the books transferred to its keeping for convenience of access by students. Smellie was buried in a small chapel attached to the ruins of St Kentigern's Church, where a wreath is laid annually on his grave. The maternity hospital which stood near Steel's Cross for many years was aptly named the William Smellie Memorial Hospital. It was replaced in December 1992 by a large maternity unit in Law Hospital, known as the William Smellie Maternity Unit. *Motherhood*, a statue in bronze executed by Denis Peploe, was presented in 1954 to the town of Lanark by Emeritus Professor Samuel J. Cameron of the Chair of Midwifery in the University of Glasgow in memory of Smellie. Since the closure of the Memorial Hospital the statue has stood in the entrance foyer of the Health Centre in South Vennel.

Robert McQueen, later Lord Braxfield, son of John McQueen of Braxfield, Sheriff-substitute at Lanark, was born in Lanark in 1722 and went on from the grammar school there to the University of Edinburgh. He was called to the Bar in 1744, raised to the Bench with the title Lord Braxfield in 1776, and became Lord Justice-Clerk in 1788. He died in 1799. Due mainly to Lord Cockburn writing of him in his *Memorials of his Time* in 1856 as the very devil incarnate and as a criminal judge who could not be condemned more severely, few men of historical importance have acquired a worse reputation than he has. Cockburn

2.4. Lord Braxfield.

called him the Jeffreys of Scotland. Famed for his savage sentences and his coarse jokes at prisoners' expense, he was portrayed as showing undisguised glee in rejecting the last despairing claim of a wretched culprit and sending him either to the gallows or to Botany Bay, the penal settlement in Australia to which criminals found guilty were often sent. This impression of Braxfield became firmly fixed in oral tradition and led to his being referred to as the 'Hanging Judge'. John Gibson Lockhart in his seven-volume biography of Sir Walter Scott, completed in 1838, relates how Braxfield once said to a culprit of some ability 'ye're a very clever chiel, man, but ye would be nane the waur o' a hangin''. In accordance with the same tradition R. L. Stevenson in his last great novel modelled his fictional Lord Justice-Clerk Weir of Hermiston on him.

An entirely different picture of Braxfield as a man and as a *criminal* judge from that painted by Cockburn who, it should be remembered, was only a boy when Braxfield died, can be obtained by going back to contemporary records such as the biographical note in the *Scots Magazine* of 1801. William Roughead and C. M. H. Millar, writing in the *Juridical Review* of 1922 and 1979, respectively, have found that those who actually knew Braxfield took a much more favourable view of him than Cockburn did. Thus, Robert Dundas of Arniston knew Robert McQueen as a boy and 'soon grew exceedingly fond of his company and conversation'. Likewise, Dr. John Erskine, a fellow student at the University of Edinburgh, refers to 'Robbie McQueen whose honesty and good nature made him a general favourite'. McQueen, as a senior member of the Bar, seemed also to have been kind and helpful to junior members. For example, he was very kind to James Boswell, giving him generous praise whenever he had pleaded well, while his kindness to young Walter Scott at the beginning of his career led Scott, when he was admitted as an advocate, to dedicate his thesis – written in Latin and dealing with the law relating to the disposal of the bodies of executed criminals – to him. Again, a lawyer, Alexander Young of Harburn, a contemporary of McQueen, wrote in a memoir: 'This, however, I will take it upon me to say that he was one of the most kind, benevolent, cheerful and agreeable men I ever knew, most hospitable and attentive in an eminent degree to all his neighbours'.

Similar sentiments were expressed by John Mowbray of Harwood, another contemporary. Likewise, the portrait of Braxfield painted in the *Scots Magazine* of 1801 is completely different from that drawn by Cockburn. The biographical notice says that 'The Lord Justice-Clerk was an affectionate husband and tender parent; he had a warmness of temper and benevolence of heart which made him highly susceptible of domestic attachment. As a companion and friend he was peculiarly beloved by such as stood in these relations to him ... His engaging, we may say, fascinating manners rendered him a most agreeable member of society. The company was always lively and happy of which the Lord Justice-Clerk was a member'.

A trial for murder in which Braxfield was shown at his best was that of Sir Archibald Kinloch in 1795. Braxfield's charge to the jury showed sound reasoning and foreshadowed the later notion of diminished responsibility. His final words were: 'But, gentlemen, I think that in all events a verdict of not guilty is not the proper verdict for you to return. I think you ought to return a special verdict, finding that the pannel was guilty of taking the life of his brother but finding also that he was insane at the time'. (*Pannel* was the old word for the person at the bar of the Court.) About the same time, James Niven was charged with murder for killing a man accidentally. Requiring further information, Braxfield and the Bench deferred pronouncing judgment. Eventually the case was remitted to a trial by jury, which returned a majority verdict of 'not guilty'.

Again, at the famous trial of Deacon Brodie in 1788 soon after Braxfield had been made Lord Justice-Clerk, he displayed not only his depth of legal knowledge but also his great patience and humanity. Thus, at one stage of the trial he said:

A'hm ane o' thae folk wha are aye for ge'in fair play tae paynels, an' ah'l never allow ony advantage to be taken o' them. But, jist the same, ah'm for ge'in fair play to the evidence.

Then in his address to Brodie before passing sentence of death on him he said:

Ah wish ah could be of ony use tae you in yer melancholy

situation. You, William Brodie, frae yer education and habits o' life, canna but ken a' thing aboot yer present situation which ah could suggest tae you. It's much tae be lamented that thae vices, which are called gentlemanly vices, are sae favourably looked upon in the present age. They hae been the source o' yer ruin; and, whatever may be thocht o' them, they are sic as assuredly lead tae ruin. I hope you'll improve the short time which ye hae noo' tae live by reflectin' upon yer past conduct, and endeavourin' tae procure, by a sincere repentance, forgiveness for yer money crimes. Goad aye listens tae those wha' seek him wi' sincerity.

The reports of these trials are not in keeping with the malevolent attack by Cockburn, who was very selective in the trials that he chose to describe. He seemed to have based his opinion on some of the sedition trials of 1793–1794 and made no reference to those that did not suit him.

The famous sedition trials came about in the following way. The outbreak of the French Revolution in 1789 seemed to many liberally minded men in many countries to presage the dawn of a new age. In Scotland, where there was much unrest and a desire that the parliamentary franchise should be given to every man of twenty-one and over, hopes ran high not only among politicians but also among intellectuals such as Dugald Stewart, the philosopher, who visited Paris about that time and came home very impressed. However, in 1793 the French declaration of war on Britain, the execution of Louis XVI and the enthronement of a prostitute in Nôtre Dame seemed to indicate that the French Revolution with all its talk of liberty and reason was nothing other than a murderous attack on established order, private property and the Christian religion. The sympathy shown in Scotland for the French Revolutionaries upset the Government, which then branded its opponents as potential traitors and began prosecuting them for 'sedition', a crime unknown in Scottish law until 1795 when the expression of political opinion was muzzled by a new Treason Act and a Sedition Act. The Government was, of course, justified in its apprehension: a plot to seize Edinburgh Castle, the banks and the judges had been uncovered in 1794.

Braxfield played a prominent part in these trials for sedition. In some of them Cockburn's opinion cannot be upheld in any way. For example, in the trial of Charles Sinclair in 1794 there was a long debate between counsel and Braxfield about the indictment and the nature of the alleged crime, which led to the trial being postponed three times and then dropped. It is clear that to be tried by Braxfield did not necessarily entail a savage sentence. It often did, however, as in the famous trial of Thomas Muir, an Edinburgh advocate, who was sent to Botany Bay for fourteen years for distributing a classic radical text by Tom Paine. Cockburn relates that, as one of the jurors at this trial passed behind Braxfield on the Bench, the latter said to him, 'come awa' and help us to hang ane o' thae damned scoondrels'. However, none of the scoundrels was hanged. Any attempt to alter the British Constitution, which Braxfield as a judge had sworn to defend, was regarded by him as bordering on treason, and its perpetrators had to be punished as severely as the law would permit. Cockburn, who was a boy at this time, recalls the harshness of the sentences but seems to forget the seriousness of the situation. When the sedition trials were discussed in Parliament, Lord Mansfield, the Lord Justice-General, said: 'I have not the pleasure of personal acquaintance with the Lord Justice-Clerk, but I have long heard the loud voice of fame, that speaks of him as a man of pure and spotless integrity, of great talents, and with a transcendent knowledge of the laws of his country'.

It is as a judge of criminal cases that Braxfield has been criticised. The intellectual capacity, knowledge of civil and feudal law, and absolute integrity that he displayed in civil cases are unquestioned. Early in his career at the Bar McQueen distinguished himself as one of the counsel for the Crown in many intricate feudal cases that arose after heritable jurisdiction was abolished in 1747 (after the '45 Rebellion); Highland chiefs then lost both their authority and their estates. Even Cockburn conceded that 'within the range of feudal and civil branches, and in every matter depending on natural ability ... he was very great'.

As regards Braxfield's personal qualities, all are agreed that his speech was often coarse and ribald and inappropriate for a judge. On one occasion he said to two opposing advocates: 'Ye maun jist pack up yer papers and gang hame. The tane o' ye's riftin' punch. The tither's belchin' claret. There'll be nae guid got oot o' ye the day'. He himself drank heavily, especially claret, but was always perfectly alert in the Court. It must be remembered that, in passing judgment on great historical figures, it is wrong to apply modern standards to their different conditions. In eighteenth century Edinburgh many people in public life drank too much, swore too often and blushed at nothing. According to Cockburn, a notorious saying of Braxfield was the reply he gave in one of the sedition trials when the accused in defence of innovation remarked that Jesus himself was an innovator. Braxfield replied: 'Muckle he made o' that; he was hangit'. In the official report of the trial no mention is made of Jesus. Of course, since anecdotes both true and false would circulate about a man like Braxfield, this story may just have been a jocular invention.

Braxfield was one of the last judges, if not the last, to speak in Lowland Scots in his daily work. On one occasion he said to a man standing trial: 'Ha'e ye ony coonsel, man?' 'No', said the man. When he then said, 'dae ye want to ha'e ony appointed?', the man replied, 'I only want an interpreter to make me understand what your Lordship says'. Another anecdote told about him relates to old James, a manservant who had been long in his service. One day James gave his master notice that he would leave at the next term. 'What's wrang noo, James?' said Braxfield. 'Nothing but your Lordship's temper' was the reply. 'Hoots man, what needs ye mind o' that?' said his master, 'Ye ken weel it's nae sooner on than it's aff.' 'Very true,' replied James, 'but it's nae sooner aff than it's on!'

John Glaister, senior, born into a Lanark family in 1856, held with great distinction the Chair of Forensic Medicine in the University of Glasgow from 1898 to 1931. He wrote many books, several of which became authoritative, dealing not only with various aspects of forensic medicine but also with dissimilar subjects ranging from social bionomics to Chaldean discoveries. Special mention should be made here of his book *William Smellie and his Contemporaries: a Contribution to the Literature of Midwifery in the Eighteenth Century*, published in 1894. The book was a contribution to the history of midwifery and provided a biography of Smellie, giving a most exhaustive and original résumé of Smellie's life's work in reforming obstetric medicine. It deals at length with the development and use of forceps. When Glaister was a pupil at Lanark Grammar School, he discovered a collection of large sheets of paper lying on the top of a cupboard. These were obstetric drawings and part of the library that Smellie had bequeathed to the School. The fascination of these drawings led the youthful Glaister to think of making medicine his career. Glaister was in great demand as an expert witness at High Court trials in Scotland. His analytic mind, fully stored with sound scientific knowledge, made him a formidable witness to defending counsels. His opinions were probabilities. When he was under cross-examination and a suggestion contrary to his expressed opinion was made, he would reply, 'Yes, it is possible but highly improbable' or 'Yes, it is possible but I do not know of such a case'. Glaister was a founder and the leader in Scotland of the burial reform movement, which was responsible for the opening of a crematorium in Glasgow in 1895, the first in Scotland and the second in Britain. He was succeeded in his Chair by his son John Glaister, junior, who was deeply involved in the famous Ruxton murder trial in 1936. John Glaister, senior, died in 1932.

The most important civic event of the year in Lanark is the Lanimers held each year in June. Originally, the Lanimers (Land March Day) was simply the annual inspection of the march stones defining the boundary of the burgh, a duty imposed on burghs from the time of their foundation by David I and his successors. The burgh records of 1588 refer to the Lanimers as being 'ancient and yearly'. However, since 1893, when a Lanimer Queen was chosen for the first time, the Lanimers has become an elaborate festival lasting for a week. The celebrations begin on a Sunday with the 'kirkin'' of the Lord Cornet or Standard Bearer in St Nicholas' Church. Monday sees the beginning of the perambulation of the marches, on Tuesday evening the Lanimer Ball is held, on Wednesday the Lord Cornet leads a cavalcade to inspect the remainder of the boundary, and on the morning of Thursday, Lanimer Day itself, the proceedings come to a climax when a procession of the Lord Cornet, his predecessors in office, the Lanimer Queen-elect with her Court, bands and decorated vehicles with tableaux, many of them elaborate, winds its way in the presence of great crowds down the High

Street to St Nicholas' Church, where the Queen is crowned under the statue of Wallace. To be chosen as Lord Cornet or Queen or as the lady who crowns the Queen is regarded as a signal honour. In the afternoon sports are held in Castlebank Park and in the evening the Lord Cornet makes a public declaration that the march stones are in their true positions. Further events on Friday and Saturday complete the week's festivities. In bygone years Lanimer Day was the day after the Whitsun Fair, which was held on the last Wednesday of May but, since the time when the Calendar was changed by omitting eleven days, the earliest and latest possible dates for Lanimer Day are Thursday, 6th June and Thursday, 12th June. A short digression on the Gregorian calendar may be permitted here. The adjustment made to the calendar by a decree of Pope Gregory XIII in 1582, in order to compensate for the fact that the seasons had got out of step with the sun by ten days, was accepted by the Roman Catholic countries but was not accepted in Scotland and England until 1752, by which time the discrepancy had increased to eleven days. When 3rd September was replaced by 14th September, rioting mobs in England shouted 'Give us back our eleven days!'. Since by the same decree the beginning of the year was changed from 25th March to 1st January, a change made in Scotland in 1600, care is often required in dating events. For example, the date of the foundation of Biggar Kirk is January, 1545 in the old style of reckoning but is 1546 in the new style. Such is the importance of the Lanimers to Lanarkians that, when on two occasions in the 1980s a General Election was proposed for the Thursday of Lanimer Day, the Prime Minister was asked to avoid that date! The enthusiasm of the Lanarkians, who spare no effort either timewise or moneywise to ensure the success of the celebrations, is truly remarkable. For example, in 1997 the cost borne by the Lanimer Committee was £20,077, of which sum about £7914 went for the hire of the bands, their travelling expenses and meals.

One of Lanark's most cheerful traditional events is *Whuppity Scoorie* which is enacted on the evening of 1st March each year when a large number of children, assembled at the Cross and waiting for the bell of St Nicholas' Church to start ringing at 6 p.m., race round the church three times, whirling round their heads tightly rolled balls of paper each attached to a string about two feet long. The first to complete the three circuits is given a monetary prize. The original intention of the procedure was to beat off evil spirits at the end of winter and so to ensure a good harvest later. The ringing of a bell, involving as it does the clanging of metals, was often thought in European folklore to be efficacious in driving away evil spirits.

Another ancient custom still carried out in Lanark is the Het Pint. By a bequest, originally made for educational purposes by James, Lord Carmichael in 1662, a pint of ale used to be dispensed annually to citizens in need. Today £1 is given to each applicant at a traditionally happy ceremony on New Year's Day. The fund is now administered by the Community Council, which is also responsible for Whuppity Scoorie and the ringing of the bells on Hogmanay.

Apart from the A73 which passes right through Lanark, the main roads leaving the town are the A72, which leaves the A73 at Steel's Cross (NS 876439), the A706 which leaves the A73 as Hope Street at the western end of the Bloomgate (NS 880437), and the A743 which begins as St Leonard Street at the top of the High Street.

The A73 as Bannatyne Street passes the railway station, the bus station, the Roman Catholic Church of St Mary and then, as Ladyacre Road, passes the Clyde Valley Tourist Information Centre before turning left/east along Hyndford Road at the Auction Mart. The railway came to Lanark in 1855, the line branching from the main Glasgow to Carlisle line at Cleghorn two miles away. The arrival of the railway led to the building of several hotels in the neighbourhood of the station and to the making of Lanark with its beneficial air into a holiday resort.

St Mary's Church, an inspiring structure in neo-Gothic style built in 1910, replaced a church erected in 1859 largely by the generosity of Mr Robert Monteith of Carstairs but which was burnt down in 1907. Mr Monteith erected the church in memory of his young daughter Caroline who died in 1853 and as a thanksgiving for his own remarkable recovery from a fever. £35,000 that he had laid aside for Caroline's dowry was used for this purpose. He also built a presbytery for the Vincentian fathers whom he brought over from Ireland to run the Church. Robert Monteith (1812–1884) was the only son of Mr Henry Monteith, a very wealthy textile magnate from Glasgow whose beneficence to the village of Carstairs is referred to in Chapter 9. Educated at the University of Glasgow and at Trinity College, Cambridge, Robert became a member of a brilliant and exclusive set in Cambridge. He made the acquaintance of Thackeray and became a lifelong friend of Tennyson. Having become acquainted at Trinity with Roman Catholicism in an intellectual way, he was later greatly influenced by John Henry (later, Cardinal) Newman and in 1846 was received into the Roman Catholic Church. He became prominent in its affairs at a high level and took part in the First Vatican Council of 1870. He was undoubtedly the most intellectual Scottish Catholic of his day.

Lanark Auction Mart was set up about 1840 by Mr John Lawrie, who in 1862 took his nephew Mr James Symington into partnership. They moved from a site near the foot of Hope Street to the present site in 1867. Early in the twentieth century the business was acquired by Mr William Elliot, father of the Rt. Hon. Walter Elliot P.C., C.H., M.P., whose widow Baroness Elliot of Harwood was chairman of the company for many years. Until the middle of the nineteenth century the buying and selling of cattle was done either privately or at the annual fairs held in burghs in accordance with their charters. Lanark was originally allowed to have four annual fairs and a weekly market, but from about the end of the eighteenth century seven fairs were allowed. Then there were also the great Michaelmas trysts for the sale of cattle and to a lesser extent of sheep held at Crieff until 1770 and afterwards at Falkirk from where as many as 100,000 head of cattle went annually to England. However, after the extensive building of railways in Scotland in the middle of the nineteenth century, the trysts at Falkirk gradually diminished in importance – the last tryst was held in 1901 – as auction marts to which cattle could be taken by rail sprang up all over the country. Now, of course, much of the transport is by road. The Lanark mart, now covering 12½ acres (5 ha.) of ground, is one of the largest and best known in the country, with dealers coming from all over Britain to the special sales of cattle and sheep held from time to time. During 1997, for example, something like 7,000 calves, 32,000 cattle and 264,000 sheep were handled in the Mart. At a special sale in October 1997 a record price of £85,000 for a

2.5. Old St Kentigern's Church.

blackface ram lamb was obtained. Sales of agricultural machinery
are held every three or four weeks. The ordinary sales on Mondays
are well patronised, as is a shop for the sale of top quality farm
produce which is open every weekday. The octagonal auction
room close by Hyndford Road still contains the original ring and
fittings.

Across from the Mart on Hyndford Road stands the old Church
of St Kentigern already mentioned. Originally belonging to the
Crown, the church of which the present ruins are thought to be
those of its fifteenth century successor was conveyed along with
its lands and teinds to the monks of Dryburgh by a charter
granted by David I sometime between 1150 and 1153. Around this
time landowners sometimes presented land to parish churches
to provide them with extra income; one such donation was made
to the Church of St Kentigern by a certain Jordanus Brac and
consisted of land, later known as Braxfield, lying between the
churchyard wall and the Clyde. Since the church stood outside
the burgh of Lanark but within the parish, it was, as mentioned
before, referred to as the 'Out Kirk'. At the time of the Reformation (1560) the church was stripped of its revenue but it
continued in use as the Parish Church of Lanark. The fabric

steadily deteriorated and by 1668 was in such a bad state that the church had to be abandoned in favour of the Church of St Nicholas. Built of whinstone from Jerviswood in the valley of the Mouse, the ruins are of a church in the Early English style of architecture with large pointed windows as in the nave of Dunblane Cathedral, in the crypt and choir of Glasgow Cathedral and in the transept of Dryburgh Abbey. The site of the belfry is visible outside the west wall; the bell was removed to St Nicholas' Church where it still hangs.

Blind Harry in his poem on Wallace refers to him passing

on fra the Kyrk that was without the town

and asserts that it was here that he first saw Marion Braidfute, heiress of Lamington, who became his wife. Harry writes:

Upon a day to ye Kyrk as sche went,
Wallace hyr saw, as he hys eyne can cast,
Ye prent off luff hym punzett at ye last,
So, asprely, throuch bewte off yat brycht,
With gret uness in presence bid he mycht,
He knew full weyll hyr kynerent and her blud,
And quhew sche was in honest eyss and gud.

The graveyard surrounding St Kentigern's Church is now of considerable size. Among the monuments in the older part is the large Martyrs' Monument erected in 1881 to commemorate four Covenanters who were executed, one of them being Robert Baillie of Jerviswood, eleven who were fined without trial, four who were imprisoned and outlawed as rebels, one of them being John Bannatyne of Corehouse, fourteen who were condemned as traitors and had their possessions forfeited but who fled and escaped, and twenty-two who were outlawed and declared fugitives.

A short distance from the Martyrs' Monument is the Murray Chapel, gifted to Lanark in 1912. It is Romanesque in style, with round-headed arches and chevron (inverted V) decoration, is beautifully designed with stained-glass windows, and is frequently used for funeral services.

About ⅝ mile (1 km.) east of the western entrance to the churchyard the A73 passes Lanark Loch on the left/north.

2.6. Martyrs' Memorial, Lanark.

Originally developed from a swamp between 1832 and 1840, it provided the town with a water supply from 1850 to 1881 when a new supply of excellent water was obtained from Lochlyoch at the foot of Tinto Hill. The loch now provides fishing and boating and is part of Lanark Moor Country Park, which includes play and picnic areas. Most of Lanark's present water supply comes from the neighbouring reservoirs of Lochlyoch and Cleuch.

Close by Lanark Loch is the clubhouse of the well-known Lanark Golf Course. This, which developed from a course of six holes laid out in 1851, is thought to be the 17th oldest golf course in Great Britain. Extensions and modifications having been made over the years, the course became one of eighteen holes in 1897. The present first and eighteenth holes have remained unchanged since 1851. The ground consists of ridges, mounds and hollows of sand and gravel deposited by the melting waters of the last ice sheet about 10,000 years ago and which form the nearest inland equivalent of coastal links. The course, with a length of 6425 yards (5875 m.), is regarded as first-class in the opinion of many who are competent to judge, and is a great credit to the club members who over the years have spared no expense in maintaining its good condition. In recent years it has been regularly used by the R.&A. as one of the regional qualifying courses in the run-up to the Open Championship. Alongside the 18-hole course there is a nine-hole course, used by beginners and those who do not wish to hinder better players on the main course. Both were owned by the Lanark Common Good Fund and have recently been sold to the Golf Club for £350,000.

Beyond the entrance to Lanark Loch Park the A73 runs along the edge of Lanark racecourse, where horse-racing took place for several hundred years before it ceased in the late 1970s. The major trophy awarded annually was the famous Silver Bell. Traditionally, the Bell is said to have been presented by William the Lion when he instituted racing in Lanark in 1160, but this assumption cannot be true for an investigation made about 1890 showed that the Bell was made in Edinburgh around 1608–1610. Silver bells were fashionable as prizes at race meetings in the early seventeenth century but, when racing was reintroduced in Lanark in the early eighteenth century after having been abandoned from around 1630 because of religious strife in the country, silver bells

2.7. The Lanark Silver Bell.

were regarded as unfashionable and were replaced by tankards, cups or plates. The Silver Bell then seemed to have been forgotten about until it was unearthed when the Council offices moved from the Tolbooth to Hope Street in 1836. Realising then that the Bell was a valuable antique, the Council decided that it be awarded as the main prize at the race meetings. These meetings were later taken over and run by the Lanark Racecourse Company until the racecourse closed in 1979. The Hamilton Racecourse Company tried on different occasions to have the Silver Bell competed for at Hamilton Park, but Clydesdale District Council, strongly supported by the residents of Lanark, would not permit this. It is hoped by many that racing may be revived in Lanark and the Silver Bell competed for again. As an indication of the value placed on the Silver Bell, winners of it were not allowed to keep it for a year, as is the normal practice, but were given instead a smaller-sized replica. Each name was inscribed on a shield which hung from a Victorian stand surmounted by the Bell; the oldest shield is dated 1628. Only three exceptions are known to have been made to the retention rule; these were made on the occasions when Lord Rosebery, Lord Hamilton of Dalzell and King George VI were the winners.

An event of international importance took place on Lanark racecourse from 6th to 13th August, 1910, when the first Scottish International Aviation Meeting was held there. (The first meeting of this kind had been held in Rheims in August, 1909.) Nineteen pilots took part, one of whom, B. Dickson, flying in a biplane, made the first-ever passenger flight in Scotland on 8th August, 1910. Another pilot, J. B. Drexel, broke the world altitude record by attaining a height of 6750 ft. Two other world records were broken when an endurance record of 3 hours 11 minutes and a speed record of 75 m.p.h. were attained. Unfortunately, an attempt to set a distance record failed, when a plane set off for Edinburgh but ran out of fuel and returned to Lanark on a farm cart. About 200,000 spectators attended during the week, and such was the importance attached to the event that the Caledonian Railway Company opened a new station close to the racecourse (known as Racecourse Station) on the branch line from Lanark to Douglas and Muirkirk; this line was closed in 1964.

Continuing eastwards from Lanark racecourse, the A73 passes Winston Barracks which were set up by the War Office a few

2.8. Scottish International Aviation Meeting, Lanark, 1910.

years prior to the outbreak of World War II in 1939. The property, which includes a number of dwelling houses which appear to have been substantially built, now stands abandoned. The A73 now drops down to cross the Clyde at Hyndford Bridge about 2½ miles (4 km.) from Lanark railway station and built in 1773. An account of the district beyond this point will be given in later chapters.

The A743 begins as St Leonard Street, so named because of the Hospital of St Leonard which stood on it but of which there has been no trace for more than 200 years. The hospital and its lands were granted to Sir John de Dalzell by Robert III in 1393 on condition that three masses were said each week for the King and his family. The hospital's land included two fields in the neighbourhood and about 1000 acres (400 ha.) of land on the moor between Yieldshields in the parish of Carluke and Forth. St Leonard Street becomes Carstairs Road at NS 895442, where Stanmore Road goes off to the left/north and leads to Cleghorn. Stanmore House, situated on this road, is a school for spastic children; it belongs to Capability Scotland, formerly known as the Scottish Council for Spastics, and is a centre of excellence for the work that it does. A short distance along Carstairs Road stands St Mary's Hospital, opened in 1972. The road continues on by Ravenstruther to Carstairs, a place which will be considered in Chapter 9.

The A706, beginning as Hope Street, which was opened some-time in the 1830s, and then becoming Cleghorn Road, contains some impressive Georgian and Victorian houses and buildings. It is perhaps worth noting that it was about this time that, in preparation for the first decennial census of 1841, the numbering of houses was introduced. On the right/east side of the street stands the Lindsay Institute (the District Library headquarters), built in 1914 using a bequest by Mr Charles Lindsay, the former Council Building opened in 1836 and the Sheriff Courthouse opened in 1868. Further on, on the same side of the road, stands Christ Church, a beautiful building belonging to the Episcopal Church in Scotland, dating from 1858 and serving a wide area. A short distance up Hope Street on the left/west side stands the nineteenth century St Kentigern's Church (of Scotland), now unused and at the time of writing (late 1998) with an unknown future. In 1993 the congregation united with that of Cairns Church in Bloomgate to form the appropriately named Greyfriars Church whose congregation now worships in the Cairns Church building. The roof of St Kentigern's Church is in need of repair and the tall spire could pose a problem for anyone taking over the building. The pews have been removed from the church and eighteen of them used in the renovation made in 1996 of Kilchoan Parish Church in Ardnamurchan. The A706 leads on for about 2 miles (3 km.) to Cleghorn where it crosses the Mouse (pronounced Moose), a tributary of the Clyde rising in the neighbourhood of Wilsontown. The bridge here dates from 1661. What was once the very old Cleghorn Mill is now a dwelling house with a beautifully landscaped garden. After crossing the main Glasgow to Carlisle railway by a level-crossing, the road continues to Harelaw roundabout and ultimately via Forth to Whitburn, where it joins the M8.

The valley of the Mouse can be conveniently explored by going along Bellefield Road, which leaves the A706 at NS 882443 and leads to Jerviswood House and to Leechford Bridge, a footbridge over the Mouse. Jerviswood House, a completely and faithfully restored laird's house dating from *c.*1600 and whose present owner Mr J. Aitken was given a Civic Award in 1984 for his work on it, was the home of Robert Baillie, a Covenanter who was unjustly hanged, drawn and quartered in 1684 for his alleged part in the Rye House Plot of 1683, a plot to kill the King (Charles II) as he passed along a narrow road near Rye House at Hoddesdon in Hertfordshire. One of the quarters exposed on the Tolbooth in Lanark was removed by a young farmer of the name of Leechman from Dolphinton, for which meritorious act the Jerviswood family educated his son William for the ministry of the Church. William became Professor of Divinity in the University of Glasgow in 1744 and served as Principal of the University from 1761 until 1785. Robert Baillie's own son George fled to Holland for safety after his father's execution and while in that country became an intimate friend of William of Orange, with whom he returned to Britain at the time of the Revolution Settlement in 1690. The Baillies of Jerviswood were descended from the Baillies of Lamington and Robert Baillie was a great-grandson of John Knox.

Leechford Bridge replaced a ford across the river which was much used in earlier days. The path upstream from here passes through the Cleghorn Glen National Nature Reserve, which the Nature Conservancy Council has designated as a Site of Special Scientific Interest, and after a distance of about 1⅓ miles (2 km.), having at one point traversed the edge of a precipice about 80 ft (25 m.) high above the river, arrives at Cleghorn Bridge on the A706. The path downstream from Leechford Bridge, not everywhere well defined, passes through a very picturesque area and after a mile or so (2 km.) emerges on to Mousebank Road (on the line of the old road from Lanark to Carluke) near Lockhartmill Bridge, an iron structure replacing a bridge built in 1784 and slightly upstream from it. After crossing Mousebank Road, the path continues for about a mile (1.6 km.) to emerge on to the A73 at Cartland Bridge. Great care must be taken where the path is right on the edge of the 200ft (60 m.) – high crags and at places where the ground is falling away. Wallace's Cave is near the end of the path but, since the path down to it is decidedly dangerous, a visit is not recommended.

The remaining road out of Lanark, the A72, which drops steeply down to Kirkfieldbank after leaving the A73 at Steel's Cross and goes on to join the M74 in the Hamilton area, will provide the subject matter of Chapter 6.

3

New Lanark
and the Falls of Clyde

The village of New Lanark, which lies in a gorge of the river
Clyde, is fully a mile (1.6 km.) from Lanark railway station and
can be reached from there by going along Ladyacre Road, turning
to the right along Hyndford Road and then proceeding along
Braxfield Road. It had its origin in a visit paid in 1784 to the Falls
of Clyde by Richard Arkwright, the pioneer of cotton–spinning
on a large scale, and David Dale, a textile merchant in Glasgow,
who was Agent there for the Royal Bank of Scotland and a founder
member of the Glasgow Chamber of Commerce. Arkwright was
of the opinion that, since the Clyde below the Falls was both
voluminous and fast-moving, the right bank there would be an
ideal site for the erection of a water-powered mill for the spinning
of cotton. Within a year or so Arkwright and Dale had gone into

3.1. New Lanark and the River Clyde.

49

partnership and feued some land beside the river, mainly from Lord Braxfield, who resided just a short distance downstream, but also from the Incorporation of Shoemakers in Lanark and from Sir John Lockhart Ross of Bonnington (a naval Commander who became Admiral of the North Sea Fleet). They decided to call the mill and the housing associated with it 'New Lanark'. The partnership between Arkwright and Dale turned out to be short-lived but, after its dissolution in December, 1786, Dale carried on enthusiastically on his own. A weir had to be constructed on the river above Dundaff Linn, the smallest of the Falls with a drop of about 10 ft (3 m.), and the water led from there through a tunnel some 300 yards (274 m.) long to the giant water-wheel at the mill. Spinning began in March, 1786. Further mills along with housing were erected later and by 1793 there were 1334 workers from 200 families employed in the work. It is significant that many of these were children, 275 of them being orphans from Glasgow and Edinburgh and some of them as young as six years of age; by 1800 the number of pauper children had increased to over 400. Relative to the standards prevailing at the time, the children were well treated. Thus, in 1796, Dale could say that

there are six sleeping apartments for them and three children are allowed to each bed. The ceilings and walls of the apartments are white-washed twice a year with hot lime and the floors washed with scalding hot water and sand. The children sleep on wooden-bottomed beds on bed ticks filled with straw which are, in general, changed once a month. A sheet covers the bed ticks and above that there are one or two pairs of blankets and a bed cover as the season requires. The bedrooms are carefully swept and the windows thrown open every morning in which state they remain through the day. Of late cast iron beds have been introduced in place of wooden ones. The body clothing in use in Summer both for boys and for girls is entirely cotton which, as they have spare suits to change with, is washed once a fortnight. In Winter the boys are dressed in woolen cloth and they, as well as the girls, have complete dress suits for Sundays. Their linens are changed once a week. For a few months in Summer both boys and girls go without shoes and stockings.

The children were given porridge and milk for breakfast and supper, while for dinner they were given soup and either beef or cheese together with plenty of potatoes and barley bread. A school was set up by Dale both for the children working in the mill – they attended from 7 till 9 p.m., having worked from 6 a.m. till 7 p.m. with half an hour off for breakfast and an hour for dinner (i.e. lunch) – and for younger ones who attended during the day. In 1796 there were 507 pupils with 16 teachers, who not only taught the '3 Rs' but also gave instruction in sewing and church music.

It is interesting to note that many Highlanders, migrating from their crofts with the hope of attaining a higher standard of living elsewhere, found employment in New Lanark. In 1791, when a ship with 400 passengers emigrating from Skye to North Carolina was forced into Greenock by a storm, Dale offered employment to those who had not already entered into contracts and by doing so increased his workforce at New Lanark by about 100. Dale was very impressed with these people and, being keen to do anything that he could to discourage emigration, he set up mills at Oban in Argyll, at Stanley in Perthshire and at Spinningdale in Sutherland. He was altogether a man of great Christian piety and benevolence. The first Bible Society in Scotland was set up under Dale's leadership in Glasgow in 1805. He died in 1806 at the age of 67. An anecdote told about him by Dean Ramsay in his *Reminiscences of Scottish Life and Character* is worth quoting as an illustration of the familiarity between a master and his trusted servants that was permitted in these days. One hard winter day Dale, who was short in stature and very stout, came into the counting house and complained to an employee, Matthew by name, that he had fallen on the ice. Matthew, who saw that his master was not hurt very badly, grinned a sarcastic smile. 'I fell all my length' said Dale. 'Nae great length, sir,' said Matthew. 'Indeed, Matthew, ye need not laugh,' said Dale; 'I have hurt the sma'o'my back.' 'I wunner whaur *that* is,' replied Matthew.

Robert Owen, born in Newtown in Montgomeryshire in 1771, now comes into the picture. In 1799 he married Caroline, one of Dale's daughters, and in 1799 along with two partners took over the mills at New Lanark. When he arrived there he found himself faced with many problems. The prevalence of drunkenness was one of them and led him to introduce street patrols in the evenings. Another was the bad state of repair of many of the houses and the heaps of filth and rubbish outside them. To remedy this Owen made new regulations which were not at all popular. It was laid down, for example, that houses had to be not only cleaned but also inspected once a week, a demand that raised the wrath of the female occupants. Also, rotas for cleaning the tenement staircases and the ground around the entrances were introduced. Then, in winter a curfew at 10.30 p.m. was imposed. Owen, however, went up in the estimation of the workers in 1807 when he paid them their wages in full while the mills were closed down for a few months for economic reasons outwith the owners' control.

Since there were mounting disagreements between Owen and his partners, the partnership was dissolved in 1810. Owen found new partners but his profligate way of living led to the dissolution of this second partnership in 1813. A third partnership was formed in 1814 and lasted for ten years. During this period Owen developed his socialistic views as far as he could. Thus, for example, a Sick Fund was set up into which each worker contributed a sixtieth of his wages, a shop was opened in which goods were sold at almost cost price, free medical care was provided, and a Savings Bank was established. Furthermore, the workers made only token payments as rents of their houses. In the Institute for the Formation of Character built in 1816 the school was run on lines very advanced for their time. These included what would now be called a nursery school in which no child was forced in any way. Toys were conspicuous by their absence, Owen taking the view that a group of children left to themselves will entertain each other without 'useless toys'. There was adequate provision throughout the whole school for singing and dancing, the children being taught to sing Scottish and other traditional songs in harmony. Neither rewards nor corporal punishment were given in the school. The mills themselves were efficiently run with management techniques that were very modern at the time. The daily performance of each worker was shown at a glance by Owen's so-called silent monitor. A wooden cube surmounted by a pyramid with four faces and with a ring at its apex was suspended in front of each worker, whose performance was indicated by the colour of the square and triangular face facing him, white for

3.2. Early engraving of New Lanark.

excellent, yellow for good, blue for indifferent and black for bad. Anyone who thought that he or she had been unjustly assessed by the departmental supervisor could appeal directly to Owen.

The fame of New Lanark spread abroad – Owen was an expert on self-advertisement – and thousands came to see, examine and criticise the work that was going on. Among the visitors were the Grand Duke Nicholas, afterwards Emperor of Russia, Princes John and Maximilian of Austria, noblemen and men of learning both from home and abroad. Many of the visitors were favourably impressed but others, notably the poet Robert Southey, were not taken in by Owen's socialistic benevolence but discerned a hard authoritarianism underneath. After having been shown round the place by Owen himself in 1819, Southey concluded that 'Owen in reality deceives himself' and that his factory and colony differed 'more in accidents than in essence from a [slave] plantation'. Owen's workers were free 'to quit his service', but 'while they remain in it they are as much under his absolute management as so many negro slaves'. Southey asserted that Owen would not admit even to himself that 'his system instead of aiming at absolute freedom can only be kept in play by absolute powers'. He regarded Owen as a benevolent despot.

At home strong opposition to Owen was expressed by the Rev. William Menzies, minister of Lanark, who regarded it as his bounden duty to expose what he considered to be the non-scriptural character and the falsity of Owen's system. Owen had published a collection of essays entitled *A New View of Society* in which he claimed that human nature is basically good and can be trained in such a way that all people will ultimately become united, good, wise, wealthy and happy. He stated his firm conviction that religious belief inflicted imbecility of mind on its adherents and that religion obstructed human progress. He regarded his father-in-law David Dale as having been a genuine, good and religious man but regarded himself as a conscientious believer in the fundamental error of all religions. Mr Menzies complained that, although the Bible was taught, the Shorter Catechism was not taught in the school in New Lanark, and he raised the matter with the Presbytery of Lanark, which claimed jurisdiction over all the schools in the area. Representatives of the Presbytery visited the school from time to time and exposed any fault that they could find with the teaching. On one occasion Owen twitted Menzies in saying that his twenty years of ministry in Lanark had not produced any noticeable change for the better among the people there, whereas in sixteen years New Lanark had witnessed a change from a low state of morality to general behaviour that was sufficiently superior to attract the attention of most distinguished people both at home and abroad. Feeling in Church circles must have been running high, for on one occasion Menzies made a special journey to London to call to the attention of the Secretary of State the treasonable character of some of Owen's addresses to the workforce in New Lanark. Eventually, Owen's partners, who included two prominent and wealthy Quakers, told him that they were determined to prevent New Lanark becoming an infidel establishment. Accordingly, the teaching of dancing and singing was abandoned and the children's dress, provided by Owen and designed to give freedom of movement with consequent freedom of spirit, was discarded lest it should promote promiscuity.

Frustrated by the attitude of his partners, Owen sold his interest in the business in 1824 and went to America where he purchased an experimental cooperative movement in Harmony, Indiana.

However, there turned out to be much internal squabbling in New Harmony, as Owen called the place, with the result that Owen left in 1828. Democracy was carried too far for some in New Harmony. Apparently, partners at dances were chosen by lot and sometimes 'young ladies turned up their noses at the democratic dancers who in this way often fell to their lot'! After returning to this country Owen participated in Trade Union activity for a time, and then threw himself wholeheartedly into the Cooperative movement in which he played a noteworthy part. He died in 1858.

After Owen's departure to America the mills at New Lanark were run under the same guiding principles as before by Charles and Henry Walker, sons of John Walker, one of Owen's wealthy Quaker partners, until 1881 when the business was sold to Henry Birkmyre of the Gourock Ropework Company. The same ideas prevailed and, apart from some diversification of the company's products and the introduction of electricity in 1898, conditions hardly altered. Labour relations were extremely good and the Institute was the centre of social life in the village until 1968 when the mills closed down. One of the factors contributing to the closing of the mills was that an estimate made in 1967 of the Gourock company's assets in New Lanark made depressing reading, despite the fact that the company had spent £250,000 in modernising the plant a few years previously. The mill buildings were sold in 1970 to Metal Extractions Limited.

The condition of the dwelling houses in the village had also been an increasing worry over the years. The houses had either to be modernised or condemned after the Housing Act of 1950 deemed them uninhabitable. In 1962 Lanark Town Council reluctantly turned down an offer by the company to sell the whole village to it for the nominal sum of £250; the upgrading of the property was estimated to cost about £250,000. The Council was well aware, of course, that if the property was condemned, it would have the daunting task of rehousing something like 160 families. However, in November, 1963 a number of interested parties got together and formed the New Lanark Association, which was later able to purchase the village with the object of modernising the houses and keeping the community alive. Work progressed and three years later in November, 1966 the first of the new flats was opened, very fittingly, by Kenneth Dale Owen, a businessman in Texas and a descendant of Robert Owen. Further developments took place after the formation in 1974 of the New Lanark Conservation and Civic Trust. These included the sale in 1975 of some houses to buyers willing to restore them, and by the end of 1998 there were 20 houses owner-occupied and 45 tenanted. Ultimately, the first figure will rise to 27. In due course, the mill buildings were acquired, some of them compulsorily, from Metal Extractions and the huge task of restoration began. The permanent visitor centre now includes a reception area, a sales point, a coffee shop and a textile machinery display, while a millworker's house, a period village store and Robert Owen's house can also be visited. In what has been designated the *Annie McLeod Experience* the very latest technology has been used to show the activity of a typical day in the mill at the time of Robert Owen. The Visitor Centre, which was opened on 14th November, 1990 by the Rt Hon. George Younger, who was Secretary of State for Scotland when the negotiations for the restoration were at one of their crucial stages, was awarded a major prize for the most outstanding tourist attraction of 1990. The number of visitors in each year is about 400,000. It need hardly be said that this achievement was made possible only by the tremendous enthusiasm on the part of the people involved and by the generous financial assistance given by various public and private institutions. These included the European Economic Community's Regional Development Fund, the Council of Architectural Heritage, Strathclyde Regional Council, Clydesdale District Council, the Scottish Development Agency, the Countryside Commission for Scotland, the Scottish Development Department, the Training Agency, the Scottish Tourist Board, the Local Museums Purchase Fund, the National Heritage Memorial Fund, the Carnegie United Kingdom Trust, the Scottish Civic Trust, the Architectural Heritage Fund, the Cooperative Wholesale Society, the Pilgrim Trust, the Royal Bank of Scotland, New Lanark Community Council and the New Lanark Village Group.

    The most recent developments have been the conversion of the 'Wee Row' to a Youth Hostel with accommodation for 64 people and the transformation of Mill One into a 3-star hotel with 38 bedrooms. £3 million for the basic refurbishment was

3.3. Corra Linn.

provided by the European Regional Development Fund via Strathclyde Integrated Development Operation, the Lanarkshire Development Agency, Historic Scotland, Strathclyde Regional Council and Clydesdale District Council (the last two now merged into South Lanarkshire Council). The second phase of the development was financed by these bodies and by the Heritage Lottery Fund, which contributed £1.8 m. The hotel together with eight self-catering cottages was opened on 14th May, 1998. An arrangement has been made whereby students of hospitality management at Motherwell College may do some of their training at the hotel.

The Falls of Clyde, three of which, Bonnington Linn at NS 883405, Corra Linn at NS 883413 and Dundaff Linn at NS 881422, are within a distance of 1½ miles (2½ km.) upstream from New Lanark, have been a famous scenic attraction for more than 200 years. The fourth, Stonebyres Linn at NS 853440, is about 2 miles (3½ km.) downstream and will be described in Chapter 6. They were visited by among others Thomas Pennant, Sir Walter Scott, Robert Southey, Samuel Taylor Coleridge, William Wordsworth and his sister Dorothy, and by the artists Jacob More, who made a particularly fine painting of Corra Linn in 1771, and the famous

J. M. W. Turner, who executed a watercolour of Corra Linn in 1801 and an impressionistic oil painting, 'The Falls of Clyde', sometime between 1835 and 1840. (The word *linn*, incidentally, is derived from the Gaelic word *linne* meaning a pool and so, when applied to a waterfall, strictly means the pool at the bottom of the fall.) Although none of these falls has a height anything like that of the highest falls in Scotland, the volume of water flowing over them is the fifth greatest. The discharge of the falls, varying from about 175 cu. ft (5 cu. m.) per second to about 17,645 cu. ft (500 cu. m.) per second, has a mean discharge of about 880 cu. ft (25 cu. m.) per second. On the other hand the highest waterfall in Scotland, Eas Coul Aluin in Sutherland with a height of about 656 ft (200 m.), which is about seven times that of Corra Linn, has a mean discharge of only 9 cu. ft (0.25 cu. m.). (The falls with the biggest discharge in Great Britain is the Campsie Linn Falls on the Tay near Stanley with a mean discharge of 5470 cu. ft (155 cu. m.) per second but with a height of only 6.5 ft (2m.).) Since 1927, when the Clyde Valley Electrical Power Company harnessed Bonnington Linn and Corra Linn, the falls are far less impressive than they were previously, although after a spell of wet weather they are still worth seeing. On five days of each year that coincide with local holidays the water to the power station is turned off and the falls can be viewed in their full glory. Since the generators were replaced in 1971, the power generated has been 11 megawatts. This is seen to be a relatively small output when it is realised that, for example, the electrical power used by the University of Glasgow peaks at 6 megawatts.

From New Lanark the final section of the projected 40-mile (64 km.) long Clyde Walkway, which when completed will go all the way from Glasgow to the Falls of Clyde, leads through a gorge of the river to Bonnington Linn, the furthest away of the three falls. The path, in good condition and with safety barriers erected at viewing points high above the river, goes through the Falls of Clyde Nature Reserve, looked after by the Scottish Wildlife Trust. The upgrading of an already existing track was paid for jointly by Clydesdale District Council, Strathclyde Regional Council, the Countryside Commission for Scotland, the Scottish Wildlife Trust and the European Regional Development Fund.

After passing Dundaff Linn, the path leads to Bonnington Power Station and then climbs up high above the river to give excellent views of Corra Linn. In 1708 Sir James Carmichael of Bonnington built a pavilion containing mirrors arranged in such a way that anyone inside it was led to think that the waters of the falls were falling on to him. The remains of this pavilion can be seen high above the path, beside the surge chamber on the pipes leading the water to the power station. In 1829 Lady Mary Ross of Bonnington House on the right-hand/east side of the river built a staircase leading down to the linn of the falls. At Corra Linn the river drops about 100 ft (30 m.) in three stages with the whole cascade contained in a superbly beautiful rock amphi-theatre. The old red sandstone cliffs in the gorge below the falls rise to a height of about 130 ft (40 m.) but a softening effect is produced by the very rich foliage of trees, shrubs and ferns all around. Wordsworth was so affected by the calm beauty of the place that he wrote:

> In Cora's glen the calm how deep
> That trees on loftiest hill
> Like statues stand, or things asleep
> All motionless and still.

Dorothy Wordsworth wrote in her *Recollections of a tour made in Scotland*: 'The majesty and strength of the water, for I had never before seen so large a cataract, struck me with astonishment which died, giving place to more delightful feelings'.

About ¾ mile (1 km.) above Corra Linn is Bonnington Linn which, when the river is in spate, is the widest of the Falls of Clyde. The flow, which is divided in two by a rocky islet, has a drop of about 33 ft (10 m.). The gorge below the falls, like the one below Corra Linn, is very impressive, the old red sandstone walls rising to 80 to 100 ft (25 to 30 m.) in height and the river at one point flowing along a channel only 16 ft (5 m.) wide. A weir, over which pedestrians can cross, has been built across the river at the intake for the power station just above the falls. The weir is a tilting one and maintains a constant flow of water to the power station; any excess of water flows over the weir.

Instead of returning to New Lanark in the reverse direction, walkers can cross the weir and proceed through the Corehouse

3.4. Bonnington Linn.

estate on the left/west side of the river to Kirkfieldbank and then back to Lanark. By a long tradition walkers were allowed to walk through the estate but this privilege was formalised in 1970 when, at the instigation of the late Lieutenant-Colonel Alastair Cranstoun, the owner of the estate at the time, the original Scottish Wildlife Trust Reserve based around Corehouse was set up.

The Falls of Clyde Nature Reserve, which stretches along both sides of the river for about 2 miles (3 km.) and covers an area of about 175 acres (71 hectares) is a place of exceptional interest. The Visitor Centre, opened in 1984 in the old Dyeworks at New Lanark, was completely refurbished in 1995 and, being open all year round and with a Ranger service, is very popular with lovers of nature of all kinds; it has about 50,000 visitors each year. It provides interesting and useful information, very clearly set out, on every aspect of the gorge. It is also the starting point of a nature trail.

The birds that breed in the Reserve and are not migrants include mallards, kestrels, jackdaws, wood pigeons, dippers and four species of tit; the gorge is thought to be the only regular breeding place in Scotland of willow tits. Kingfishers reside in the gorge but do not breed there. Summer visitors include cuckoos, swallows, house martins, swifts and oyster catchers. Snipes and golden plovers can be seen in winter.

Among the animals are grey squirrels, badgers, foxes, mink and roe deer. Badger watches, arranged on a regular basis, have been very successful.

Prominent among the trees in the Reserve are alders along the water's edge, ash, birch, oak and wych elm. In the 1940s and 1950s much of the native woodland was felled and replaced for commercial reasons by conifers. However, since 1980 these conifers are being cut down to enable the woodland to return to its natural state. There are some fine Douglas firs on the Corehouse estate. In spring and early summer much of the woodland is covered with anemones, bluebells, celandine and violets, a delight to behold.

Perched on the top of a cliff above Corra Linn and on the Corehouse side of the river stands Corra Castle, an ancient keep now in ruins and in a dangerous condition. *Corra* is from the Cumbric word *corrach* or *currach* meaning a marshy plain. Corehouse is the anglicised plural of *corrach*. Corra Castle was the home of the Bannatyne family for hundreds of years. The Register of the Great Seal of Scotland has the entries 'Johannes de Bennachtyn de la Corrokys' (1362), 'Richard Bannachtyn dominus de Corhouse' (1459) and 'John Bannatyne of Corhous' (1662). A romantic story is linked to Corra Castle. James Somerville of Cambusnethan decided against his father's wishes to join the army of Charles II, who in 1651 was preparing to advance into England. However, before leaving home he went to Corra Castle to say goodbye to Martha Bannatyne, a young lady of exceptional charm, who was deeply in love with him. After he arrived at the Castle, Martha, determined to prevent James from going to fight, arranged that the drawbridge over the moat on the only accessible side of the castle could not be lowered to let him out. James was happy to stay beside Martha and by doing so probably saved his life, as most of those who went with Charles were annihilated by Cromwell at Worcester. Whether or not these details are correct, the marriage of James and Martha took place on 15th November, 1651 in the church at Lesmahagow and was followed by a great feast by the Clyde that lasted for five days. Present were one marquis, three earls, two lords, sixteen baronets and

3.5. The River Clyde and Corra Castle.

eight ministers. It was the noise and power of the water immediately below Corra Castle that impelled Wordsworth to write:

> Lord of the Vale! Astounding flood
> The fullest leaf in this thick wood
> Quakes – conscious of thy power:
> The caves reply with hollow moan;
> And vibrates to its central stone
> Yon time-cemented tower.

A short distance from Corra Castle stands Corehouse, one of
the few large nineteenth-century mansion houses in Upper
Clydesdale still in use as a private residence. The house was built
in 1827 by George C. Cranstoun, who became Dean of the Faculty
of Advocates in 1823 and a Senator of the College of Justice with
the title Lord Corehouse in 1826. He was an eminent Greek
scholar and an intimate friend of Sir Walter Scott. He died in
1850, having retired early because of paralysis that struck him in
1839. Corehouse, which includes stones taken from the old Corra
Castle, is the only remaining house in Scotland designed by the
architect Edward Blore (1787–1879), who became famous for his
work on Windsor Castle and Hampton Court Palace, and for
his completion of Buckingham Palace, whose building had been
begun by John Nash (1752–1835). The policies, which include a
riverside road from Kirkfieldbank, now overgrown in places, were
planned by a half-brother of Sir Edwin Landseer. R.A., the famous
artist. Blore, it may be remarked, was also a friend of Sir Walter
Scott, who asked him to submit a design for Abbotsford. However, Scott rejected Blore's submission because (according to oral
tradition) he preferred small cosy rooms and secret passages to
the large rooms and open staircases proposed by Blore. The final
plan of Abbotsford, based on Blore's, was prepared by William
Atkinson. In 1983 Corehouse was in such a poor, even dangerous,
condition, that Lt. Col. and Mrs. Cranstoun engaged William
Cadell to carry out a complete restoration. The work took four
years to complete and was given financial support by Historic
Scotland. The house is open to the public during August of each
year.

Finally, some lines from a poem, 'The Clyde', by the nineteenth-
century poet John Wilson, a native of Lesmahagow:–

Where ancient Corehouse hangs above the stream
And far beneath the tumbling surges gleam,
Engulphed in crags, the fretting river raves,
Chaffed into foam resound his tortured waves.
With giddy heads we view the dreadful deep
And cattle snort and tremble at the steep,
Where down at once the foaming waters pour
And tottering rocks repel the deafening roar.
Viewed from below, it seems from heaven they fell!
Seen from above they seem to sink in hell!
But when the deluge pours from every hill
And Clyde's wide bed ten thousand torrents fill
His rage the murmuring mountain streams augment
Redoubled rage in rocks so closely pent.
Then shattered woods with ragged roots uptorn
And herds and harvests down the waves are borne;
Huge stones heaved upwards through the boiling deep,
And rocks enormous thundering down the steep,
In swift descent, fixed rocks encountering, roar,
Crash, as from slings discharged, and shake the shore.

– may be quoted.

3.6. Corehouse.

4
Lanark to Carluke

The A73, which along its northerly direction from Lanark leads to Carluke and beyond, is part of the turnpike road from Falkirk to Carlisle that Thomas Telford was commissioned to design and construct in 1820.

When coaches were introduced into Scotland in the early seventeenth century, the old tracks, described by travellers as being infamous and execrable and having ruts of liquid mud and stony channels worse than the bed of a stream, had to be replaced by something better. In 1617 the Scottish Parliament enacted that the Justices of the Peace be responsible for 'mending all highways' but, as the Act proved to be ineffective, another Act introducing the idea of statute labour was passed in 1669. It laid down that every man between the ages of 15 and 70 had to work for six days in each year on the roads, which had now to be 20 ft (6 m.) wide. Again the Act did not work in practice and its failure led to the introduction of the turnpike system from about 1713 onwards. A turnpike road was administered in sections by a trust or group of private individuals, which paid for the construction and maintenance of the road and recouped its expenditure by collecting tolls at tollhouses operating tollbars or turnpikes. The collection of tolls ceased in 1878 when the Roads and Bridges (Scotland) Act made the upkeep of roads the responsibility of the local authorities. Some of the places where former tollhouses can still be distinctly seen are at Cartland Bridge, Hyndford Bridge and Fallburn road-end at the foot of Tinto.

Thomas Telford, the son of a shepherd, was born at Glendinning in the parish of Westerkirk, Dumfriesshire, in 1757 and began his working life as an apprentice to a stonemason in Lochmaben. His most notable works, all of which displayed good taste, included the building of the suspension bridge over the Menai Strait to Anglesey and in Scotland the construction of the Caledonian Canal (1803–1823), the reconstruction of the Crinan

65

Canal in 1817 and the building of about 1000 miles of road with 17 major and about 1100 minor bridges. The bridge across the Tay at Dunkeld, the Dean Bridge in Edinburgh and Cartland Bridge in Lanark, the last of which gave him particular pleasure and satisfaction, are among his masterpieces. His friend Robert Southey, the poet, aptly nicknamed him *Pontifex Maximus.* Telford also improved 15 harbours on the east coast of Scotland, including those at Aberdeen, Dundee, Peterhead and Wick and, at the Government's request, designed 32 churches and 43 manses to enable the Church of Scotland ministry to be extended to outlying parts of geographically large parishes. In 1816 he designed and built the Mound, a great earthen embankment with big wooden valves across the mouth of Loch Fleet north of Dornoch in Sutherland as a barrier preventing the sea from sweeping up the valley of the River Fleet, thus enabling a large area of land to be cultivated. Telford died in 1834 and was buried in Westminster Abbey.

As the A73 proceeds northwards from the town of Lanark it descends steadily to Cartland Bridge about a mile (1½ km.) from Lanark railway station. A short distance before reaching the bridge it passes on the right the entrance to Cartland Bridge Hotel, which was originally Baronald House, a late Victorian mansion of great magnificence. For some time a home for inebriates, it was opened as a hotel in 1962. The lands of Baronald belonged in earlier times to a branch of the famous Lockhart family, ubiquitous for centuries in this part of Scotland. It was a William Lockhart of Baronald who contributed the article on Lanark in the (First) Statistical Account of Scotland compiled by Sir John Sinclair of Ulbster in the 1790s and describing the country parish by parish. It is an invaluable work of reference.

Cartland Bridge over a most spectacular gorge worn out by the Mouse Water, designed by Telford, was built in 1822 by John Gibb of Aberdeen, who later became famous for his building of docks in London. With three graceful arches spanning the ravine and with the top of the parapet 129 ft (39 m.) above the bed of the river, the bridge is the highest road bridge of its kind in Scotland. The old red sandstone crags in the gorge rise to a height of about 200 ft (61 m.).

At the west end of Cartland Bridge two roads branch off to

4.1. Cartland Bridge.

the left. One goes down one of the steepest braes in Lanarkshire – referred to colloquially as the Mouse 'peth' – passing the entrance lodge to the Sunnyside estate and then what remains of Mouse Mill, built in 1795. The inhabitants of Lanark and of Nemphlar were obliged to have their grain ground at Mouse Mill. The road, which joins the A72 at Kirkfieldbank Bridge, gives an excellent view of the three arches of Cartland Bridge and of an old bridge across the Mouse, built in 1649 but erroneously referred to as a Roman bridge.

The other road leaving the A73 at the west end of Cartland Bridge is West Nemphlar Road, which reaches the village of Nemphlar at NS 856449 after 1 km. or so. From this point Nemphlar Moor Road proceeds for about 3 km. (2 miles) until it joins the B7056 from Braidwood to Crossford. This quiet road is a delightful one to walk along. The view over the Clyde Valley during the descent from Nemphlar is magnificent.

At one time Nemphlar was a weaving community with more than 100 handloom weavers in it in the 1850s. The industry declined and by the late nineteenth century the neighbouring Lee estate had become the main source of employment in the

4.2. 'Roman' bridge.

area. The school population in 1906 was 46 but gradually declined until the school was closed in 1966.

In medieval times Nemphlar had its chapel, brought to mind by the sites Chapel Knowe and My Lady's Well on West Nemphlar Road. There was also an association with Knights Templars about whom a few remarks should be made. After Asia Minor had been captured from the Romans by the Turks, who were Mohammedans, in 1071 and Jerusalem occupied in 1076, the Christians there were persecuted badly. The Christians in Western Europe therefore raised military expeditions to the Holy Land with the object of winning it back into Christendom. There were eight such Crusades, the first beginning in 1095 and the last in 1270. In particular, a military monastic order, known as the Knights of the Temple whose members were known as Knights Templar, was formed in 1118 to patrol and guard the route along which pilgrims travelled from the sea coast to the Temple in Jerusalem. The Templars, who came from all parts of Christendom, had one of their greatest centres in London in what is now known as Temple Church. Within this church (on the Strand) there are marble effigies of nine Templars lying as if asleep and with crossed ankles, knees or thighs according to whether they had served in one, two or three crusades. The order, which was wealthy and independent of all higher authority except that of the Pope, was dissolved by Pope Clement V in 1312.

A private house in Nemphlar has evolved after considerable modification from what was once a *bastle house*, i.e. a fortified farm house of two storeys with the animals housed on the ground floor and the humans above. The name is of the same origin as the French word *bastille* meaning a strong place. Bastle houses were built at a time when there was a great deal of raiding and plundering, especially in the Borders. The house in Nemphlar in which a stone removed from a fireplace bears the date 1607 is one of the most northerly bastle houses at present known. Occupied houses of this type can be seen today in the Dolomites where they are known in the local dialect as *basel* houses.

After crossing Cartland Bridge the A73 steadily climbs in a tortuous manner for about a mile (1½ km.) or so until it levels out at its junction on the right/east with Cartland Moor Road, which leads to the small agricultural hamlet of Cartland. Across the valley Nemphlar can be seen standing amidst farmland at a height of about 600 ft (185 m.). The village can be reached on foot by a right of way that leaves the A 73 a short distance north of Cartland road-end, descends into the valley, crosses a burn and then climbs up steeply to Nemphlar Moor Road.

From the same point on the A73 Lee Castle is seen nestling in the valley; an entrance lodge of the castle stands about a mile further along the road. Lee Castle, built for Sir Norman Lockhart between 1834 and 1845 to the design of James Gillespie Graham, incorporates an earlier building erected in 1817 by Sir Charles Macdonald Lockhart. The policies were extended in the latter half of the nineteenth century by Sir Simon Macdonald Lockhart, after whose death in 1919 the castle was for a time occupied by relatives, then rented out and in 1948 sold with some adjoining land to Mr R. B. Dick. It is now owned by Mr E. L. Peter, who has also purchased the barony of Lee.

The barony of Lee was granted originally to William Loccard in 1272. William's son Symon, who was knighted by Robert the Bruce for the distinguished part that he had played in the Wars of Independence, set off in 1330 with Sir James Douglas, generally known as the Black Douglas, and other knights on an expedition to convey the embalmed heart of Bruce to the Holy Land, absolution for the extraction of the heart from the body having been given by a papal bull. Douglas carried the heart in an enamelled silver casket hung from his neck and Loccard carried its key. Bruce always regretted that he had not taken part in any crusade against the Saracens and expressed a dying wish that his heart be taken to the Church of the Holy Sepulchre in Jerusalem. However, when the party broke its journey at Seville, Douglas was prevailed upon by King Alfonso to help him in his fight with the Moors to regain the Castle of the Star at Teba, and in doing so he was killed. His body, along with Bruce's heart, was brought back to Scotland by the now disheartened knights. The body was interred in St Bride's Church, Douglas and Bruce's heart taken to Melrose Abbey. (Bruce's body was buried in Dunfermline Abbey, where a lead casket containing it was found in 1819. The skeleton was 6 ft tall and the breast bone had been sawn apart to allow the removal of the heart.) In recognition of Loccard's service the family name was changed to Lockheart, afterwards abbreviated to Lockhart, and a heart within a fetterlock was added to Sir Symon's coat of arms. The motto of the family is *corda serata pando* (I open locked hearts). In 1989 a monument executed by Hew Lorimer to the memory of Douglas was erected at Teba in the presence of many Douglases from overseas. £15,000 towards the cost of the monument was raised by the Earl of Selkirk.

During the fight with the Moors, Loccard captured a Moorish prince or nobleman whose mother (or in some sources his wife) as was the custom at the time, offered a ransom for his release. Loccard insisted that a jewel, which the lady tried to conceal, be part of the ransom. On reluctantly handing it over, the lady informed Loccard of its miraculous powers in curing diseases both of men and of cattle. This jewel is the Lee Penny, well known for the (incorrect) account of it given by Sir Walter Scott in his novel *The Talisman*. The jewel, which is heart-shaped and of a dark red colour, is now set in a groat, a silver fourpenny piece, of Edward IV of England (1461–1483). By means of a ring with a silver chain attached, the jewel could be suspended for a time in a vessel of water the contents of which, when drunk by the sick person or animal, were believed to have a curative effect. The fame of the jewel spread far and wide and a firm belief in

4.3. Lee Castle.

its medicinal value persisted for several centuries. At one time the Church of Scotland exempted the Lee Penny from its strictures against 'cures' of a magical kind. The Lee Penny, having been carefully treasured by successive generations of Lockharts, is now in the possession of Mr Angus (Macdonald) Lockhart, owner and manager of the Lee and Carnwath Estates.

On leaving the Lee Woods and crossing the March Burn at NS 856473 the A73 enters (what was) the Parish of Carluke and at Headspoint Nursery/Café enters the village of Braidwood, an attractive village (except for an unsightly scrapyard for motor vehicles) stretching for about a mile (1½ km.) along the road.

At the bridge over the railway at Braidwood the B7056 crosses the A73 and proceeds downhill in a southwesterly direction to Crossford 4 km. (2½ miles) away. It passes through the tidy little village of Lower Braidwood and at various points gives an excellent view of the other side of the Clyde Valley with Nutberry Hill near the old border between Lanarkshire and Ayrshire in the distance. Braidwood House and its estate lie to the north of the village. At one time the residence of the Clydesmuir family, the house is now a home run by Capability Scotland for adults suffering from cerebral palsy.

Further down the road there stands on the left/east the Tower of Hallbar, a fine example of a medieval tower-house. It is designated as the Tower and Fortalice of Braidwood in the old charters and as the Castle of Braidwood in Blaeu's atlas of 1654. As its name implies, a tower-house is a tall structure in which the main rooms are built on top of each other rather than side by side. From the fourteenth until the beginning of the seventeenth century the tower-house was by far the most popular type of residence for noblemen and landowners both large and small, and struck a balance between the requirements of defence and those of domestic comfort. Unlike a castle it could not stand up to an attack by a well-equipped army but with thick walls, a roof of stone slabs and a barred doorway it could offer adequate resistance to any local skirmishing party. By the early seventeenth century, tower-houses began to be superseded by a new type of residence, the laird's house. The Tower of Hallbar, which may possibly have been built by John de Monfod about 1327 after the barony of Braidwood had been conferred on him by Robert the Bruce, but which is much more likely to date from sometime in the seventeenth century – the dates 1601 and 1666 are carved on a neighbouring building – is square with its five rooms of equal size connected to each other by straight staircases contained within the walls, which have an average thickness of 5 ft 6 inches (1.7 m.). The building is 24 ft 8 inches (7.5 m.) square, is 58 ft (17.7 m.) in height and has a stone roof. The tower was bought from a member of the famous Douglas family (see Chapter 13) by Sir George Lockhart in 1681 and was extensively repaired by Sir Norman Macdonald Lockhart in 1861. It is now in the possession of Mr Angus (Macdonald) Lockhart. It was announced in November, 1997 that the London-based Vivat Trust had been given permission to carry out a restoration of the Tower of Hallbar at a cost of £350,000. The intention is to convert the tower into a 'holiday home' with three bedrooms, a lounge and a kitchen.

It is worth remarking that in 1593 Lord Thirlestane, the Lord High Chancellor of Scotland, who had bought the barony of Braidwood from the Earl of Angus in 1588, obtained a charter from James VI giving Braidwood the status of a regality. It enjoyed this status as long as the Thirlestane family remained in possession.

After passing the Tower of Hallbar the B7056 continues down-hill to cross the Clyde at Crossford, where it meets the A72; the drop in altitude from Braidwood bridge to Crossford is about 500 ft (150 m.).

Continuing northwards from Braidwood, the A73 enters the town of Carluke at Goremire Road.

4.4. Braidwood Loch.

4.5. The Tower of Hallbar.

5

Carluke

The town of Carluke, the largest town in Upper Clydesdale with a population of 12,921 in 1991, stands at a height of 600–700 ft (183–213 m.) above sea level and until 1929 was part of the parish of the same name that sloped down from an altitude of a little over 1,000 ft (305 m.) just above the hamlet of Kilncadzow to the bank of the Clyde opposite Crossford at an altitude of about 200 ft (61 m.). The town is easily recognisable from the air since the whole of it, apart from a few houses, lies on one side of the railway line. It was for this reason that air navigators in training during World War II often flew from the South of England to Carluke, where they turned and went back. The town has expanded greatly through private housing development since the end of World War II and now houses a large number of commuters to industrial Lanarkshire and Glasgow. The cultural life of the town has been greatly enriched by the arrival of these (mostly young) newcomers, and the churches, in particular, have benefited.

The name *Carluke* is puzzling and no agreement about its meaning has been reached amongst reputable Celtic scholars. The first element *car* could come either from the Cumbric (p-Celtic) word *cair*, meaning a *fort* or *strong place*, which occurs in no fewer than 18 Scottish place names south of the Forth-Clyde Valley, or from the Gaelic (*q*-Celtic) word *carn*, meaning a cairn. The origin of the second element *luke* is unknown. The name occurs as *Carneluk* in the Register of the Great Seal of 1315, as *Carluk* in the Exchequer Rolls of Scotland in 1359 and as *Carlouk* in the Register of the Great Seal of 1440.

There is not a great deal of interesting history associated with Carluke. However, Carluke cemetery, the old graveyard now rarely used at the foot of the High Street and with its entrance on Carnwath Road, has some interesting features, despite the absolutely shocking vandalism evident within it. Of the very old church that stood in the older part of the graveyard, all that now remains is a square appendage with the date 1692 on one of its stones and built by the laird of Mauldslie at the time, and the bell-tower 40 ft (12.3 m.) high and dated 1715. Prior to the erection of the steeple, the bell was suspended from a branch of a tree. The church itself was of uncertain age but the parish minister Dr Scott, writing in the (First) Statistical Account of Scotland of 1792, says that 'the Kirk is very old and vestiges of Roman Catholic worship imply that it is pre-Reformation'. The Session minutes of 1650 make it clear that at that time the building was almost in ruins; the Kirk Session was appealing for money for repairs but this was not forthcoming to the extent required. After a visitation by the Presbytery of Lanark in 1799 the church was condemned as 'being old and frail and capable of accommodating only 454 sitters' and the construction of a new building by the heritors was resolved upon. The church was then pulled down and replaced in 1800 by the church in Mount Stewart Street known since 1929 as St Andrew's Church (of Scotland). This church, which is beautifully proportioned, was designed by Henry Bell of *Comet* fame for 2½ guineas and cost £950 to erect. In 1801 the spire, which was of an elegant light design, was struck by lightning; it was replaced in 1820 by what Dr D. R. Rankin, the historian of Carluke, called 'the present incongruous mass'.

There are at present two other Church of Scotland congregations in Carluke. Kirkton on Station Road was founded as a congregation of the Relief Church when, in 1832, certain members of the Parish Church, dissatisfied with the theological and political opinions of their minister, the Rev. (later Dr) John Wylie, seceded. As a result of unions, the Church became Carluke United Presbyterian Church in 1847, Kirkton United Free Church in 1900 and Kirkton Church of Scotland in 1929. St John's Church in Hamilton Street, originally Carluke Free Church, was founded at the time of the Disruption, that ecclesiastical cataclysm of 1843 when 474 ministers of the Church of Scotland out of 1203 seceded and constituted themselves as the Free Church of Scotland. The building in Hamilton Street dates from 1865. In 1900 the name was changed to St John's United Free Church and finally in 1929 to St John's Church of Scotland.

The old church referred to above was the successor of a church

5.1. St Luke's Church, Carluke.

of some kind situated beside the Clyde opposite or nearly opposite the present village of Rosebank and designated *Eglismalesock* (or *Eglismalescok*) in a Kelso charter of 1321; being in the Forest of Mauldslie – a royal demesne – it was popularly known as *Forest Kirk*. It should be noted that in medieval times the word *forest* did not connote an entirely wooded area as it generally does today ('deer forest' being an exception). The word is derived from the medieval Latin words *forestis silva* meaning the wood and treeless moorland outside the fenced-in estate of a castle, a laird's house or a church; many of these pieces of land were designated as royal forests in which the King's right to hunt took precedence over all other activities. Prior to 1321 Forest Kirk belonged to the Chapter of Glasgow Cathedral – the See of Glasgow was founded towards the end of the sixth century by St Kentigern, better known as St Mungo, its first bishop – but in that year Robert I (the Bruce) requested that the Chapter hand the Kirk over to the monks of Kelso in part compensation for the sufferings and losses incurred by them during the Wars of Independence. The monks of Kelso were Tironensians transferred there in 1128 from Selkirk, where they had been established by David I in 1116 or 1117. In 1144 the first of Kelso's daughter-houses

5.2. St Andrew's Church, Carluke.

was established at Lesmahagow, from where the monks exerted their influence in Upper Clydesdale.

If Blind Harry can be believed, it was at Forest Kirk that Wallace, after his success against the English at Biggar, was elected Guardian of Scotland in 1297:

> Syne couth to Braidwode fayr,
> At a counceill thre dayes soiornyt thar;
> At Forest Kirk a metyng ordeend he
> That choset Wallace Scottis wardand to be.

It is uncertain when the church by the Clyde was abandoned, but it is known that the name Forest Kirk was retained by its successor in 1574; in that year 'David Forrest was reader, Forest Kirk alias Carlouck'.

A plaque on the bell-tower in the older part of Carluke church-yard indicates that the cost of the extension of the graveyard and the erection of the wall surrounding it, incurred in 1853, was met by Thomas and James Gibb and James and John Ross, all merchants in Quebec. James Ross in particular is worthy of notice. He was born in Carluke in 1819 and at the age of 13 emigrated to Quebec where, in due course, he became a clerk with his uncle, Thomas Gibb, who had a wholesale and retail grocery business. He prospered so well that, when he died in 1888, the *Quebec Chronicle* could say that he possessed 'the most colossal fortune ever made by one individual in this city'. Besides being a merchant, he had extensive interests in railways, banking, mining, shipbuilding and lumbering. He became a Senator of Canada in 1884. James Ross was extremely generous to charity, and the Ross Bequest for 'the relief and benefit of the Protestant poor, infirm or old of the town and parish of Carluke' still provides a monetary gift to about 200 beneficiaries each Christmas.

The epitaphs on some of the tombstones in the older part of Carluke cemetery are interesting. The detail given is indeed minute. Here is an example:

> Erected by John Brown in memory of Emilia Girdwood his wife, whom he deeply regrets. She died on the 14th December, ten minutes before two o'clock a.m. in the year of our Lord 1842 aged 33 years, 7 months and 6 days. Also James

Brown son of John Brown who died on 18th May, 1843, twenty minutes past two o'clock a.m. aged 10 years 8 months and 20 minutes; also the above John Brown who died on 16th April 1846, 25 minutes past 4 a.m. aged 39 years 9 months 7 days 4 hours and 25 minutes.

Then, on the badly vandalised table-stone over the grave of the Rev. Peter Kid, minister of Carluke from 1672 until 1684, is inscribed the following epitaph in the real Covenanting style:

A faithful, holy pastor here lies hid –
One of a thousand – Mr. Peter Kid;
Firm as a stone, but of a heart contrite,
A wrestling, praying, weeping Israelite.
A powerful preacher, far from ostentation;
A son of thunder and of consolation.
His face, his speech, and humble walk might tell
That he was in the Mount and Peniel.
He was in Patmos, and did far surpass,
In fixed steadfastness, the Rocky Bass.
His love to Christ made his life to be spent
In feeding flocks and kids beside his tent.
His frail flesh could not equal paces keep
With his most willing spirit, but fell asleep.
His soul's in heaven, where it was much before,
His flesh rests here in hopes of future glore.
Passenger! ere thou go, sigh, weep, and pray -
Help, Lord, because the godly do decay.

Near the steeple of the old church there can be seen the vandalised tombstone of Dr D. R. Rankin, the author of *Notices Historical, Statistical and Biographical relating to the Parish of Carluke from 1288 to 1874*, a very scholarly local history printed privately and without the author's name on it in 1874. Born in Carluke in 1805 and qualifying as a medical doctor in 1829, Rankin laboured faithfully in Carluke for more than half a century, not only rendering devoted service to his patients but also acting as their guide, counsellor and friend. He had a great interest in geology, especially in palaeontology, and was a keen collector of fossils, some of which are now housed in the Royal Scottish

Museum in Edinburgh. He was also intensely interested in archaeology and made no fewer than nine contributions to the *Proceedings of the Society of Antiquaries of Scotland*. When anything of archaeological interest was discovered in the parish, he examined it in minute detail and wrote up an account of it with meticulous care. Rankin was highly thought of by some of the leading scientists of his day. The famous T. H. Huxley on one occasion broke his journey to the North at Carstairs, where he spent the night in the Inn with the intention of spending the next day with Rankin but, unfortunately, Huxley's evening meal so upset his stomach that sickness prevented him from going to Carluke. Though eccentric in many ways, Rankin was a man of absolute integrity who expressed his views in no uncertain manner. For example, in his condemnation of smoking, he wrote as follows in an unpublished manuscript:

> The disgusting and wasteful practice of smoking tobacco, for example, is beyond comprehension, since it is known to be unnecessary to health and to conduce in no degree to the welfare of its votaries – while by the indulgence they add not a little to the discomfort of friends and neighbours if not to all with whom they come into contact. The abominable reeky and sickening compound produced by the smoker, so openly and thoughtlessly, he ought in fairness be forced to swallow, or in failing that duty, should be sent to prison or to a place set aside for the purpose, like the leper houses of old.

After Rankin died (of paralysis) in 1882, the Rankin Memorial Library and Town Hall were erected by public subscription. However, as part of the redevelopment of the town around 1980, these buildings along with the adjacent property were demolished and replaced by a supermarket and shops. This complex has been designated *Rankin Gait*; the old word *gait* simply means roadway. A clock on a plinth with a plaque bearing an inscription to the effect that Rankin's life was devoted to the art of healing, the advancement of knowledge and the promotion of sound learning, was erected in his memory. I am sure that he would not have approved of the clock, which is minute in size when compared with the original one on the steeple of the Town Hall.

Having referred to Carluke churchyard, I think it is appropriate to say something about the customs observed at funerals in bygone days. Dr John Wylie, the parish minister from 1818 until 1873, in his article on Carluke in the New Statistical Account of Scotland, published in 1845, describes the customs invariably observed at the funeral of anyone aiming at any degree of re-spectability, but which were dying out at the beginning of his ministry. From the time the mourners gathered at the home of the deceased person for the 'bidding to the burial' at 10 o'clock in the morning they mingled worship with entertainment until the 'lifting' – a word still in use today – at 2 or 3 o'clock in the afternoon when the coffin was removed to the churchyard. The mourners were treated with 'services' interspersed with numerous lengthy prayers and graces. The 'services' were as follows:

1st service: Bread and cheese with ale or porter,
2nd service: A glass of rum with 'burial bread',
3rd service: Pipes already filled with tobacco handed out to
                all around.

The 4th, 5th, 6th and 7th services were of port, sherry, whisky and unspecified wine, respectively, with cake. The 8th service (if it could be called so) was an expression of thanks for the whole proceedings.

For a time in the late 1820s the snatching of recently buried bodies from their graves for sale to anatomists in Glasgow and Edinburgh was quite widespread and caused great indignation throughout the country. The celebrated case of Burke and Hare is well-known. These Irish criminals made their living by selling the bodies of people whom they had suffocated to anatomists for dissection. Burke was hanged but Hare, having turned an informer, escaped punishment. Body-snatching took place in Carluke where, according to oral tradition current in the 1920s, a stonemason called Telfer (or Telford?) Ritchie was deeply in-volved. One of his escapades is something like the following.

Some people in Wishaw were suspicious when they saw a non-local, luxurious-looking horse-drawn cab heading south-wards through the town. Thinking that it was going perhaps to Carluke to collect a body, they decided to ambush it on its way back. When they did this and found some earth on the floor of

5.3. Dr Daniel
Rankin.

the cab, they forced the driver, who was accompanied by a
Glasgow doctor, to turn back towards Carluke. The captors
scoured the roadsides as they went along and soon found a
woman's body in a shallow grave; she had been buried in Carluke
a few days previously. The prisoners were taken to the Crown
Inn (later the Crown Hotel and now a block of flats) in Carluke
and held there while someone went to Lanark to fetch the fiscal.
In the meantime an angry mob had gathered and was trying to
force its way into the inn. To avoid an unpleasant scene, the
fiscal kept the cab waiting at the front door of the inn and
arranged for the prisoners to leave by the back door and be taken
to Lanark on horseback. It would appear that Telfer Ritchie, after
he had helped the two men to exhume the body, had somehow
heard of the suspicions of the Wishaw people and had immediately set out to overtake the cab. When he did so, the two men

hastily reinterred the body in a field close to the road. All three men were charged but the sentences passed on them have not been remembered.

At NS 849508 at the top of Chapel Street and not far from the churchyard stands the High Mill, whose tower, 32 ft (9.8 m.) high and of diameter 27 ft (8.2 m.) at the base, is a well-known landmark. Built in 1797 as a windmill, the mill was powered by steam from sometime in the 1830s until sometime before World War I when steam was replaced by gas. The mill ceased to operate in the 1930s but, fortunately, most of the original machinery was left in place. The High Mill Trust, set up in 1988, hopes to restore the mill to working order as a visitor attraction.

Reference has already been made to the Covenanter, the Rev. Peter Kid. He was only one of many in Carluke who were involved in the struggle against the forces of the Crown in the latter half of the seventeenth century.

At the Battle of Kilsyth on 15th August, 1645, which was Montrose's last and greatest victory and one at which the Covenanters were routed and almost all their foot-soldiers killed or taken prisoner, Mr John Weir, minister of Carluke, along with other ministers from the Presbytery of Lanark, was in attendance on the Covenanters' army to give counsel and spiritual comfort to the soldiers. However, when the ministers realised the danger facing them at Kilsyth, they took fright and, in the words of Dr Rankin, 'sought safety in desertion and flight, not to their several charges in the Church, but inside the walls of Berwick'. (Why they fled to Berwick is not clear.) However, after the defeat of Montrose at Philiphaugh a few months later, they returned to their flocks and immediately began with their Kirk Sessions to take disciplinary action against any who had helped or had been associated with the Royalists in any way! Later, during Cromwell's occupation of the country, the Church was left relatively free and good civil order was enjoyed, but after the Restoration in 1660 much hardship and injustice once again prevailed; in 1662, seven Carluke people, including Sir Daniel Carmichael, the laird of Mauldslie, were fined without either accusation or trial.

The Pentland Rising of 1666 involved many in Carluke. Gavin Hamilton, one of the first ten executed for treason for being present at Rullion Green, was an elder in the Kirk of Carluke in 1645 and remained in office till his execution in Edinburgh on 7th December, 1666. His head, after having been publicly exposed with the heads of three others, was interred in Hamilton churchyard, where a stone marks the spot. Then in the outbreak of 1679, which was suppressed by the King's army at Bothwell Bridge, Walter Lockhart of Kirkton commanded a troop of soldiers, while William Keagow in Kilkeagow was later charged with treason but died in prison in Edinburgh before the day appointed for his trial. In 1683 eight people including Sir Daniel Carmichael of Mauldslie and Walter Lockhart of Kirkton were accused of 'rebellion and other treasonable crimes'. Finally, in 1685, Thomas Young of Carluke and several others were 'hanged at Mauchline on one gibbet without being suffered to pray at their death'.

Carluke became a burgh of barony in 1662 when Charles II granted a charter to Walter Lockhart of Kirkton erecting the lands of Kirkton into a barony and the neighbouring pendicle of Kirkstyle into a free burgh of barony. Kirkton House, part of which dated from 1618, was situated on the south side of what is now Station Road at its junction with the present Victoria Avenue. The noted Major Weir, a seventeenth-century character of whom something will be said later, was born and brought up in Kirkton House. An old tradition, long since died out, asserted that on one occasion King Charles I spent a night in Kirkton House and that the troops and others accompanying him were encamped where the Children's Home and Kirkton Church now stand. The evidence for this tradition is very flimsy and hangs simply on the fact that in the poll-tax list of 1695 – almost 50 years after Charles' death – the land east of Kirkton House was designated *roialdikes* (later written as Royal Dykes). There is much stronger evidence for the story that a band of forlorn Highlanders, retreating from Derby in December, 1745, paid an unwelcome visit to Kirkton House and helped themselves to whatever they wanted. The occupier at this time was the widow of Captain Walter Lockhart who, at the time of his death in 1743, was paymaster of the armed forces in Scotland. The house was demolished and replaced by the present ranch-type house in 1959.

In the poll-tax list of 1695, the name Kirkstyle was replaced by the name Carluke. Since only six families are enumerated in this list, the population at that time must have been very small. By about 1780 there were 33 houses in the High Street, known at the time as the *Worn Way* and the only street in the village. Kirkton Street and Stewart Street were opened in 1823 as part of the new Stirling to Carlisle turnpike road, now the A73; their junction with High Street formed the Cross. At this time the parish school and schoolhouse were situated where the Royal Bank now stands at the Cross, having moved from very inadequate premises about halfway down the left/north side of the Worn Way in 1789. However, objections by parents that their children were exposed to danger from traffic on the new road led to the demolition of the school and the erection of a new one on Wellgreen in 1841. There are now six primary schools in the town, including a Roman Catholic school and one for handicapped children. Carluke High School, in Carnwath Road since 1978 and with 1335 students in September, 1998, is the largest school in Upper Clydesdale and the second largest in South Lanarkshire. Under its rector, Mr Russell Rodger, who retired in 1996, it has grown up into a secondary school of high standing.

5.4. High Mill, Carluke.

In the early nineteenth century, and for many years before, home-weaving was the major industry in Carluke. However, as the Industrial Revolution progressed with hand-labour being replaced by work done by machines, weaving gradually died out. Fortunately, another source of employment sprang up in the mid-1830s when the mining of ironstone was commenced by the Coltness Iron Company at Mayfield on the Milton Lockhart estate in 1835. Then in 1838 the Shotts Iron Company erected blast furnaces for the manufacture of iron at Castlehill (on the A73 about a mile (1.6 km) north of Carluke), using coal from a mine opened there by the Company in the previous year. The limestone required came from Craigenhill about a mile (1.6 km) south of Kilncadzow. The marketing of the iron was greatly facilitated by the opening of the Caledonian Railway in 1848. Unfortunately, the ironstone industry in Carluke began to wane when the demand for haematite rather than ordinary iron ore increased, with the result that the furnaces closed down sometime during the period 1884–1886. Nevertheless, bricks are still being made from the blaes left from former ironstone workings at a brickwork opened at Mayfield in 1947. This brickwork replaced one opened in 1880 at Hallcraig on Jock's Burn and near the present golf course. Eight million bricks from Hallcraig were used in building the railway through Glasgow Central Low Level Station.

Large-scale coalmining continued in the Carluke area until the 1950s, and between the two World Wars was the principal occupation of working men in the town. Coalmining operations on a small scale have been conducted at various places in the district at different times. The earliest known reference to the mining of coal in Carluke is the following petition to the Kirk Session of Carluke Parish Church: '25th August, 1650. The qlk day Claud Hamilton of Garein desired liberty to sett ther water of Coalheugh upon the Sabbath morning, qch was granted because it was ane work of necessity'.

The village of Law owes its existence to the coalmining industry. The placename does not appear on the Ordnance Survey map of 1857–1859, the centre of the community at that time being only a row of workers' dwelling houses known as Brackenhill Row. The village grew along with the industry – at one time there were at least 10 pits producing 2000 tons of coal a day – and was a sizeable community when coalmining died out. Since then it has expanded greatly with much private housing development taking place. The population in 1991 was 3009 (including Law Hospital). The village stands on Law Hill, originally known as the Law of Mauldslie, which rises to an altitude of 663 ft (202m.); a marvellous view can be obtained from there on a clear day.

Reference has been made to the laying of the Caledonian Railway in 1845–1848. It is noteworthy that this led to the establishment of the Roman Catholic community in Carluke. Due to the Famine in Ireland in 1846 many Irishmen came over to work on the construction of the railway and, when the work was completed, settled down in the ironstone and coal industries that had opened up not long before.

Passing on now from industries that have died out, we consider the main present-day sources of employment in the town and surrounding area.

In Clyde Street and not far from the Cross stands the factory, originally known as Clydesdale Preserve Works, of R. & W. Scott Ltd, whose jams, jellies and marmalades have made the town of Carluke known all over the world. It was in 1880 that the two

5.5. The Cross, Carluke, c.1900.

brothers Robert and William Scott, originally stone-masons in Uddingston, set up the factory to preserve the fruit from their small fruit-growing business near Crossford that was surplus to local requirements. The company prospered and by the early twentieth century had established itself as a market leader in jams, jellies and marmalades. However, after World War II the jam industry declined due to the advent of canteens in works and schools which led to families becoming less dependent on bread and jam for their sustenance. The arrival of various fish and chicken spreads for sandwiches also contributed to the disappearance of the 'jeelly piece' of earlier days. Diversification therefore became necessary and so in 1954 the production of cooking chocolate, now known under the trade name *Scotbloc*, was begun. Cooking chocolate, it may be noted, is made from a different fat – hardened palm kernel oil – from the one used for eating chocolate, and can be used over a wider range of temperature than eating chocolate when this is used for cooking purposes. The chocolate side of the business has grown tremendously and the firm is now not only a manufacturer of chocolate for the home-baking market but is also a supplier in bulk to the confectionery and bakery industries. A consequence of the increasingly international aspect of the business was the setting up in 1986 of a partnership with the German company Schwartauer Werke GmbH. This partnership heralded a major enlargement of the factory which began in 1990 and is still going on. About 100 staff and workers are now employed. With the retiral of Mr Kenneth Scott, the last of the Scott family in the firm, in 1995, the firm is now completely owned by the German company and trades under the name Renshaw Scott. The firm for many years now has put considerable effort into the export side of its business. Exporting at one time to more than 50 different countries, it is widely recognised as an inter-national trader in jam, marmalade, chocolate and chocolate products.

With a staff (March 1998) of 1876, comprising 66 doctors, 925 nurses, 380 administrative and clerical staff and 505 others, Law Hospital is the biggest source of employment in the Carluke area. With the advent of World War II in September, 1939, Law Hospital was one of seven new hospitals built to deal primarily with wounded soldiers, civilian casualties and the chronic sick evacuated from areas thought to be vulnerable to air attack. The other hospitals were at Ballochmyle in Ayrshire, Bridge of Earn in Perthshire, Killearn in Dunbartonshire, Peel in Selkirkshire, Raigmore in Inverness and Stracathro in Angus. The site of Law Hospital on 84 acres of land about 2 miles (3 km) northwards along the A73 from Carluke Cross, though bleak and exposed, was chosen because of its isolation from any built-up area, its proximity to Law Junction station (now closed) on the main Glasgow to Carlisle railway line, and the fact that a completely new sewerage system for the area was about to be opened. The first patient, a soldier from Winston Barracks in Lanark, who was suffering from severe abdominal burns, was admitted to the hospital on 25th October, 1940. In due course not only many British and Allied soldiers were admitted but also victims of the Clydebank blitz of 1941, some German prisoners-of-war and elderly chronic sick from the South of England. When the beds were not being fully used in this way, local civilians were admitted; until this time those in the area requiring major surgery were sent to Glasgow, usually to the Royal Infirmary. Then, in 1946, the hospital became a general hospital open to all and in 1948 was incorporated in the National Health Service. Since then it has, of course, been modernised in many ways although its external appearance has hardly altered. A maternity unit was added in 1992 to replace the William Smellie Hospital in Lanark and was appropriately designated the William Smellie Maternity Unit; something like 1500 babies are born in it each year. Since 1994 the hospital has been managed by Law Hospital N.H.S. Trust. The hospital is due to be replaced by a large general hospital, at Netherton in the Motherwell area, but the move is unlikely to take place in the present century.

Since 1956 the Scottish National Blood Transfusion Service has had a centre, popularly known as the 'Blood Bank', located in the grounds of Law Hospital. In the early 1980s the Scottish Antibody Production Unit was split off from the Blood Transfusion Service as a separate agency. The two centres at Law serve a population of about three million in the West of Scotland by distributing blood and blood products to more than 20 hospitals. Something like 150,000 pints of blood are handled annually. When the hospital moves to Netherton, the Blood Bank will probably be moved to Glasgow.

Something must now be said about a few natives of Carluke who have distinguished themselves in one way or another.

Major-General William Roy, founder of the Ordnance Survey, was born on 4th May, 1726 at Miltonhead, Carluke, where his father John Roy was factor to the Hamiltons of Hallcraig, an estate on Jock's Burn and near the present-day golf course. William and his brother James were educated at the parish school in Carluke and at the Grammar School of Lanark. There is no mention of William in the records of Glasgow University but there is mention of James, who matriculated in 1742, was awarded a Forfar bursary and in due course became minister of Prestonpans.

Nothing definite about William's post-school career is recorded until 1746 when he became a young military engineer working as a civilian in Fort Augustus under Lt. Col. David Watson, who was assisting General Wade in his plans to subjugate the Highland clans after the '45 Rebellion; these plans included the opening up of new roads and communications. Since maps at that time were practically non-existent, a map of the Highlands had to be made, and it was in its preparation that Roy made his mark. The map on a scale of 1 inch to 1000 yards was at first confined to the Highlands but later extended to the Lowlands. In Roy's own words, it was 'rather to be considered as a magnificent military sketch than a very accurate map of the country'. Angles were measured but distances were only estimated. The manuscript is in the British Library but photocopies are held by the Universities of Glasgow, Edinburgh and Aberdeen.

Roy's next work was in the South of England where, in anticipation of a French invasion, he made a military survey of Kent and Sussex. In 1755 he ceased to be a civilian (and eventually in 1781 he became a Major-General). In 1759 he served in Germany and took part in the Battle of Minden. Having by then gradually acquired a position of recognised eminence as a surveyor, he was appointed in 1765 to the newly established post of Surveyor-General of the Coasts and Engineer for making and directing military surveys of Great Britain. It was around this time that Roy conceived the idea of a national survey. A memorandum written by him in 1766 and now in the Royal archives in Windsor Castle urged the making of 'a General Military map of England' which could be executed 'at a modest Expence'. Unfortunately, this idea did not come to fruition until after Roy's death in 1790.

In 1778 Roy published in the *Philosophical Transactions* of the Royal Society, of which he had been elected a Fellow in 1767, a lengthy paper entitled 'Experiments and observations made in Britain in order to obtain a rule for measuring heights with a barometer'. Atmospheric pressure diminishes with altitude and, if the law connecting these two variables is known, a barometer can be used to estimate differences in altitude. The difficulty, of course, is to determine the law, and this is what Roy tried to do in his paper. Apart from the difficulty of thinking out plausible assumptions to be made, all sorts of complications entered into the matter. Roy handled them with meticulous care and with perfect logical precision. For example, he performed experiments on the pressures of various mixtures of air and water-vapour and practically discovered the well-known law of partial pressures formulated by the chemist Dalton in 1803. Roy verified his rule by determining a large number of altitude differences by baro- meter and then comparing his estimates with the correct values obtained trigonometrically. Thus he found that the difference in altitude between a point near Carmichael House and the top of Tinto was 1642.5 ft when measured barometrically and 1645.5 ft when measured trigonometrically.

In 1785 another important paper by Roy was published by the Royal Society and gained him the Society's Copley Medal. When an area has to be surveyed, it is divided up into triangular regions formed by suitable landmarks; then, provided that the length of one side of any one triangle is known, all the other lengths can be determined by simply measuring angles and applying the rules of elementary trigonometry. It is of vital importance to know this one length as accurately as possible, since all the calculated lengths depend on it. Roy measured one such base-line of length 27,404 ft on Hounslow Heath, and of three measurements made, no two differed by more than 3 inches. The work and all the complications involved in it are lucidly described by Roy in his Royal Society paper (95 pages in length). For example, in inves- tigating the effect of temperature changes on the lengths of his measuring rods, Roy devised the method of measuring the coefficient of linear expansion of a metal for long known as the method of Roy and Ramsden.

Roy's last paper, published by the Royal Society in 1790, dealt with the following problem. The South of England had been accurately triangulated using the Hounslow base-line and the same had been done for Northern France by the French authorities, but it was necessary to determine the relationship between the two sets of triangles or, what is essentially the same thing, to find the position of the Paris observatory relative to the Greenwich one. The calculations involved were most laborious and Roy showed himself to be a master of trigonometry both plane and spherical. He even investigated the errors that could be introduced through not allowing for the flattening of the Earth at the Poles. It was while correcting the proofs of this paper at his home in Argyle Street (off Oxford Street) in London that Roy died on June 30th, 1790. Shortly after his death, his planned survey of Great Britain was begun; and the work so assiduously carried out by him formed the basis from which it developed. The Ordnance Survey Department is the direct outcome of Roy's ideas and labours.

Roy had a lifelong interest in Roman remains and, being not only a shrewd and capable observer but also a superb draughtsman, his sketches of remains are trustworthy and of permanent value. His investigations are incorporated in his book *Military Antiquities of the Romans in Britain* which was published posthumously by the Society of Antiquaries in 1793. The value of the book, which is an archaeological classic, resides in its careful plans which preserve for us features of sites that have long since been mutilated by agricultural developments or altogether destroyed.

A monument to Roy's memory, in the form of an Ordnance Survey triangulation pillar with plaque, was unveiled at Miltonhead in 1956 by Major-General J. C. T. Willis, the Director of the Ordance Survey at that time. Although situated off the beaten track, the monument became badly vandalised and had to be rededicated in 1987. The plaque had been removed but, after it was found in a local scrapyard, it was refurbished by The Royal Engineers and re-attached to the pillar.

Kirkton House has already been referred to as the birthplace of Major Thomas Weir whose name is prominent in any historical account of witchcraft in Scotland. A son of Thomas Weir (or Vere) of Stonebyres, he was born in 1599. Witchcraft was prevalent in Scotland in the latter half of the sixteenth century and in the earlier half of the seventeenth and was frowned upon by both Church and State. In order to stamp it out the Scots Parliament passed an Act in 1563 making its practice punishable by death, an enactment in keeping with the teaching of the Old Testament which says in Exodus 22.18, 'Thou shalt not suffer a witch to live'. The number of convictions made over a century has been estimated to have been as high as 80,000, but of these no more than 1300 led to executions. Major Weir, who was Commander of the Edinburgh City Guard in which capacity he escorted James Graham, Marquis of Montrose, to the gallows in 1649, and who was a member of an extremely narrow Presbyterian sect, was highly respected in Edinburgh. Unfortunately, in his old age he suffered from senile dementia and began accusing himself and his sister Grizel of being servants of the Devil. He was eventually charged with incest, adultery and bestiality, witchcraft being implied, and burned at the stake on 11th April, 1670. Grizel was hanged in the Grassmarket on the following day. The house in West Bow occupied by Major Weir and his sister remained uninhabited for more than a century as local residents were convinced that the building was haunted by evil spirits.

It is noteworthy that in more modern times three men from Carluke were awarded the Victoria Cross, two of them in World War I and the other in World War II.

Lance-Corporal William Angus was the first to bring this distinction to the town. When dawn broke on June 12th, 1915 a patrol near Givenchy in France, in which Angus was serving, realised that their officer, Lieut. James Martin, also from Carluke, was lying wounded close to the enemy's position about 70 yards (64 m.) away. Although warned that it could mean certain death, Angus volunteered to save the officer. Crawling on the ground and clearing a path to make the return journey easier, he had just reached the wounded man when the Germans noticed him and started firing and throwing grenades. However, using a rope,

5.6. Unveiling the Roy Monument.

he was able miraculously to drag the officer back to the British line although in the process he lost an eye and sustained 42 other wounds. Lieut. Martin in due course recovered from his wounds. When Angus returned to Carluke on 4th September, 1915, he was given a tumultuous welcome in the Market Square and presented with a clock and a cheque for £1,000 which were handed over by Lord Newlands. He was also presented with a gold watch and chain by the grateful Lieut. Martin. After Angus's death on June 14th 1959, his family presented all his medals including the Victoria Cross to the Scottish United Services Museum in Edinburgh Castle, where they remain as a public tribute to his bravery.

Sergeant Thomas Caldwell won his award almost at the end of the War. On the morning of 31st October, 1918, the platoon of the Royal Scots Fusiliers of which he was a member came under heavy machine-gun fire from a farm near Oudenarde and suffered many casualties. After running over more than 100 yards (92 m.) of open country, Caldwell brought the farm under fire, captured 17 of the enemy and so removed the obstacle to his platoon's movement. Caldwell emigrated to Australia, where he died in 1969.

Lieut. Donald Cameron, R.N. was awarded the Victoria Cross for his leadership in a midget submarine attack on the German battleship *Tirpitz* as she lay moored in a Norwegian fjord on 22nd September, 1943. When the anti-submarine net across the

5.7. Carluke's three VCs.

fjord was opened to allow a coaster to enter, Cameron surfaced, passed through the boom in early light and then submerged again. He then sailed by dead reckoning towards the battleship but, unfortunately, was spotted when he surfaced momentarily. However, he dived again, sailed close to the battleship and set two charges timed to go off an hour later. After destroying his secret equipment, Cameron scuttled his vessel and baled out. He and the other two members of his crew were rescued by the Germans. When the explosion took place at 8.12 a.m. the battleship was lifted five feet out of the water and, although it did not sink, it was rendered useless as a fighting ship for the remainder of the War. It is noteworthy that the German officers and crew, in admiration of the bravery and consummate skill shown by Cameron and his men, treated their prisoners surprisingly well. Cameron died in 1961.

When the new housing scheme in the Crawforddyke area of Carluke was completed, three of the roads were named after Angus, Caldwell and Cameron. A fourth in the same district was named after Sergeant Arthur Ramage, D.C.M., M.M. and Bar, Croix de Guerre and three times mentioned in despatches, whose military career was sufficiently distinguished for him to have been at one time recommended for a Victoria Cross. He was awarded the Military Medal for rescuing several severely wounded soldiers in September, 1915. For a similar rescue in 1916 of an officer under a hail of enemy fire a Bar was added to his M.M. In the same year he gained a Distinguished Conduct Medal for conspicuous gallantry and devotion to duty during the reconnaissance of a farm held by the Germans. Ramage was killed at the 3rd Battle of Ypres on 1st August, 1917.

Another native of Carluke worthy of mention is John Gibson Jarvie (1883–1964), who was the pioneer of hire-purchase in Britain. The second son of John Jarvie, for many years the local veterinary surgeon, he studied art in Glasgow, London and on the Continent before abandoning it in favour of commerce. After being secretary to a prominent financier in the City of London, he went in 1913 to America where he gained wide business experience and saw hire-purchase in operation. On his return to Britain in 1919 he developed a hire-purchase business which, as the United Dominions Trust, became Britain's largest credit finance house. Its high standing was recognised in 1930 when the Bank of England made a substantial capital investment in it. Jarvie remained as its Chairman until his retiral in 1963 when he became President of the Company.

6

'The Orchard Country':
Lanark to Garrion Bridge

After the A72 breaks away from the A73 at Steel's Cross in Lanark it descends in a steep and tortuous way down the famous Kirk-fieldbank Brae to cross the Clyde by a bridge built in 1959 and to enter the village of Kirkfieldbank. This bridge replaced the nearby Clydesholm Bridge designed and built in 1699 under the supervision of John Lochoir (Lochore in modern spelling) using stones from Headsmuir on the Lee estate. The road now enters the 'Orchard Country' which stretches along the valley of the Clyde for about 7 miles (11 km.) to a little beyond Garrion Bridge. The fruit-tree blossom when out in April, May and June is a wonderful sight and attracts many visitors. The road is very tortuous.

It is not known for certain when fruit-growing was introduced into the Clyde Valley. There is no documentary evidence for the oft-quoted assertion, which may of course be true, that the Romans did so in the second century A.D. Although Merlin in the sixth century sang about the orchards of Clyde and the Venerable Bede in the eighth century wrote of the 'appleyards of Lanark', it is likely that fruit-growing on a reasonable scale was first started by the monks of Kelso, who settled in Lesma-hagow in 1144 (see Chapter 14) and who, belonging to the Tironensian order, would have a particular interest in farming and horticulture. For centuries thereafter apples, pears and plums were grown on the slopes of the valley, while on the flatter ground on either side of the river fruits such as raspberries, gooseberries and strawberries were produced in large quantities. Much of this was sent to Glasgow and also to English markets by a special goods train which was filled up every evening during the season in the sidings at Braidwood railway station (no longer in existence) up the hill from Crossford. Raspberries were not cultivated before the fifteenth century; they were regarded as inferior blackberries. Gooseberries came a century or so later, and when strawberries were introduced about 1869 the Golden Age of fruit-growing on Clydeside began. The growing of strawberries became a profitable enterprise and the acreage of land devoted to this rapidly increased. In the early 1920s strawberry plants became the victim of a disease which spread so rapidly that entire fields of them were ruined. Strawberry growing ceased to be profitable and often ended in a complete loss. A soil fungus, not known to occur in any host plant other than the strawberry, attacked the root system and ultimately killed it. The central vascular cylinder, which is normally white, became red and led to the disease becoming known as the Red Core disease. In an attempt to overcome the disease a great deal of research work was carried out from 1930 onwards at the West of Scotland Agricultural College at Auchincruive in Ayrshire under the leadership of Robert D. Reid, a native of Carluke. To breed new varieties of strawberry strongly resistant to Red Core disease was not at all easy and it was 1944 before such new varieties were released. The need was urgent, for by this time the acreage of land under strawberries had been reduced to about a quarter of its one-time peak. The most strongly resistant variety appeared in 1947 with the name Auchincruive Climax. It was initially very successful but after four or five years its resistance began to diminish. It was, however, established by Daniel Carmichael of Roadmeetings, Carluke, that an excess of moisture encouraged Red Core disease, which could therefore be controlled by adequate draining.

Although the climate in the valley is generally milder than that in, say, Carluke town, which has an altitude about 500 ft (152 m.) higher than that of Crossford, the valley can suffer from severe frosts which, if they come after the blossom on the fruit-trees is past, can have a disastrous effect on the crop. The decline in the strawberry industry together with the dependence of the crop of apples, pears and plums on frost-free conditions after the blossom had appeared, led growers to start producing their crops in glass-houses, the chief crop being tomatoes but with lettuces, sweetpeas, late chrysanthemums, carnations and bulbous early spring flowers being cultivated as well. The growing of tomatoes commercially was pioneered in the latter part of the

nineteenth century by Andrew Gilchrist of Lesmahagow, grandfather of the late Sir Andrew Gilchrist, diplomat and novelist,
who in his retirement lived at Arthur's Crag, Hazelbank. His
idea, which was novel at the time, was to grow tomatoes in
greenhouses heated by cheap coal which was plentiful in the
district. A tremendous increase in the acreage of land under glass
came in the 1920s and 1930s when, as I can clearly remember,
the cost of erection of the standard type of glass-house was 30/-,
i.e. £1.50 per foot! When the account of Carluke for the Third
Statistical Account of Scotland was written in 1952, there were
32.7 acres (13.2 ha.) covered by glass in the parish.

The next grievous setback for the growers was the arrival of
foreign competition which by the 1980s had become very serious
indeed and had forced the closure of many orchards and glass-
houses. There are three aspects of the situation. Firstly, because
of advances in technology, tomatoes grown abroad can be chilled
and stored and so made available all through the winter. Secondly,
even in summer and autumn Clyde Valley growers cannot produce fruit in the vast quantities often demanded by the
supermarkets. Thirdly, because of subsidies given by, for example,
the Dutch government, fruit from abroad can be sold cheaply.
The growing of tomatoes in the Valley has therefore been replaced
by the growing of lettuces and leeks and by the provision of
shrubs and bedding plants for the excellent garden centres that
have sprung up all along the Valley and on the A73 at Braidwood.
A good example of the initiative taken by the growers facing
adverse economic conditions was the setting up with some external funding in October, 1992, when the tomato industry was
declining rapidly, of a co-operative known as *Scotland's Tomatoes*.
Six tomato growers abandoned the business rivalry that had
existed between their families for generations and decided to
compete collectively against the Dutch growers and to supply
supermarkets with Scottish tomatoes. In 1993 the group captured
10% of the Scottish market, with sales 23% above target giving
a turnover of £1.7 m. The tomatoes are dearer to buy than the
Dutch ones but are fresher through being on the shelves within
a few hours of being picked. The stronger the intensity of the
aroma from the stalk of a tomato, the shorter the time since
the tomato was picked.

With the object of stimulating the production of tomatoes in the Clyde Valley, *Scotland's Tomatoes* is now funding a three-year research project with the University of Glasgow to investigate the health-giving qualities of tomatoes. Since different varieties of tomatoes contain different levels of flavonoids, anti-oxidants that help to prevent cancer and heart disease, one of the aims of the research is to identify the varieties that are most beneficial. It is also hoped to monitor the effects of different growing conditions, storage and handling.

After crossing the Kirkfieldbank bridge, the A72 turns to the right to go through the western part of the village. Kirkfieldbank, with many beautifully kept gardens, was at one time a weaving village and some of the old weavers' cottages can still be seen. The road to the left/east at the end of the bridge splits at different points and leads to Douglas or to Lesmahagow or to the Corehouse Nature Reserve. To reach the Reserve, fork to the left at NS 870435, continue on past Byretown farm and then along a privately maintained road liberally endowed with potholes to arrive at the West Lodge of Corehouse. An alternative route is to avoid the fork to the left and after climbing up the steep hill to carry on to NS 874411, where a road to the left leads to the West Lodge. On either route a splendid view of the town of Lanark on the opposite side of the Clyde is obtained.

At Linnville at the western end of Kirkfieldbank the B7018 road for Lesmahagow goes off to the left. Anyone in the Valley with time to spare should go along this road, which climbs most of the way, to the point NS 833431, where a National Trust for Scotland notice board indicates a path to Blackhill Viewpoint, and then climb about 130 ft (40 m.) to the viewpoint at NS 832435 at a height of 951 ft (290 m.). The view from here on a clear day is magnificent in every direction and includes Tinto Hill, Goatfell in Arran and Ben Lomond. The line of the Clyde Valley is visible beneath and it is noticeable how steep the sides of the valley are. The remains of a stone-walled Iron Age fort and of a later settlement can be seen on the summit of the hill, the oval-shaped fort measuring about 508 ft (155 m.) by 354 ft (108 m.) with a wall up to 16 ft (5 m.) in thickness and 20in. (0.5 m.) in height in places, and the settlement on sloping ground to the south-east of the fort measuring about 256 ft (78 m.) by

190 ft (58 m.). Within the fort and at the highest point of the
hill there are the grass-covered remains of a round cairn 59 ft
(18 m.) in diameter and 35 in. (0.9 m.) high. An Ordnance Survey
triangulation pillar has been erected on the top of the cairn.

The fruit farm of Linnmill near where the B7018 leaves the
A72 provided the material for the book *Linmill Stories* by Robert
McLellan, published in 1990. The author, who stayed with his
grandparents on their farm between 1912 and 1922, gives in the
local dialect a vivid account of what life in the Valley was like
at that time. The speech in the rural parts of Clydesdale was
then Lowland Scots, clearly articulated and in marked contrast
to the slovenly English so often heard nowadays. Another source
of information about the way of life in the Valley during the
years 1911–1915 is the privately published correspondence of Gavin
Scott of Hillend and latterly of Hallhill to his son George, a
medical officer in Malaysia. The farm of Hallhill, pronounced
locally as Ha'hill, stands at the junction of the B7086 road for
Auchenheath, which leaves the A72 at NS 841443, a point known
locally as 'the Check', and the road, known as 'the Cut', that
climbs up the gorge of the Nethan from Crossford. The correspondence, which deals with all aspects of country and village
life both serious and trivial, was put together in five booklets
and published by Mrs Ruth Richens, daughter of John Scott,
second son of Gavin, under the title *Your loving father Gavin
Scott. Letters from a Lanarkshire farmer.* John Scott, after being
a joiner – he was attracted to this trade by the smell of wood
shavings – went to the University of Glasgow to study for the
ministry of the Church but was deflected into Philosophy by Sir
Henry Jones, Professor of Moral Philosophy in the University,
and ultimately became Professor of Logic and Moral Philosophy
in Cardiff. Also very distinguished was the eldest son, Gavin,
who took second place in the strongly competitive entrance
examination to the Indian Civil Service. The Scott family was
renowned in the district for its academic achievements. Altogether, seven of the family (of 11) graduated at the University
of Glasgow.

At NS 853440 is Stonebyres Linn, the fourth of the Falls of
Clyde as mentioned in Chapter 3. The drop of about 80 ft (24 m.)
into a deep pool takes place in three steps that immediately

follow each other, in this respect unlike Corra Linn. When in spate the river is one tremendous mass of falling water, so much so that Dorothy Wordsworth and other visitors of discrimination have rated Stonebyres more highly than Corra Linn. When the Clyde was sufficiently clean for salmon to come up it – and this condition seems to be returning – the fish could get no further than Stonebyres. If it is true that a salmon has been seen further upstream, it may have reached there through the Biggar Gap where, when flooding is heavy, the waters of the Clyde can merge with those of the Biggar Water, which flows into the Tweed near Broughton. A similar situation can arise at Garvald beyond Dolphinton, where the waters of the Medwin, a tributary of the Clyde, can merge with those of the West Water, which ultimately flows via the Lyne into the Tweed. As at Bonnington and Corra Linn, a hydro-electric power station was erected at Stonebyres in 1927. It generates a power of 6 megawatts.

After passing through the village of Hazelbank with its neat

6.1. The Clyde Valley Country Estate.

and beautifully kept gardens and with old orchards on the rising ground behind it, the A72 approaches the village of Crossford. On the opposite side of the Clyde, and with a suspension footbridge at NS 829460 leading over to it, is the Clyde Valley Country Estate opened in 1989 in a delightful setting on the former Carfin estate. Carfin House, built in the early nineteenth century and known to have been occupied by a family of Nisbets in 1824, belonged to a family of Steels in the 1870s, at which time it was known as Holmhead House. When it was bought by James Noble Graham of port wine fame in 1880, the name 'Carfin' was restored. Graham spent a vast sum of money on the house and the grounds, employed a considerable number of staff both indoor and outdoor – there were six gardeners – and was highly thought of in the neighbourhood. The house, I have been told by old people, was really beautiful. Unfortunately, through no fault of his own but due rather to economic conditions prevailing after World War I, Graham found himself in dire financial straits in 1923. However, he was able to keep the house until his death in Oporto in 1928. Unfortunately, too, Graham lost a son in the war for whom he had extensively renovated the neighbouring Stonebyres House, in bygone days a seat of the Vere family, which he had purchased from Miss Monteith-Scott in 1906. This house was resold to Miss Monteith-Scott in 1924 but, after her death late in 1933, was demolished in 1934 and its grounds broken up into small holdings. From 1935 a tomato-growing concern was run on the Carfin estate by Youngs of Troon. Eventually, in 1957 Carfin house was demolished except for the coach-house and the stable. The renovated stable is now a first-class restaurant while the coach-house has been converted into a number of small shops. What was the walled garden is now a garden centre with a coffee shop. A cast-iron fountain in the form of a stork and dating from Graham's time has been restored. The grounds also include a pony-trekking establishment and a narrow-gauge railway that runs for a short distance along the side of the river. The footbridge across the river already referred to and built in the mid-1880s has also been restored at great expense. Its restoration was awarded a Certificate of Approbation by the Commission for the Restoration of Rural Scotland in 1993, and in the same year the Saltire Society gave the whole restoration project a Saltire Conservation Commendation. There are ample parking facilities on the estate and on the A72 side of the suspension bridge.

The road bridge over the Clyde at Crossford dates from 1793 and replaced a ford a short distance downstream. The village, of course, takes its name from this ford. With the decline in the fruit-growing industry, most of the residents, as in the other villages in the Valley, commute to work elsewhere. The population in 1991 was 591.

As regards the Church in Crossford, congregations of the United Secession Church and of the Free Church were set up in 1832 and in 1870, respectively. In 1847 the former became Crossford United Presbyterian Church and then in 1900, when the union of the Free and the U.P. Churches to form the United Free Church took place, Crossford had two U.F. Churches. After much strife and bitterness they joined together in 1917 as Crossford U.F. Church. Finally, by the Union of 1929 the congregation entered the Church of Scotland.

The building used, that of the former Free Church, was extensively renovated in 1950 in accordance with plans prepared by Basil Spence, famous for his design of Coventry Cathedral. A new pulpit was erected and a pipe organ installed. The organ was given by the 1st Lord Clydesmuir, who also paid the architect's fees. On the day when the church was re-opened, Lord Clydemuir played the organ and Basil Spence read a lesson.

At NS 823471 at the northern end of the village, the A72 crosses the Nethan, a tributary of the Clyde, which rises on Nutberry Hill near the former county boundary between Ayrshire and Lanarkshire, flows through Lesmahagow, passes Craignethan Castle and after tumbling through a heavily eroded gorge enters the Clyde at NS 826472. The large house clearly visible on the opposite side of the Clyde is Orchard House Nursing Home. The house was built early in the nineteenth century and was added to in Victorian times. It became a nursing home in 1988. The gorge of the Nethan is of considerable scientific interest and, as the Nethan Gorge Reserve, is looked after by the Scottish Wildlife Trust. The footpath up through the gorge leaves the A72 on the north side of the bridge and leads to Craignethan Castle; the walk takes 30–40 minutes. The road ('the Cut') on the south

6.2. Craignethan Castle.

side of the Nethan climbs steeply up through the gorge, gives a beautiful view of the Clyde Valley and leads to Kirkmuirhill and the M74. After this road levels out, a road going off to the right/west leads to Craignethan Castle, whose fabric was carefully restored in the 1950s and 1960s to give a building of exceptional interest and merit.

The castle was built about 1532 as a tower-house by Sir James Hamilton of Finnart, an illegitimate son of James Hamilton, 1st Earl of Arran. Sir James, for many years a firm friend of James V, who appointed him superintendent of the royal properties, was responsible for enlargements to the palaces of Falkland and Linlithgow and for improvements to the palace of Holyroodhouse and the castles of Edinburgh, Stirling and Rothesay. From the fourteenth to the sixteenth centuries tower-houses were regarded as the appropriate residences for noblemen and landowners both large and small. In this case the tower-house is of unusual proportions, 52 ft (16 m.) in the north to south direction, 69.6 ft (21.2 m.) in the east to west direction and rising to a height of 34.8 ft (10.6 m.) above the bottom of the parapet. It stands in a rectangular close – *close* is the old word for a courtyard – of dimensions 163 ft by 90 ft (49.7 m. by 27.4 m.) and is surrounded by a defensive system with towers, the one at the south-east corner being the best preserved. Standing on a spur of land, bounded on the north by the Craignethan Burn and on the east and south by the Nethan, and with the ground falling very steeply to the water, the castle was naturally inaccessible except from the west. To overcome this deficiency a massive rampart 16 ft (4.9 m.) thick and rising vertically to a height now unknown from a great ditch about 32 ft (10 m.) wide was built across the neck of the spur. On the outer/western side of the ditch there was a vertical wall. At a date not later than 1579 and during the ownership of the 2nd Earl of Arran, a half-brother of Sir James, a large outer courtyard was built on the west side of the ditch with a low wall on the north, west and south sides and with towers at the north-west and south-west corners. Although the courtyard could be protected by gunfire from gunloops arranged along the walls and on the towers, it could only contend with minor attacks and, unlike the tower, could not withstand a real siege, in which event the courtyard could be quickly abandoned.

In 1540 Sir James Hamilton was accused of having plotted against the life of James V in 1528 and, after his trial and execution for treason, his possessions including Craignethan Castle were forfeited to the Crown. A few years later James Hamilton, 2nd Earl of Arran, obtained possession of Craignethan. He was appointed Regent of Scotland on the death of James V in 1542, was created Duke of Chatelherault in France in 1549 and was altogether a man of great influence and power; indeed, from 1536 until his death in 1575 he was heir presumptive to the Scottish throne. The fortunes of the powerful Hamilton family in the middle years of the sixteenth century need not be recounted here; the relevant parts are succinctly related in the excellent HMSO booklet on Craignethan Castle, which should also be consulted for details of the building. Suffice it to say, however, that, because of the support given by the Hamiltons to Mary, Queen of Scots, the demolition of their castles was ordered by the Privy Council in 1579. At Craignethan the great rampart was knocked down into the ditch and the north front ruined. The south front and the corner towers of the outer courtyard were, however, spared.

In 1659 Anne, Duchess of Hamilton sold the ruins to Andrew

Hay, who built a new home for himself in the outer courtyard using stones from the original buildings. Then, sometime around 1730 the property was sold to Archibald, the 1st (and last) Duke of Douglas. Decay of the older part continued until the beginning of the nineteenth century when, recognising the architectural and historical importance of the ruins, the 12th Earl of Home repaired them. In 1949, his descendant, the 14th Earl of Home, the late Lord Home of the Hirsel, handed over the ruins to the Secretary of State for Scotland to be held in trust for the nation. The mammoth task of consolidating the fabric, which began soon afterwards, led in 1962 to the unearthing of a caponier which had lain buried in the ditch under the rubble that came from the demolition of the great rampart. The caponier was a stone-roofed gallery built between the two walls of the ditch and with loopholes through which gunners could shoot at any attacker trying to cross the ditch. It was entered from the south-west tower. The idea of a caponier is Italian in origin, the name itself coming from the Italian word *capannata*, meaning a small hut. The caponier at Craignethan is the only one surviving in Britain.

In the nineteenth century Craignethan Castle became famous because of the belief that it was the Tillietudlem Castle of Sir Walter Scott's *Old Mortality*. Scott was certainly very impressed with the castle though he denied the assertion that he was at one time interested in the idea of making it a residence for himself. The fictional name 'Tillietudlem' became so strongly associated with the castle and the area around it that the halt on the Caledonian Railway Company's branch line from Ferniegair to Brocketsbrae – closed in 1951 – and the hamlet around it both adopted the name.

The A72 after crossing the Nethan at Crossford runs for fully a mile (1.6 km.) at a distance of about 500 yards (457 m.) from the Clyde with very rich land in between. As it passes the large garden centre at Sandyholm where at times customers can be seen picking their own fruit, it leaves the former Clydesdale District and enters the former Hamilton District. On sloping ground on the other side of the Clyde there can be seen the mansion house of Waygateshaw with its tower dating from the sixteenth century and set in 27 acres (11 ha.) of ground. Major Weir, referred to in Chapter 5, was associated with this house.

The estate was owned by the Lockhart family from 1539 or earlier until 1720.

An avenue leaving the A72 at NS 811488 was the principal approach to the mansion house of Milton Lockhart, now demolished, and crosses the Clyde by a magnificent bridge with ribbed arches like those of the old Bothwell Bridge. At the north end of the bridge are a gatehouse and watch towers on which there is some beautifully carved ropework; these are now listed buildings. The view of the river from the bridge is a fine one, enhanced by Clyde's Mill Fall just upstream, where the broad river sweeps over broken rocks in a fine rapid. Milton Lockhart, standing on a beautiful site overlooking the river chosen by Sir Walter Scott, was built in 1829 for William Lockhart, a half-brother of John Gibson Lockhart, son-in-law and biographer of Scott, and distantly related to the Lockharts of Lee. The house, designed by the architect Burn of Edinburgh, was considered to be one of his best. After standing empty for many years and steadily deteriorating, the house was bought by a Japanese businessman in 1987 and dismantled stone by stone for re-erection at Hokkaido in Japan as a tourist attraction. The stones were later sold to a company concerned with quarrying and the house

6.3. Milton Lockhart Bridge.

rebuilt with certain modifications near Tokyo with the name Lockheart Castle. As well as being the firm's headquarters, it is part of an exhibition centre relating to stones and stonework.

William Lockhart, who built the house, was a generous, unostentatious and truly good man. Although he is long since dead, it is right to say a little about him – and likewise, a little later, about the two Lords Newlands of Mauldslie – for his beneficence is still (unknowingly) being enjoyed by a large number of people. At the time of his death in 1856 he had been M.P. for Lanark for 16 years and was Dean of Faculties of the University of Glasgow, an appointment which at that time was not an honorary one as it is now. In 1835 he agreed to the mining of ironstone on his estate (in the parish of Carluke) on generous terms, a gesture that led to works for the manufacture of iron being set up in the district and which, in turn, led to the Caledonian Railway passing through Carluke. It was after the death in 1922 of the widow of William Lockhart's nephew Major-General David Blair Lockhart that the house and estate began to decline.

When Sir Walter Scott came in 1829 to help choose the site of Milton Lockhart, he made the acquaintance of John Greenshields, who lived in a small thatched cottage known as Willans standing by the side of the Clyde almost opposite the site actually chosen, and who was a sculptor of growing repute. Greenshields was born in Lesmahagow in 1794 but spent the whole of his life from infancy at Willans. He began his working life as a stonemason but very soon became engaged in his spare time in making small works of art such as greyhounds and lions for ornaments on gateways. In 1827 he completed a statue of Lord Byron the comments on which by Flaxman, a sculptor of recognised eminence in London (and designer of a bronze statue of Sir John Moore which was erected in George Square, Glasgow in 1819), so encouraged Greenshields that he decided there and then to devote his life to art. There followed statues of George Canning, of the Duke of York and of George IV, which were also very favourably commented upon when exhibited.

When he met Scott in 1829, Greenshields was thinking of making a group-statue of the eight characters in the *Jolly Beggars*, a cantata of love and liberty by Robert Burns, inspired by beggars and vagrants who frequented a tavern run by Agnes Gibson (Poosie Nancie). When Scott expressed the opinion that the subject was grotesque and unsuitable for statuary, Greenshields said 'Ah, but you're wrang there, Sir Walter, an' if we baith live twa or three month, ye'll be on my side. Fitness, Sir, Lo'd bless ye, the picture's matchless'. Greenshields clearly had a mind of his own and, as he said to someone at the time, 'Sir Walter is the foremost of story-tellers as all the world knows and might, if he liked, have been a capital hand at the chisel, but he has evidently looked at the delineations of Burns, in this instance, from a wrong point'. In due course the group of figures was completed and conveyed to Edinburgh, where it was admired by many, including Scott, who sent a message to Greenshields to say how astonished and delighted he was. 'Tell John', he said to Greenshields' brother, 'that he has taught me to read Burns in my old age. Say to him that the group is faultless'.

After Scott's death in 1832 Greenshields made from memory a statue of him sitting in the library in Milton Lockhart. J. G. Lockhart who, in his biography of Scott, describes the statue as a most meritorious work, made the suggestion, which was accepted, that it be labelled *sic sedebat*. The statue now stands in Parliament Hall in Parliament House in Edinburgh.

Other well-known works by Greenshields are a statue of Sir John Sinclair of Ulbster, a great agriculturalist famous for organising the production of the (First) Statistical Account of Scotland, which was erected in Thurso in 1832, a statue of James Watt with his arm resting on the cylinder of a steam engine made in 1833 and now in the University of Strathclyde, and a statue of Sir Walter Scott now standing on the top of a high pedestal in George Square in Glasgow. Greenshields agreed rather reluctantly to design this statue, which was made from Greenshields' model after his death by Mr. Handyside Ritchie of Musselburgh. A stucco statuette of Sir John Sinclair made by Greenshields in 1832 was presented to the Royal Society of Edinburgh in 1875 by D. R. Rankin, the historian of Carluke and a close friend of Greenshields.

One of the last pieces of work executed by Greenshields is the statue on the top of the monument at Glenfinnan, where the Jacobite standard was raised in 1745. In 1834 Greenshields was commissioned by Angus Macdonald of Glenaladale to execute a statue of Prince Charles for erection on the monument which, incidentally, was the tower of a shooting-box that remained after the building was demolished. Greenshields was given very little detailed information about the appearance and dress of the Prince but, knowing that there was an oil painting of the Prince hanging in the library of Lee Castle, the home of the Lockhart family in the neighbouring parish of Lanark, he went to Lee one day to examine the portrait. Unfortunately, on the day of his visit none of the family was at home, but the housekeeper took him into the library where, despite the fact that the position of the painting had been previously indicated to him by some informed person, probably D. R. Rankin, his eye fixed on a fine painting of George Lockhart, a Jacobite who had fought in the '45, which was hanging next to that of the Prince. Convinced that this was the painting for which he was looking, he studied it in detail and in due course faithfully reproduced its features on his model for the statue. When the error was eventually pointed out to him by the well-informed friend already referred to, Greenshields, who was normally very particular about accuracy, was defiant and declared firmly, 'Well, be as it may, I shall stand by that model; it is a thousand times more fit than the Prince in pantaloons'. In the actual painting of the Prince, he was portrayed as a light, handsome figure, armed and in tights, jacket, plaid and glengarry, all in tartan. Lockhart, however, was depicted in his painting as armed but wearing a short velvet tunic, tastefully scalloped and filled in with silk between the shoulders and elbows, a velvet cap and a kilt. These features of Lockhart's attire are clearly visible in the statue as it is today. The statue is 8 ft (2.5 m.) in height. In most older books it was either stated or implied that the statue was of the Prince but, after the story just related came to light, someone invented the notion that since the monument was in memory of the men who fell in the '45, it follows that the statue is one of a typical Highlander and not of the Prince.

Greenshields died in 1835 at the age of 40. Since he had risen to prominence within seven or eight years, there can be little doubt that had he lived longer he would have become preeminent indeed.

A short distance beyond the entrance to Milton Lockhart the tortuous A72 reaches the village of Rosebank, refurbished as a model estate village, much of it in mock Tudor style, by the 1st Lord Newlands (1825–1906), whose seat was Mauldslie Castle on the opposite side of the Clyde. Since his Lordship's time there has, of course, been much private building of houses at both ends of the village and on the sloping ground above it. The neat and tidy gardens, many of them beautifully kept, add to the beauty of the landscape and make Rosebank a most attractive village. Originally most of the villagers were employees on the Mauldslie estate but now they are mainly commuters to larger centres of population. The Popinjay Hotel, designed by the architect Cullen of Hamilton, replaced the single-storeyed Rosebank Inn in 1900. It is a first-class hotel with a beautiful lawn at the back that stretches down to the river. A popinjay was a multi-coloured parrot-like effigy used for practice in archery; its use is described in Scott's *Old Mortality*.

At a short distance beyond Rosebank the A72 passes the Gothic-style West Gatehouse of Mauldslie Castle with a bridge across the Clyde immediately behind it. Mauldslie Castle, now demolished, was built in 1793 by Thomas Carmichael, 5th Earl of Hyndford, from a design by Robert Adam of Edinburgh. It had a magnificent situation on the north bank of the Clyde, was in baronial style and was regarded as a wonder of its time. It was purchased in 1850 by James Hozier of Newlands and Barrowfield, an advocate in Glasgow, belonging to a family of brewers or maltmen that had come from Stirlingshire about the end of the seventeenth century. Their original name was Maclehose. James Hozier was succeeded on his death by his son Colonel William Wallace Hozier (1825–1906), who was granted a baronetcy in 1890 and raised to the peerage with the title Baron Newlands of Newlands and Barrowfield in 1898. A generous benefactor of worthy causes, he was a loyal churchman who did a great deal for Dalserf Parish Church. It seems somewhat strange that with his estate being in the parish of Carluke he (and his son after him) worshipped in Dalserf rather than in Carluke Parish Church, where the 'Mauldslie Loft' still exists. As already mentioned, Lord Newlands enlarged the village of Rosebank, and it was he who built the West Gatehouse and bridge in 1861. It is worthy of note that his brother Colonel Sir Henry Hozier was the father of Clementine Hozier whom Winston Churchill married in 1908.

On his death in 1906, Lord Newlands was succeeded by his son James Henry Cecil Hozier (1851–1929) who, like his father, was very public-spirited and beneficent. He was a man of ability, having won prizes in German and Italian at Eton, obtained a second class in Classical Moderations at Oxford and entered the Foreign Office by competitive examination. He was Unionist M.P. for South Lanark from 1886 until 1906 and was Lord Lieutenant of the County of Lanark from 1915 until 1920. Devoted to Balliol College, Oxford, of which he was elected an Honorary Fellow in 1907, he founded the Jowett Scholarship there in 1904 and in 1908 the Newlands Fellowship at the University of Glasgow which was used to supplement the income of those able students who had won Snell Exhibitions taking them from Glasgow to Balliol. Lord Newlands, who had married Lady Mary Cecil, daughter of the 3rd Marquis of Exeter, in 1880, died in 1929, leaving no issue. He was buried on Mount Pisgah on the Mauldslie estate. His heir was his nephew Sir James Baird who, unfortunately, was unable to keep up the estate. The castle was eventually demolished in 1935.

It is fashionable nowadays for writers to portray the domestic and outdoor staff of the large estates of bygone days as slave labourers, poorly paid and not very happy. It is undoubtedly true that there were estates where this state of affairs existed, but Mauldslie was certainly not one of them. The same can be said about Milton Lockhart and Carfin. During the time of the 2nd Lord Newlands the staff at Mauldslie included 11 indoor staff, 4 laundrymaids, 4 dairymaids, 5 gardeners, 2 coachmen, 2 carters, 1 forester, 1 shepherd, 1 mole-catcher and 1 painter. Altogether, they formed a very happy community, bearing no resentment to the laird because of his wealth and knowing that he would come to their rescue in any time of trouble.

On a site to the south of where Mauldslie Castle stood, sewage purification works for both Carluke and Law were set up by the former County Council of Lanark in 1941. Ten miles of main outfall sewers convey the whole of the sewage to Mauldslie, where the purified effluent passes into the Clyde. Access to the works is by the arched gateway at the West Lodge and the bridge over the river. These are now owned by South Lanarkshire Council. The lodge itself was sold to a private individual, restored and made into a most attractive-looking house.

Continuing on from the entrance to Mauldslie, the A72 passes the entrance lodge of the former Dalserf House. This mansion, built around 1700, stood in a beautiful situation on the left bank of the Clyde surrounded by gardens and orchards. Originally the property of the Hamiltons of Dalserf, it passed through the female line to the Henderson-Hamiltons. Having suffered badly from underground mine workings, the house was demolished sometime in the 1950s.

Dalserf Village is now little more than the few seventeenth-century cottages on the side road leading down from the main road to the Parish Church. The village, however, was much larger and busier in the eighteenth century than it is now. The existence of a ford across the Clyde brought many passers-by, while coal-mining in places such as Ashgill and Canderside on the higher ground above the village brought employment to it. In 1775 the population was about 1100. When Garrion Bridge was built in 1818, the ford ceased to be used, and as the nineteenth century progressed the coal mines became either exhausted or unprofitable. As a result the population of Dalserf decreased; at the same time that of Rosebank increased.

There is much Covenanting lore associated with Dalserf. For example, Jon Simpson was killed at Rullion Green in 1666 and, a few weeks after returning home from the battle there, Robert Scott of the Shaws was seized in his home, and taken to Glasgow where after trial he was sentenced to be hanged and to have his head and right hand cut off for public display in Glasgow. He and eight other Covenanters are commemorated by a stone with a quaint epitaph on it in Glasgow Cathedral. Thirteen years later Jon Frame died of wounds inflicted on him at Bothwell Bridge. In addition to those who suffered the extreme penalty, there were others who were subjected to gross injustice such as having heavy fines imposed on them for trivial offences or having dragoons billeted on them without payment. In 1666 James Hastie of Sandie-holm, who was ill-treated for many years, had all of his possessions stolen from him by William Hamilton of Raploch, one of the most notorious persecutors of Covenanters in Lanarkshire.

Dalserf Parish Church is interesting. It was built in 1655 but was enlarged and thoroughly renovated in 1894. The cost of these alterations was largely borne by the 1st Lord Newlands who contributed more than £1000 (the equivalent of at least £120,000 nowadays) to it. A further restoration costing £32,000 was made in the 1970s. The gallery is reached by three outside stairs while two doors give admission to the sitting accommodation on ground level. This caused a difficulty in the days when the offering was taken at the church door rather than during the service, but it was got over by having the 'plate' at the kirk gate. In the graveyard surrounding the church there are two things of interest. One is a memorial to the Rev. John Macmillan, the leader of the Cameronians referred to in Chapter 11, who ended his days in Dalserf parish, where he died in 1753. The other interesting thing is a hogback stone found on the south side of the church in 1897, but now resting under one of the west windows of the church. A hogback stone is a special type of tombstone invented in the tenth century by Scandinavian communities in Yorkshire and Cumbria. It is a solid block of stone carved into the shape of a house with a convex roof and gable ends. A Christian tradition at one time of keeping the relics of saints in house-shaped shrines led some better-off people to erect tombstones of this shape. Five fine examples of hogback stones of the tenth century can be seen in Govan Old Parish Church, Glasgow.

Garrion Bridge, already referred to, was built in 1818 to a design by Telford. There was formerly a toll-house at the north-western end of the bridge. On the right side of the river just upstream from the bridge there was a meal-mill that stood for generations but which was converted into a dwelling house sometime in the 1980s. There was a meal-mill either here or in the vicinity at the time of Robert the Bruce, for one of the Kelso charters indicates that the King granted the monks of Lesmachute (see Chapter 14) ten merks sterling annually from the revenue of his mills at Mauldslie for the continual support of lights at the tomb of St. Machute.

Garrion Tower, overlooking the confluence of the Garrion Burn with the Clyde on the right bank of the river, is an en-largement made in 1840 of a small fifteenth- or sixteenth-century tower-house which was then almost in ruins. There is evidence

6.4. Garrion Bridge.

that the house was used as a summer residence for the Arch-
bishops of Glasgow before the Reformation and for some time
afterwards. In Brown's *History of the Parish of Cambusnethan* of
1859 it is maintained that the house was built by Archbishop
James Beaton between 1509 and 1539, but the Third Statistical
Account of Scotland (1960) gives the date of its building as 1484.
It may be noted that D. R. Rankin in his book on the history of
Carluke, printed in 1874, describes the ecclesiastical connection
as 'downright fable'. The house is still used as a dwelling house
and is well maintained.

7
Lanark to Biggar via Symington

The route lies along the A73 to about a mile (1.6 km.) short of the village of Symington and then along the A72 to Biggar. The first 2 miles (3 km.) or so to Winston Barracks have already been described in Chapter 2. After passing the barracks the A73 is met at an acute angle by the A70 road from Edinburgh to Ayr and the two roads run together for about half a mile (rather less than 1 km.) until they have crossed Hyndford Bridge, a bridge of five arches built over the Clyde in 1773 by Alexander Stevens. After the building of the bridge, fords and ferries within 1.5 miles (2.4 km.) on either side of it ceased to be used. Indeed, according to oral tradition, the bridge was built by the country lairds to enable them to get to Lanark more conveniently for their social activities! The old tollhouse at the east end of the bridge, though boarded up, is still standing. There are two objects of interest to be seen before the river is crossed. At NS 906418 the remains of a crannog or lake dwelling can be seen among trees. Originally an artificial islet near the edge of a small loch, it now appears as an almost circular mound of about 25 yards (23 m.) across surrounded by a ditch of varying width. When the crannog was excavated in 1898, many objects of metal, glass, pottery and stone, as well as animal bones and a great deal of rubbish, were found. The collection is now in the National Museum in Edinburgh. Some of the objects are of Roman origin and date from the end of the first century A.D. If, as is very probable, these came from the Roman fort at Castledykes about 2 miles (3 km.) away (and to be described below), then, since the fort was rebuilt and re-occupied during the Antonine period, which began about A.D. 140, and since no remains from this period have been found in the crannog, it would seem that the crannog fell into disuse early in the second century A.D.

The other object of interest is Castledykes fort just referred to. The extensive complex of a fort with temporary camp sites and enclosures is situated on a plateau, which overlooks on the south a flood-plain of the Clyde, about 2 miles (3 km.) in a northerly direction along the A70 from its junction with the A73. The largest complex of Roman remains in Lanarkshire, it is now largely occupied by the farmstead of Corbiehall. A fort was built here at the time of Agricola's campaigns in the early '80s A.D. (in the Flavian period) but, like the fort at Crawford, was abandoned for a time and then reoccupied about A.D. 142 during the Antonine period. Its fine strategic position illustrates Agricola's renowned skill in choosing sites for his forts. This fort covers an area of 8.9 acres (3.6 ha.) when measured externally. Although the site of the fort is to a certain extent covered by trees, most of its perimeter can be traced on the ground, the thick rampart rising to a height of 5 feet (1.5 m.) in places.

At NS 926416, rather less than a mile (1.6 km.) along the A73 from Hyndford Bridge, a side road breaks off to the left and leads to the village of Pettinain about 2 miles (3 km.) away. This pleasant little village, situated on the crest of a hill at an altitude of about 700 ft (214 m.), retains much of its original character. The church, standing on or near the site of an earlier one – there was a priest in Pettinain in the year 1147 – dates from about the end of the seventeenth century. The belfry dates from 1692 and the bell bears the date 1695. Unfortunately, the church is no longer in use. In 1995 it was decided by the Church of Scotland authorities that the churches at Pettinain, Covington and Carmichael should together form the Parish Church of Cairngryffe with Carmichael Church as the place of worship. Cairngryffe Church is linked with that at Symington and both are served by the one minister. The future of the church buildings at Pettinain and Covington is at present unknown.

In its early days Pettinain Church seems to have been associated with (the old) St Kentigern's Church in Lanark, and in 1150 David I transferred both of them to the abbot and canons of Dryburgh Abbey, who remained in possession until the Reformation in 1560. In 1606 the whole of the property of Dryburgh Abbey was transferred to John, Earl of Mar, who sold it to Sir James (later, Lord) Carmichael sometime between 1634 and 1640. As a consequence, the Carmichael family had the right to present a minister to Pettinain Church, whenever a vacancy occurred, until

1874 when the law of patronage, which gave this power to the laird of a parish, was abolished by an Act of Parliament. In 1696 communion cups were presented to the church by John, 2nd Lord Carmichael, later Earl of Hyndford. The 6th Earl of Hyndford, on whose death in 1817 the title became extinct, resided mainly at Westraw in the parish of Pettinain, although he had a magnificent residence at Mauldslie in Carluke.

The highest hill in the parish of Pettinain is Cairngryffe Hill, which rises to a height of 1,115 ft (340 m.). The igneous rock felsite of which the hill is composed has a fine crystalline structure which for long made it admirably suitable for road surfacing. However, the mineral is not so suitable for main roads nowadays as the very heavy lorries at present in use polish the road-surface and make it slippery. Until Cairngryffe Quarry was taken over by the Cloburn Quarry Co. Ltd a few years ago, Strathclyde Regional Council extracted about 125,000 tons of the reddish-coloured mineral for the roads each year. As a consequence many of the roads in the rural part of Clydesdale are red in colour.

At NS 943398 the A73 passes the end of the rhododendron-lined drive leading to the ruins of Carmichael House, at one time the home of the Carmichael family. The so-called Eagle Gateway into the drive used to be very conspicuous because its stonework was adorned by two eagles and two pineapples carved in stone, and about 250 years old; they were stolen in mid-August 1997. The public road to the village of Carmichael leaves the A73 further on at NS 952387 and climbs up steadily before descending to the village, which consists mainly of a few houses clustered round the church and the school.

In the article on Carmichael written in 1838 for the New Statistical Account of Scotland, Vol. VI, published in 1845, special mention is made of the parish school in Carmichael. Due to the excellent teaching of the dominie, a Mr. Lithgow, and two assistants, pupils came from over a wide area, 32 of them being boarders either with the headmaster or with other people in the village. The subjects taught included Latin, Greek, French, English, Geography and Drawing. Some of the fees per quarter were, when expressed in modern coinage: English and Writing 15p., Arithmetic 17½p., English grammar 20p. and Latin 25p. (It should be noted that at this time a typical wage for a ploughman was

£20 per annum and a stone of oatmeal per week.) The writer of the article commended the teachers for their attention to the religious and moral training of the pupils and to their health and comfort.

The Carmichael family has included some very distinguished members. In 1701 John, the 2nd Lord Carmichael, was created Earl of Hyndford. He had a distinguished political career and was a Commissioner for the Treaty of Union signed in 1707. Despite the fact that he favoured the Union, the people of Carmichael raised a petition against it. The earl was Chancellor of the University of Glasgow from 1692 until his death in 1710. The third earl, who was born in 1701 and succeeded his father in 1737, was the most distinguished member of the family through his outstanding diplomatic career. When Frederick the Great, the King of Prussia, invaded Silesia in 1740, the earl was sent as envoy extraordinary and plenipotentiary to that monarch, and it was through his good offices that preliminaries for peace between Empress Maria Theresa and Frederick the Great were signed at Breslau in June, 1742. In recognition of the part that he had played in these negotiations, George II appointed him a Knight of the Thistle, while the King of Prussia permitted him to add the Eagle of Silesia to his paternal coat of arms with the motto *ex bene merito*. In 1744 he became Ambassador to Russia, in which capacity he helped to accelerate the signing of the Treaty of Aix-la-Chapelle in 1748. After being ambassador in Vienna from 1752 until 1764, he died in 1767. A recently restored monument to his memory stands on Carmichael Hill; it is clearly visible from the path going up Tinto Hill from Fallburn farm. When the 6th Earl of Hyndford died in 1817 the title became extinct and the property devolved on Sir Windham Carmichael Anstruther of Anstruther and Elie in Fife, who was descended from a daughter of James, 2nd Earl of Carmichael. The present laird, Richard Carmichael of Carmichael, became 30th Chief of the Carmichaels and 26th Baron after the death of his cousin in 1980. The estate that he inherited had been reduced in size over the years from about 19,000 acres (7,700 ha.) to about 2,300 acres (930 ha.) mainly because of a succession of inheritance tax payments. However, the use of improved agricultural techniques has given it a new lease of life and it now includes a sawmill, a deer farm and a roadside café. Recently, a visitor centre, including a heritage centre, a museum of wax models of famous characters in Scottish history, literature and science, a restaurant and facilities for pony trekking and horse riding, has been set up on the estate about 3 miles (5 km.) along the A73 from Hyndford Bridge. The laird has also been able to enlist the interest and support of Carmichaels living overseas, with the result that the Third International Clan Carmichael Gathering held in 1990 was very successful.

Carmichael Church, founded early in the twelfth century and dedicated to St Michael, can trace its history back to Robert de Jedworth, who was its rector from 1296 until 1361. The patronage of the church, that is, the right to present a minister to it, was granted to the famous Douglas family by Robert the Bruce but was transferred to the Carmichael family in the eighteenth century. This privilege was removed by Disraeli's Government in 1874. The present church was built in 1750 with the pre-Reformation outside stone staircase, leading to the Carmichael loft, transported from the former church, which stood on a hill about a mile (1.6 km.) to the south-east. Extensive alterations were made in 1904 in accordance with plans made by Sir John Lorimer, later to become famous for his design of the Scottish National War Memorial in Edinburgh Castle. At the same time a magnificent stained-glass window was installed in memory of Sir Windham Robert Carmichael Anstruther, who died at the age of 26 and whose trustees paid for the renovation of the church. The window contains the figures of Noah and of St Columba together with the coat-of-arms of Glasgow, to the see of which the church was originally attached. Other windows in the church depict Faith, Hope, Charity, Justice, Truth and Peace. A number of brasses and tablets commemorating members of the Carmichael family are to be seen in the church. In particular, there is a marble slab outlining the career of John, the 3rd Earl of Hyndford. In 1914 an attempt was made to set fire to the church by some suffragettes, who broke in through the vestry window. Fortunately, relatively little damage was done. Finally, it should be noted that at the gateway of the church there is a stone stair and a 'loupin' on stane'. These were used for mounting and dismounting by ladies who rode on horseback behind their

7.1. Tinto.

husbands and servants. As explained in reference to Pettinain
Church, Carmichael Church is now designated Cairngryffe Parish
Church.

The view to the south from the long straight stretch of the
A73 beyond the Carmichael roadend which, like the railway over
the Moor of Rannoch, is supported by tons of brushwood laid
down on the underlying bog, is dominated by Tinto Hill, 2320
ft (707 m.) in height. A prominent landmark, seen from much
of Lanarkshire, Tinto looks from many viewpoints like an isolated
hill. It is, however, one end of a ridge 4 or 5 miles (6 or 8 km.)
long with its other end, known as Tinto End, near the highest
point on the B7055 road from Douglas Water to Wiston. The
usual route up the hill is by a well-defined path starting at the
cattle grid beside the car park at Fallburn farm (NS 965375) a
short distance from what was once Thankerton tollhouse. The
climb is fairly gentle except for the last four or five hundred feet
(120 or 150 m.) of altitude and takes 1½ to 2 hours to accomplish.
A second route begins at a small parking space at NS 985353 on
the A73. The path, which is initially not easy to find, goes round
the north and west sides of Wee Hill, 1262 ft (385 m.) in height,
and ascends Scaut Hill, 1922 ft (586 m.) in height before turning

west and climbing to the summit of Tinto. A third and much steeper route begins at Millrig farm, Wiston (NS 954323), goes up the west side of the West Burn and after passing to the east of Pap Craig zigzags to the summit. A fourth route begins at NS 925331, where the B7055 meets the side road from Roberton, proceeds to Howgate Mouth, the cleft in the Tinto ridge, and then follows the stone dyke boundary right up to the summit.

On the summit of Tinto there is an enormous cairn 150 ft (46 m.) in diameter and rising to a height of almost 20 ft (6 m.). It can be seen by the naked eye from a distance of about 12 miles (19 km.). It is thought to be a Bronze Age cairn dating from about 1500 B.C. The view from the top of Tinto on a clear day, including the Pentlands, the Border hills, the Lowthers, the hills of Cumbria, Goat Fell in Arran and the more southern of the Grampians, is truly magnificent. An indicator erected a number of years ago was vandalised but has since been repaired. A well-known verse about the top of Tinto is as follows, but I have no idea of what it means.

On Tintock-tap there is a mist,
And in that mist there is a kist,
And in that kist there is a caup,
And in that caup there is a drap;
Tak up the caup, drink off the drap,
And set the caup on Tintock-tap.

At NS 962367 a short distance to the left/east of the path from Fallburn and about 0.68 mile (1.1 km.) from what was Thankerton tollhouse, there is a very impressive Iron Age hill-fort. It is almost circular, measuring 210 ft by 180 ft (64 m. by 55 m.) with double ramparts and ditches. The inner rampart rises to 10 ft (3 m.) above the bottom of the inner ditch.

The dome of Tinto is a mass of red felsite (as at Cairngryffe), estimated to go down to a depth of about 3,500 ft (1067 m.).

At Thankerton tollhouse a side road going off to the left/north-east from the A73 passes through the neat little village of Thankerton and then emerges back on to the A73 at NS 974372. The name of the village, like those of some others in the area, is of feudal origin. When David I succeeded to the Scottish throne in 1124, he had already spent much of his youth at the English

Court and through his wife Matilda had held the earldom of Northampton. He had therefore had first-hand experience of the Anglo-Norman system of government and had come to admire it greatly. As soon as he became King he therefore began what might be called the Norman Conquest of Scotland, an endeavour that was continued by his grandson Malcolm IV, who succeeded him in 1153. As explained in Chapter 1, large tracts of land were granted to lords in return for services rendered. Many Norman families, who had settled in England, were probably quite happy to get away from the troubles that beset England after the death of Henry I in 1135, and to settle in Scotland. Thus, for example, William de Somerville came from Yorkshire to be lord of Libberton. Likewise, there was an influx of Flemings to whom David I and Malcolm IV gave estates in the upper part of Clydesdale that had anciently belonged to the See of Glasgow. The principal member of this group was Baldwin, Lord of Biggar and Sheriff of Lanark. Others, some of whom have left their names attached to their 'touns', are Hugh of Pettinain (Houston in Renfrewshire), Lambin (Lamington), Lambin's brother Robert (Roberton), Wice (Wiston), Simon Loccard (Symington), Colbanus (Covington) and Tancard (Thankerton and Thankerton by Bothwell). On entering his new possession the incomer built not only a castle (motte) for his own protection but a church for his retainers. The boundaries of what later became the barony and the ecclesiastical district were identical and the parochial system resulted.

From the village of Thankerton the view across to the other side of the Clyde includes Quothquan Law, a conspicuous hill 1,099 ft (335 m.) in height. On the top of the hill there is an Iron Age fort made up of two parts, an enclosure measuring 394 ft by 230 ft (120m. by 70 m.) and containing the rocky knoll of the summit, together with an extension to the north-west measuring 328 ft by 131 ft (100 m. by 40 m.). The wall of the upper enclosure has almost completely disappeared. The entrance to the fort is from the north-east.

The bridge across the Clyde at Thankerton, which was built in 1778 by the Gentlemen of the County, i.e. the J.P.s, replaced a ferry where boats were available for hire by travellers. The approach road is still known as Boat Road. The road across the bridge leads to Wolfclyde on the A72 between Symington and

7.2. Quothquan Law.

Biggar, while a road turning off to the left from this road passes through the small village of Quothquan to meet the B7016 from Carnwath to Biggar at Libberton. The parish church in Quothquan has been a ruin since 1780 or earlier, although the bell, which was cast in 1641 by James Montieth of Edinburgh, is still there. When the church was joined with Libberton Church in 1699, the congregation hid the bell in the Clyde until they had been assured that it would not be removed to Libberton. The Chancellors of Shieldhill (see Chapter 9) are buried in the aisle of Quothquan Church.

It is almost obvious to anyone looking at the Clyde from a point about half a mile (1 km.) or so from Thankerton Bridge along the road to Quothquan, that the river downstream from there must have changed its course at some time in the past. This happened in or about 1638 when, after the extensive flooding caused by a violent storm had subsided, the river was found to have adopted a new channel to the west of the original one. As a result of this change a piece of land originally on the west side of the river belonging to Carmichael of Bonnington was trans-ferred to the east side of the river. Carmichael assumed that this piece of land was still his property and continued to cultivate it much to the annoyance of Chancellor of Shieldhill, who regarded the river, which was originally the boundary between the Car-michael and Shieldhill estates, as still being the boundary. In 1688 Chancellor of the time, thinking that the time was ripe for him to establish his claim to the land, gathered together about 80 men who, armed with scythes, pitchforks, swords and pistols, cut down all of the growing corn on the land; about 80 bolls of corn were lost. Since the tenants were kept in their houses under guard, the episode was regarded as a riot and Chancellor was ordered to pay 300 merks to Carmichael as compensation for damage done. In 1695 the Lords of Session finally determined that the land should remain part of the Carmichael estate.

A rather longer but very commendable route to Thankerton leaves the A73 at the Eagle Gateway (NS 943398) by a side road on the left/north which climbs up a little and gives a view of the Tinto hills that makes the detour well worthwhile. This road, after crossing the main Glasgow to Carlisle railway line, leads to the village of Covington and thence to Thankerton.

On the left/east side of the road at Covington Mains farm there is a small cairn with a plaque on it to commemorate an overnight stay by Robert Burns at the farm in November, 1786. It was unveiled in 1986 on the bicentenary of the visit. Burns was on his way to Edinburgh on a 'pownie' provided by a George

Reid who had arranged for the poet to make a detour from Hyndford Bridge and spend the night with Archibald Prentice at Covington. Mr James MacKay in his definitive biography of Burns tells the story of what happened. Prentice arranged a dinner party for some of his neighbours who, having read and been impressed by the Kilmarnock edition of Burns' poems, were keen to meet the poet. The signal of his arrival was the hoisting of a white sheet fixed on a pitchfork perched on the top of a cornstack in the farmyard. A most memorable evening was enjoyed by all; the guests were greatly impressed by the poet's conversation, while he himself was so touched by the warmth of the hospitality afforded him that he said in a letter to a friend, 'For Mr Prentice no words can do him justice. Sound sterling sense and plain warm hospitality are truly his'. The value that Prentice attached to the visit is indicated by the following incident for which there is documentary evidence. As Burns was preparing to leave on the morning after the party some boys, passing by on their way to Covington school, saw his pony tethered to a gate. Prentice ordered the boys to hold the stirrup for the visitor to mount on, saying 'You'll boast of this till your dying day.' The boys were

7.3. Covington Tower.

afraid of being late for school, but Prentice assured them that he would settle the matter with the dominie. One of the boys, recalling the event, when he was over 80 years of age, said, 'I think I'm prouder of that forenoon frae the schule than a' the days I was at it'.

The next two objects of interest on the road are Covington Tower with its dovecot and the nearby Covington Church.

Covington Tower, with walls 11 ft (3.4 m.) thick and with traces of a dry moat surrounding it, is now a ruin, stones having been removed from it at various times for building purposes. One such stone with carving on it is incorporated in the north wall of the church. The tower was built by the Lindsays in the early fifteenth century and was occupied by that family for two and a half centuries. The Lindsays, who were descended from the Lindsays of Crawford and who were mixed in with the famous Flemings of Biggar by marriage, were at one time a wild lot, stealing cattle, for instance, and putting their neighbours into a state of alarm. An old couplet that has been handed down says:

Who rides so fast down Coulter Brae,
The Devil or a Lindsay?

However, one John Lindsay of Covington was a witness to the charter of foundation of St Mary's Church in Biggar in 1546. Sir William Lindsay, the last Baron of Covington, died some time prior to 1688 after squandering the family's assets. Before long his descendants were reduced to working as labourers. The following anecdote about Sir William was current in the middle of the nineteenth century.

Sir William had at one time a serious illness and was eventually thought to be dead. However, when the relatives and servants assembled (in Covington Tower) to place the bearded knight in his coffin, Isabella Somerville, his great grand-daughter, whispered to her mother 'The beard is wagging! The beard is wagging!' Sir William had only been in a trance or 'dead faint' of some kind. When he rallied, the family explained that they thought that he had died and that they had made arrangements for his funeral, which included the killing of an ox to feed the mourners. He replied, 'All that is as it should be. Keep it a secret that I am in life and let the folks come'. In due course the mourners arrived for the funeral and, after a delay presumed to be due to the late arrival of the clergyman, Sir William himself, pale in countenance and dressed in black, suddenly appeared leaning on the arm of the minister of Covington. After explaining to the bewildered mourners what had happened, he called on the minister to conduct an act of devotion giving thanks for his recovery and for his escape from being buried alive. The day was then given over to merrymaking with Sir William himself presiding over the carousels.

Beside Covington Tower there stands a particularly good example of a circular or beehive type of dovecot (or, doocot) containing over 500 nesting boxes arranged in nine circular rows and dating from the sixteenth or seventeenth century. Since there are no dove-holes in the dovecot, the pigeons probably entered and left by a louvre, no longer existing, over a hole in the roof. The dovecot has been restored by the Biggar Museum Trust. Pigeons were introduced into this country by the Normans as a valuable source of meat and eggs. It has often been stated that pigeons were the only source of fresh meat in winter when salt meat was the mainstay of people's diet. However, domestic records from houses such as Hopetoun House, South Queensferry, show that in the eighteenth century pigeons appeared on the dinner table from early April until October or November but that they rarely appeared between mid-November and late March. The records also reveal that during this latter period not only fresh meat of various kinds was eaten but also fish, eggs and vegetables. Eighteenth century cookery books abounded with recipes for cooking pigeons. One of them, *Art of Cookery* by Hannah Glasse, published in 1747, contained 24 different recipes. Not only the more obvious methods were used, such as roasting, stewing, boiling and pickling, but also the French methods of preparation, fricassée, ragoût, compôte and bisque. According to Nigel Tranter, one of the Popes decreed that pigeon flesh was not to be regarded as red meat and could therefore be eaten at times of fasting, in Lent and on Fridays. Pigeons were also valued for their droppings, which were used as a fertiliser for the fields. The droppings, being rich in potassium nitrate, could also be mixed with black earth and sulphur to make gunpowder. The keeping of pigeons was a privilege enjoyed only by the landed proprietors, and laws were passed from time to time to protect their rights. Thus, it was enacted in 1424 that 'destroyers of pigeon houses' be regarded as thieves and in 1503 that parents of children committing such an offence were to be fined and the children given up to the judge to be 'leschit, scurgit and doung according to his fault' (lashed, scourged and rebuked). Then in the reign of James VI penalties became very severe – eight days in the stocks and a fine of £10, a third offence being liable to incur the death penalty.

Covington Church, part of which dates from the fifteenth century, stands on what has been an ecclesiastical site for about a thousand years. It originally contained a gallery, which was entered by an outside stair as in Dalserf Church described in Chapter 6. The gallery was removed in 1903 to make way for a new window, and a transept added to compensate for the loss of seats. A further renovation was carried out in 1934. Covington Church was united with St John's Kirk in Thankerton sometime between 1702 and 1720. This ancient edifice, situated at NS 984359, where a short side road leaves the A73 to join the A72 as it approaches Symington, has entirely disappeared although the graveyard around it is still maintained. Covington Church, like that of Pettinain, was closed in December, 1995 and the future of the building is unknown.

Continuing southwards the road comes to Newton of Coving-ton, where a row of six nineteenth century cottages with their original thatched roofs now covered with corrugated iron is noteworthy. The school on the opposite side of the road was closed in 1976. Its canteen is now the church hall. Further on, near Covington Mill farm on the west side of the road, there stands a monument to the Covenanter Donald Cargill, who was captured at the farm by the notorious Irvine of Bonshaw (near Lockerbie) and taken to Edinburgh, where he was executed on 27th July, 1681. Having been evicted from his charge of the Barony Church in Glasgow, he spent some years as a wandering field preacher and in 1679 was wounded at Bothwell Bridge. By the Declaration of Sanquhar of June, 1680 he, with Richard Cameron and Hackston of Rathillet, one of those who had murdered Archbishop Sharp of St Andrews in May, 1680, disowned Charles II. In the following September at a meeting held at Torwood, near Stirling, he excommunicated the King, the Duke of York, the Earl of Lauderdale and other leading opponents of the Covenanters. Shortly afterwards a reward of 5,000 merks was offered for his capture. Cargill's last sermon was preached on Dunsyre Common on the day before he was apprehended.

From the A73, before the A72 splits off from it, sand and gravel works can be seen by the side of the Clyde; they can be seen more clearly by looking across the river from the road leading from Thankerton Bridge to Wolfclyde. The gravel consists of pebbles mainly of greywacke and basalt with sandstone and felsite in lesser quantities. The deposits cover an area of about 20 acres (8 ha.).

Not far from where it leaves the A73, the A72 passes on the right/south St John's Kirk already referred to and the long-established Tinto Hotel, recently extended and with much to commend it. It then skirts the village of Symington, named after Simon Loccard, an Anglo-Norman who flourished in the reign of Malcolm IV (1153–1165) and William I (1165–1214) and the first owner of whom there is any record. Loccard is known to have witnessed the gift, made before 1164 by Wicius of Wiston, of the Church of Wiston to the Abbey of Kelso for the safety of the souls of Malcolm and his brother William. The Loccard family remained in Symington for a long time, their names appearing as witnesses in various early charters. They subsequently became the owners of the Lee estate in the parish of Lanark, an estate that is still owned by a Lockhart. (Lee Castle, as already mentioned in Chapter 4, is at present owned by Mr E. L. Peter.) At one time many of the residents of Symington were weavers but now they tend to be either people working elsewhere or elderly people who have chosen the village as a delightful place in which to retire. Until the railway stations at Thankerton, Symington, Lamington, Abington, Crawford and Elvanfoot were closed in 1965, these villages were well served by the Tinto Express from Carlisle, or latterly from Lockerbie, which reached Carstairs at 8.30 a.m. in the morning and arrived in Glasgow at 9.25 a.m. Passengers for Edinburgh changed at Carstairs and by joining a train that had left Lanark at 8.20 a.m. reached Edinburgh at 9.10 a.m. For the return journey the train left Glasgow at 4.45 p.m. and reached the Tinto villages before or just after 6 o'clock. After it was withdrawn the 'Tinto' was greatly missed by a number of commuters.

Little or nothing of the early history of Symington Church is on record, although it is known that it was rebuilt in 1761 and enlarged in 1821. In the churchyard around it, in the south-eastern part of the village, there is a watch tower that was built in the earlier part of the nineteenth century when the snatching of bodies for dissection by anatomists in Glasgow and Edinburgh had to be guarded against.

The A72 on heading towards Biggar crosses the Clyde at Wolfclyde, where a small motte with no remaining trace of any bailey stands at NT 019363 about 100 yards (90 m.) along the side road to Thankerton. The mound is about 8 ft (2.5 m.) in height and the top is roughly circular with a diameter of about 39 ft (12 m.) The motte, guarding a crossing of the Clyde, was possibly the castle of Alexander de Cutir whose name is preserved in the place name Coulter. Here also are to be seen the pillars of the viaduct that carried across the Clyde the Symington to Biggar to Broughton railway line which functioned from 1860 until 1950; it was extended to Peebles in 1864 and ran through delightful countryside. Coulter railway station, serving the village of that name about a mile and a half (2.4 km.) away, was at Wolfclyde.

7.4. Symington Church.

The view in a south-easterly direction from the A72 between Symington and Biggar is dominated by the Coulter Hills, the highest of which is Culter Fell 2.454 ft (748 m.) in height. This range of hills gives way in a north-easterly direction to the Hartree Hills, which rise to a height of 1427 ft (435 m.) before ending due east of Wolfclyde. The estate of Hartree was owned for 200 years or so by a family of the name of Brown. A Richard Brown is mentioned in a deed dated 1409, while Andrew Brown of Hartree was a witness to the foundation charter of the collegiate church of Biggar in 1546. In the 1630s John Dickson, a lawyer by profession, took over and was the progenitor of the family of Dickson of Hartree and Kilbucho. He was raised to the Bench with the title of Lord Hartree. A distinguished successor of Lord Hartree was Lt. Colonel William Dickson, who was on active service in Egypt around 1800 and who, a year or two later, represented the burghs of Linlithgow, Peebles and Selkirk in Parliament. At a later date he was promoted to the rank of Brigadier-General. He is reputed to have been a free, hearty, individual whose addiction to good wines and whisky caused his face to gradually acquire a more and more rubicund appearance. On one occasion in London the Prince of Wales, later George IV and a somewhat stupid character, said to him, 'Well, General, how much did it cost you to paint your nose?' The reply was 'I really canna say; I ha'e na yet counted the cost as I consider the work still unfinished!' The present hotel at Hartree replaced a tower-house that stood a short distance away.

About a mile (1.6 km.) east of Wolfclyde the A72 joins the A702, the main road from the M74 to Edinburgh via Biggar, and after running over it for about 2 miles (3 km.) and passing through Biggar, parts from it at Toftcombs.

8
Biggar

Biggar, a small market town with a population of 1994 in 1991 and standing at an altitude of about 700 ft (214 m.) amidst delightful rural scenery, still retains the medieval characteristic of having a wide main street, the High Street, on which markets and fairs were held, with closes leading from it to parallel back streets, North Back Road and South Back Road. The wide tree-lined High Street with well-kept buildings, some of them dating from the seventeenth and eighteenth centuries and built of whinstone from neighbouring quarries, together with substantial villas, erected beyond each end of the street, give the town an attractive appearance. With a pleasing hinterland as well, it is the home of many retired people.

For centuries Biggar was dominated (beneficently) by the Fleming family which, having settled there in the twelfth century, was influential in the history of Scotland from the time of Robert the Bruce until that of Mary, Queen of Scots. The Flemings emigrated from Flanders to England during the reigns of William Rufus and Henry I. Unfortunately, they favoured the wrong side in the civil war in which Stephen and Henry II contended for the throne and as a result were banished from England by the victorious Henry (1154–1189). Some of them found refuge in Scotland. The first owner of Biggar of whom there is definite knowledge was Baldwin Flandrensis, later known as Baldwin of Biggar. He was appointed Sheriff of Lanarkshire in 1162 by Malcolm IV (1153–1165), who had succeeded his grandfather David I as king; Lanarkshire at that time included what later became Renfrewshire. Baldwin's name appears in several charters dating from the latter part of the twelfth century. The royal castle in Lanark was his headquarters for the administration of Clydesdale. The mound of Baldwin's motte in Biggar of about 1150 can be seen near where the B7016 from Carnwath meets the A702.

The traditional story of how the Flemings acquired their motto

'Let the deed shaw' is as follows. Robert the Bruce met John Comyn, who had a claim to the Scottish throne, in Greyfriars Church in Dumfries where, in the course of a heated argument, Bruce forgot where he was and smote Comyn to the ground. Realising his misdeed, Bruce excitedly ran out of the Church to join some friends including Robert Fleming and Roger Kirkpatrick. 'I doubt I have slain Comyn', cried Bruce. 'Doubt', said Kirkpatrick. 'Then I'll mak siccar.' Fleming and Kirkpatrick then ran into the Church and plunged their swords into the dying man. When they emerged, Bruce asked if Comyn was dead, whereupon Fleming, holding up his bloodstained sword, exclaimed 'Let the deed shaw'. These words are said to have been adopted from then on as the motto on the crest of the Fleming family. However, present-day historians do not accept the story, arguing that Fleming and Kirkpatrick spoke either Gaelic or Norman French rather than Lowland Scots.

The next Fleming who must be mentioned is Robert, Lord Fleming, in whose time James II erected Biggar into a free burgh of barony. The charter, written in Latin, was given under the great seal in Edinburgh on 31st March, 1451 and states that 'the King, because of the great respect he had for Robert Fleming of Biggar in the district of Lanark, made the lands of Biggar a free burgh of barony, and also granted to the tenants and inhabitants the free power of selling in the said burgh. And he has granted that in the said burgh they should have a cross and a market on Thursday every week'. The charter was renewed (in Lowland Scots) by James V in 1526, James VI in 1588, Charles I in 1634 and Charles II in 1662. The cross was removed in 1823.

The Flemings were devout and one of them, Malcolm, Lord Fleming, was responsible for founding Biggar Kirk, for a time known as St Mary's, in 1546. Founded under a charter granted by Cardinal Beaton, the church was dedicated to the Most Blessed and Immaculate Virgin Mary and stands at NT 041379 on the site, on rising ground north of Biggar High Street, of an earlier church dedicated to St. Nicholas and referred to in the records of Paisley Abbey. A piscina, a perforated stone basin near the altar in churches for carrying away water used in rinsing the sacred vessels, now set into the south wall of the chancel of the present building, and a stone lamp now in the vestibule, survive from that church.

The present church was the last of forty collegiate churches to be built in Scotland between the twelfth and sixteenth centuries. A collegiate church was erected primarily for the saying of prayers and masses for the souls of its founder, his family, his ancestors and his successors, by a staff sufficiently adequate to provide services more elaborate than would be possible in an ordinary parish church. Malcolm, who was killed at the battle of Pinkie in 1547, died before the building of the church was completed, but his son John continued the work and added a nave for the use of parishioners. The college consisted of a provost, eight prebendaries, four choirboys and six poor men. The charter of foundation, very long and written in Latin, makes interesting reading. It stipulates, for example, that the four boys have unbroken voices, that they be skilled in plainsong and descant, that their heads be shaven and that they wear crimson gowns. When their voices broke or if they behaved in a disorderly and incorrigible manner, the provost and prebendaries could dismiss them. The six poor men, commonly called the 'beid men', were admitted on the grounds of poverty, frailty and old age. They were to be furnished annually with white linen gowns and white cloth

8.1. Biggar Kirk.

hoods. They were to attend high mass and vespers every day and on the death of the founder they were to sit at his grave and pray devoutly for the welfare of not only his soul but also those of his progenitors and his successors.

The architecture of the church is Gothic although a doorway in the south transept is early Norman and the battlemented tower and crowstep gable are typically Scottish. The building is cruciform in plan and is beautifully proportioned. On the outside wall there can be seen the remains of iron 'jougs' by which offenders were fastened to the wall for lengths of time dependent on their misdemeanours, and just inside the church is a cutty stool or stool of repentance dated 1694 on which those guilty of indiscipline had to sit facing the congregation and make expiation for their offences. The coat of arms of the Fleming family is exhibited on the front of the gallery of the church. The church was restored in 1871 and again in 1935, when the plasterwork inside the building was wrongly removed in an attempt to give the impression of age. The same seems to have happened to the nave in 1990, when the outside stonework was repaired. The window openings are filled entirely with stained glass, dating from the 1870s onwards and including work by William Wilson R.S.A. The most recent work is by a local artist Crear McCartney and was completed in 1991.

In the graveyard there are some interesting tombstones, including one near the church door of the forebears of the great William Ewart Gladstone (1809–1898), who was four times Prime Minister. His great-grandfather John Gladstone, born in 1694, was a maltman, a burgess of Biggar and owner of Mid Toftcombs. When the Relief Church in Biggar, which was founded in 1783 by two great-uncles, John Gladstone and Richard Tweedie, of Gladstone, was pulled down and rebuilt as Gillespie Church on almost the same site in 1879, Gladstone contributed to the cost. A story that has been handed down tells of Gladstone badly upsetting the elders of Biggar Kirk by describing its architecture as 'debased Gothic' in style. His explanation that he had only used an art term that implied no insult was of no avail. 'Well, well', said one of the elders 'airt or no airt, Mr Gladstone should have written about the auld kirk in a ceevil mainner'.

When Malcolm, Lord Fleming, who founded Biggar Kirk, was

8.2. Gladstone Cottage, 1905. Home of John Gladstone (1694–1758).

killed at the battle of Pinkie in 1547, he left two sons and five daughters by his wife Janet Stewart, an illegitimate daughter of James IV by the Countess of Bothwell. One of these daughters, Mary, was chosen along with Mary Beaton, Mary Livingstone and Mary Seton to be a playmate of the young Mary, Queen of Scots, who was born in 1542, and to be trained with her in all the branches of learning relevant at the time. Since the country was in a very unsettled state, the Queen lived successively in a number of castles and for three weeks on the lonely island of Inchmahome in the Lake of Menteith but, after the battle of Pinkie, it was felt that she would be safer abroad. Accordingly, it was decided to send her to France with her aunt Lady Fleming, widow of Malcolm, as governess. In the summer of 1548 the Queen set sail for France accompanied by her four playmates, all of noble descent and of comparable age to herself, together with Lady Fleming and a train of noblemen. From then onwards the Four Maries, whom Lady Antonia Fraser in her book *Mary Queen of Scots* describes as 'those romantic concomitants of her adventures', became prominent. Mary Fleming, having a royal connection through her mother, not only held the highest status among the Maries but also was regarded by the historian John

Leslie as 'the flower of the flock'. The Queen and the four Maries returned to Scotland in 1561.

Around this time an amusement practised at the Scottish Court on the eve of Epiphany was to cut a cake in which a bean had been concealed and to distribute the slices to the company present, the person finding the bean being designated the King or Queen of the Bean. On the following day a banquet was held at which the King or Queen of the Bean was saluted as King or Queen of the realm and regarded as sovereign for the day. Thus, on 5th January, 1563 the bean was found by Mary Fleming, who therefore acted as Queen for a day. Thomas Randolph, Queen Elizabeth's ambassador, was so captivated by Mary that he said that she was fit to be a queen but not just for one day. He likened her to Venus for beauty, Minerva for wit and Juno for worldly wealth. In describing her dress, he said that 'she was that day in a gowne of cloath of silver; her head, her neck, her shoulders, the rest of her whole body so besett with stones that more in our whole jewell house were not to be found'. Even the historian George Buchanan, a crabbed bachelor with purely academic interests – he was the finest Latin scholar of his time – wrote some Latin verse in which he sang the praises of Mary Fleming whom he called Queen Flaminia. The four Maries, of whom, unfortunately, no contemporary portraits exist, obviously added beauty and vitality to the Court life at the time. In describing the pretty sight of them riding with the Queen to Parliament in 1563, Randolph referred to them as 'virgins, maids, Maries, demoiselles of honour or the Queen's mignons, call them what you please'. He was obviously greatly captivated. The radiant youth and vitality of Mary Fleming also struck Sir William Maitland, the Queen's secretary, who married her in the Chapel Royal at Stirling on 6th January, 1567.

The well known ballad –

> Last night the Queen had four Maries
> Tonight there'll be but three
> There's Mary Seton and Mary Beaton
> And Mary Carmichael and me

– was mistakenly associated with the four Maries by Sir Walter Scott, despite the fact that there is an error among the surnames.

According to Lady Antonia Fraser, the ballad had its origin in a scandal at the Court of Peter the Great in Russia when Mary Hamilton, a maid of Scottish origin, was executed for the murder of an illegitimate child she had had by Peter.

At the Gala Day held in Biggar each summer, Mary Fleming's action as Queen for a day is commemorated by the crowning of a local schoolgirl as Fleming Queen.

Little more need be said here about the Fleming family except to record its demise. A detailed history can be found in the book *Biggar and the House of Fleming* by William Hunter, published in 1862. When Charles Fleming died unmarried in 1747, his estates went to his niece Lady Clementina who, in 1735, had married Charles, second son of the 9th Lord Elphinstone. When she died in 1790 (and was buried with her forefathers in Biggar Kirk), the connection of the direct line of Flemings with Biggar came to an end. Eventually, her grandson Charles, who was an Admiral, owned the estates but, as he fell heavily into debt, the ancient possessions of the Flemings in Biggar came under the hammer about 1830 and were sold to five or six different people.

With reference to Lady Clementina's burial in Biggar Kirk – she was the last Fleming to be buried there – it may be noted that in pre-Reformation days it was a strong desire of all ranks of people, especially kings, nobles and priests, to be buried in the hallowed ground within a church, where religious exercises were performed daily and where they could lie in calm and undisturbed peace until the end of time. After the Reformation the clergy tried with the utmost vigour to repress this custom, thinking that it savoured of Roman Catholicism and superstition. An Act of the General Assembly passed against it in 1588 was ratified in 1643. The lairds, whose ancestors were buried within the walls of the parish churches, were very upset and were often at loggerheads with the clergy over it. There was serious trouble with, for example, the Chancellors of Shieldhill and the Baillies of Lamington (see Chapters 9 and 11). The Flemings, however, seem to have continued the practice.

The principal residence of the Flemings after the days of the motte already referred to was Boghall Castle, the ruin of which at NT 041370 can be seen from Station Road, Biggar. As the name suggests, it stands in the middle of a bog. Little or nothing

8.3. Boghall Castle, Biggar.

is known of its early history, although excavations made by Biggar High School in 1970 revealed that the first tower was erected in the fifteenth century and was square, not unlike Covington Tower. Later, in the sixteenth century, a curtain-wall with corner towers was added. The castle was besieged and taken in 1568 by the Regent Moray and then in 1650 by Oliver Cromwell. A restoration of the castle was made in 1670 but, after its transference to the Elphinstones in 1747, it became more and more deserted and neglected, and gradually fell into ruin. In its heyday royalty, including Mary, Queen of Scots, were entertained at Boghall. For instance, James VI stayed there for several days in January, 1595 and is said to have enjoyed the sport of hawking.

As we enter the town of Biggar by the A702 from Symington, one of the first things to be noticed is the small hump-backed bridge over the Biggar Burn at the foot of the town and known as the Cadger's Brig. The tradition is that before the Battle of Biggar, which Blind Harry describes in detail and to which he assigns the date 1297, Wallace, whose troops were encamped on the slopes of Tinto, knowing that the much larger English force was stationed in Biggar, dressed himself up as a pedlar or cadger and, having crossed this little bridge, worked his way into the

8.4. Cadger's Brig, Biggar.

English camp, where he gathered vital information about, for example, where the King (Edward I) and his generals were located. On the following day he attacked and routed the English army. Historians tend to give no credence to Blind Harry's story. Although Harry is being treated with more respect nowadays, a battle at Biggar on the scale related by him would have been impossible. The little bridge, which was built no earlier than the sixteenth century, probably got its name from the cadgers who would have crossed it when they brought their produce to the weekly market for sale.

At the top of the town the noticeable building with the clock on it is the Corn Exchange, built in 1860 to the design of the well-known Edinburgh architect David McGibbon. It replaced the old Meal House which had become infested by rats and mice and was a most uninviting place in every way. The Corn Exchange is now used for performances by the Biggar Theatre Workshop. In front of the building is a sundial executed by Ian Hamilton Finlay, who lives near Dunsyre; it was unveiled by Lady Tweedsmuir in 1970 to mark the European Conservation Year. The inscription on the sundial is

Azure & Son
Islands Ltd
Oceans Inc.

Meaning? The Mercat Cross at which people met to buy or sell local produce stood on a knowe in front of the old Meal House. The top of the Mercat Cross is now built into the rear gable of the Corn Exchange. Each year on Hogmanay a huge bonfire is lit on the site of the Mercat Cross to burn out the old year and bring in the new one. Usually, an enormous crowd gathers to witness the conflagration.

The Parish School in Biggar, built in Kirkstyle in 1847, is now the Municipal Hall. After the passing of the Education Act of 1872 the school was known as the West Public School and continued as such until 1900, when it was replaced by a new building on the site in John's Loan occupied until then by a school known as the South Public School, and renamed Biggar High School. This designation now applies to the new secondary school built further along John's Loan, the 1900 building being known as Biggar Primary School. In 1998 the High School had 605 pupils.

Across the road from the present High School stands the Kello Hospital, endowed by and named after three medical doctors who practised in Biggar in the nineteenth century. It is used nowadays mainly for elderly and less seriously ill patients,

The town of Biggar is well endowed with clubs and societies of a sporting or cultural nature. Of these pride of place must go to the Biggar Museum Trust, founded in 1971 when it took over the Gladstone Court Museum created by Mr Brian Lambie in 1968 and owned by him. Largely due to Mr Lambie's great ability and enthusiasm, the Trust has enlarged its activities to include the running of the Moat Park Heritage Centre, Greenhill Covenanters' House, Biggar Gasworks Museum, the Albion Motors Museum and the John Buchan Centre at Broughton; the first and last were formerly churches. The Trust has also taken over Hugh McDiarmid's cottage and three other disused churches, namely, the parish churches of Walston and Lamington and the Episcopal Church of Holy Trinity in Lamington. The administration of all these activities, which is done voluntarily, is obviously a considerable task, and it is a great credit to the town of Biggar that it has been able to provide such a large number of enthusiastic people willing to carry out the work, for example, of manning the museums some of which are open daily, Sundays included, from Easter until the end of October.

The Gladstone Court Museum at NT 042380 reconstructs life as it was in a small town in Victorian and Edwardian times with a bank, a schoolroom, a library and the shops of a bootmaker, a chemist, a dressmaker, an ironmonger, a photographer, a printer and a watchmaker.

The Moat Park Heritage Centre, occupying the former Moat Park Church at NT 040378, was opened by H.R.H. The Princess Royal in June, 1988 and is the flagship of the Biggar Museum Trust. It contains an extraordinarily fine collection of geological, archaeological and historical exhibits relating to Upper Clydesdale together with memorabilia portraying aspects of church, school and agricultural history. A lucid explanation is given of how the Clyde and Tweed valleys were formed millions of years ago and there are beautifully made models of early dwellings, mottes, castles and farmhouses. A noteworthy exhibit is a piece of Victorian patchwork, measuring about 9ft by 8ft (2.7 m. by 2.4 m.) with over eighty coloured figures stitched meticulously into place, made by Menzies Moffat (1828–1907), an eccentric Biggar tailor, at the time of the Crimean War. Queen Victoria and Prince Albert, depicted at the centre, are surrounded by British, French and Turkish commanders and various well-known personalities of the time. The work, which took seven years to complete, used 1000 hanks of silk and 5000 pieces of cloth.

Moat Park Church built in 1865 and Gillespie Church built in 1879 on the High Street were United Free Churches from 1900 until 1929, when they both became congregations of the Church of Scotland. After their union in 1946 to form Gillespie Moat Park Church, the Moat Park building was used as the place of worship and the Gillespie building became a church hall. Finally, in 1977, Gillespie Moat Park Church joined with St Mary's Church to form Biggar Kirk, and in 1979 the Gillespie building was renovated as the Gillespie Centre and Moat Park sold to the Museum Trust.

Biggar Gasworks at the foot of the town, dating from 1839 and closed down after the advent of North Sea gas in 1973, was reopened as a museum in 1985 and so preserved for future generations to see. As the first public gas company in the World was set up in London in 1812, Biggar as a small town did well in having a gasworks by 1839.

Greenhill Covenanters' House is the seventeenth-century Greenhill farmhouse at Wiston, removed from there, where it was in a state of dereliction, and rebuilt stone by stone between 1975 and 1981 at Burn Braes, Biggar (NT 040382). It is used as a museum of Covenanting times. The relics include furniture and dolls from this period as well as a collection of rare books and documents relating to the 'Killing Times'. One of those who signed the National Covenant, a copy of which is exhibited, was John Fleming (1589–1650), 2nd Earl of Wigtoun and Lord of Biggar and Cumbernauld, son of the 7th Lord Fleming who, as a great favourite of James VI, was created Earl of Wigtoun in 1606. John Fleming fought with his tenantry from Biggar under General Leslie in the civil wars in England. The Flemings also allowed conventicles to be held at Boghall Castle.

The Albion Archive, housed at 9, Edinburgh Road, Biggar, contains the complete records of the Albion Motor Car Company, which was founded in 1899 by Thomas Blackwood Murray and his brother-in-law Norman Fulton. John L. Murray, the father of Thomas, encouraged them in their enterprise and enabled them to set up business with a bond for £1300 on his farm at Biggar as security. John L. Murray, incidentally, was an architect as well as a farmer and was responsible for the building of many of the Victorian houses on Biggar High Street as well as Hartree House, Culter Allers House and the old County Buildings in Hamilton. The Albion company eventually became the largest manufacturer of trucks in the British Empire. It is now part of the Leyland DAF organisation. Between 1899 and 1972, when the name Albion was dropped, the firm built something like 165,000 vehicles at its works in Scotstoun, Glasgow. The Museum Trust organises in August of each year the Biggar Car Rally at which there is a large turnout – 300 or so in 1998 – of veteran and vintage vehicles. The object of the exercise is to commemorate the fact that the prototypes of some of the earliest cars in the country were tried out in the neighbourhood of Biggar. The first phase of the development of an Albion Motors Museum in Biggar was completed in the Summer of 1998. In 1990 the Trust was able to acquire a magnificent Albion Dog Cart Car dated 1901, which, along with several other acquisitions, forms the nucleus of the Museum.

The John Buchan Centre at Broughton about 6 miles (10 km.) from Biggar was formerly the Free Church there. It was while acting as supply minister in that church that Buchan's father met in 1874 his future bride, Helen Masterton, the local innkeeper's daughter. John Buchan was born in Perth in 1875 but he retained a warm affection for Tweeddale and particularly for Broughton, where his childhood holidays were spent. The Centre, containing a great many memorabilia, traces the life of Buchan as author, Member of Parliament, Lord High Commissioner to the General Assembly of the Church of Scotland and as Governor-General of Canada.

Hugh MacDiarmid's (C. M. Grieve's) cottage near Candy Mill, about 3 miles (5 km.) to the north along the A702 from Biggar, where the poet lived and worked from 1951 until his death in 1978, was taken over by the Museum Trust in 1991, the centenary of his birth. The cottage, Brownsbank by name, contains a unique collection of memorabilia and is occupied by a writer-in-residence, who is sponsored by the Scottish Arts Council and South Lanarkshire Council. A bronze head of Hugh MacDiarmid executed by Benno Schotz was presented in 1998 to the Museum Trust by the Scottish Arts Council, and is on permanent display in the Moat Park Heritage Centre.

It is clear from all that has been said that the Biggar Museum Trust has done an extraordinarily fine piece of work since its inception. The enthusiasm of those in charge remains undiminished and there is little doubt that further great successes will attend their efforts.

Mention must be made also of Biggar Little Theatre, the headquarters of the Purves Puppets, on Broughton Road. Opened in 1986, this is a complete Victorian puppet theatre in miniature. In addition there is an exhibition, a tearoom and space for outdoor Victorian games.

A native of Biggar, who is hardly ever heard of, was George Meikle Kemp (1795–1844), the architect of the Scott Monument in Princes Street, Edinburgh. He was an architectural genius although he had little formal training in architecture. The son of a shepherd, he was born in a little cottage near the farm of Hillridge in the parish of Biggar on 26th May, 1795, but a few days after his birth went with his parents to live in Walston, where he remained until 1802. After living for short periods elsewhere, the family moved finally to the Clachan of Moorfoot, where George helped his father with the sheep before becoming an apprentice joiner at Redscaurhead between Eddleston and Peebles in 1810. Four years later he began work as a millwright in Galashiels, where he remained for a year, during which time he took the opportunity to make a detailed study of the architecture of the neighbouring abbeys of Dryburgh, Jedburgh, Kelso and Melrose. After gaining further experience in Edinburgh, Manchester and Glasgow, where he made a special study of the Cathedral and attended classes at Anderson's University, the forerunner of the University of Strathclyde, he paid working visits to London, where he sketched St. Paul's Cathedral, and to France, where he was greatly impressed by the magnificence of the great cathedrals such as that at Amiens. His next employment was as a draughtsman with the eminent Edinburgh architect William Burn, who designed Carstairs House and Milton Lockhart in Carluke. His work included the preparation of working drawings for the mansion house of Bowhill, near Selkirk, which was being built by the Duke of Buccleuch, and the construction of a wooden model of a palace that the Duke was contemplating building at Dalkeith.

After the death of Sir Walter Scott on 21st September, 1832, it was decided at a public meeting held in Edinburgh that a fund should be set up for the erection of a memorial to him. A few years later the committee concerned invited submissions for the design of the memorial and in due course had a good response, which included submissions from George Kemp and from distinguished architects such as William Playfair, Sir William Allan and David Roberts, R.A. The committee recommended that the design by George Kemp, which was of an imposing monument beautifully proportioned and with all its details derived from Melrose Abbey, be accepted. However, there being opposition to the recommendation on the grounds that Kemp was a humble carpenter, the committee advertised again. They received a few more submissions but, after consulting William Burn, who declared 'his admiration of Mr. Kemp's design, its purity as a Gothic composition ... and more particularly the constructive skill exhibited in the combination of the graceful features of that style of architecture ... and the perfect solidity which it would possess when built', they recommended on 28th March, 1838 that Kemp's submission be accepted. The foundation stone was laid on 15th August, 1840, Kemp being appointed to supervise the erection, which to begin with involved excavation to a depth of 52ft (almost 16 m.) before solid rock was reached. Tragically, on the dark and foggy evening of 6th March, 1844, about seven months before the completion of the monument, Kemp, while walking home along a bank of the Union Canal, slipped into the water and was drowned. He was buried in St. Cuthbert's Churchyard, Edinburgh, his coffin being carried there by workmen from the site of the monument. Under the supervision of Kemp's brother-in-law, Thomas Bonnar, R.A., the work of erection was completed on 26th October, 1844, although it was not until 17th August, 1846 that the formal dedication took place.

Kemp was also the architect of Millburn Church, Renton in Dunbartonshire which, disused since 1990, has now fallen into such a state of disrepair that trees are growing up through the roof. With a spire reminiscent of the Scott Monument it is a grade A listed building. Its future is uncertain, but a local housing association is considering the possibility of turning it into a community museum.

On 1st October, 1932 a monument to Kemp was unveiled at Redscaurhead by a daughter-in-law; it is a gable wall of Gothic design built against the workshop in which Kemp served his time as a carpenter. On 27th May, 1995, the bicentenary of Kemp's birth was marked by the unveiling of a simple monument of Cairngryffe stone bearing a bronze plaque on the braeface at Burn Braes.

Another native of Biggar worthy of mention is Dr John Brown (1810–1882), essayist and author of the minor classic *Rab and his Friends*, a collection of entertaining essays on the human nature of dogs, which was read in the first instance before an audience in Biggar in 1859. Born in the Old Secession manse in Biggar, John Brown became a much-loved medical practitioner in Edinburgh and a great personality there. His friends included Thackeray, Ruskin and Mark Twain. When Gladstone was elected Rector of the University of Edinburgh in 1859, he nominated him as his Assessor on the University Court. There is a plaque to the memory of Dr Brown on the wall of the Municipal Hall in Biggar.

9

Carluke to Biggar via Carnwath

The route from Carluke to Carnwath along the A721 climbs steadily from an altitude of about 630 ft (192 m.) at the foot of Carluke
High Street to an altitude of about 950 ft (290 m.) at the hamlet
of Kilncadzow, with local pronunciation Kilcaigie, 2¾ miles (4.4
km.) away. The view from Kilncadzow to the south is indeed a
fine one, and it can be enhanced by climbing up a short distance
to the top of the hill that rises to a height of 1050 ft (320 m.)
above the village. From here on a clear day, Goat Fell in Arran,
the Arrochar hills, Ben Lomond, the nearer Grampians, the nearby
Pentlands, the Border Hills and the Lowthers can all be seen.

The side road going southwards from Kilncadzow and leading
ultimately to Lanark passes the remains of the limestone works
at Craigenhill, which were in operation from 1850 until 1890.
Craigenhill lime was used all over Scotland for agricultural purposes. After about a mile (1.6 km.) from Kilncadzow the road
reaches the main Glasgow to Carlisle railway, where before electrification there was a signal box and a level crossing. The road
now makes a detour to enable it to cross the railway by the
bridge near Fullwood farm. Near this bridge the railway reaches
a minor summit of about 750 ft (229m.). The walk from here to
Lanark can be a very enjoyable one except for the very steep hill
that has to be climbed from the valley of the Mouse into Lanark.

At NS 897483, a short distance along the A721 from Kilncadzow,
a side road veers off to the right/south which, after passing
Collielaw farm but just before reaching the A706 from Lanark
to West Calder at Cleghorn, passes on the left/east part of the
remains of a Roman temporary marching camp. Such camps
were erected by the Army when making a sojourn of perhaps
one, two or three nights. The Cleghorn camp, on the right bank
of the Stobilee Burn, which runs into the Mouse, is 623 yards
(570 m.) north-west of Cleghorn Mill, where the Roman road
from Castledykes to Bothwellhaugh crossed the Mouse. The

northern half of the defences are still visible in Camp Wood, the surviving rampart being a bank covered by grass and heather about 12 ft (3.7 m.) thick and 2.3 ft (0.7 m.) high. The ditch is 6 ft (1.9 m.) in width and 16 inches (0.4 m.) in depth. The rampart crosses the side road from Kilncadzow at about 330 yards (302 m.) from its junction with the A706. The area enclosed by the camp is about 47 acres (19 ha.), sufficient to accommodate two marching legions.

The A721, after the side road referred to has left it, begins to climb again with the land on either side of it being such that, just as the walker or motorist reaches the highest point on the road, a panoramic view of the Pentlands, the Culter hills and Tinto suddenly appears. This view is one of the best obtainable from a road in Clydesdale. About a mile (1.6 km.) further on, the roundabout at Harelaw, 5 miles (8 km.) from Carluke, is reached.

About 4½ miles (7.2 km.) along the A706 in a northerly direction from Harelaw the village of Forth stands at about 900 ft (275 m.) above sea level and looks over a wide expanse of moorland towards the Pentland Hills. The coal-mining industry flourished here in the nineteenth century and in the first half of the present century but, as the seams of coal became exhausted, the industry died out in the early 1950s. It was, however, replaced in 1966 by opencast coal-mining in quite a big way. When this in turn died out the affected ground was landscaped and sold to the Forestry Commission. With a population of 2560 in 1991, Forth is still a thriving community, though many of its residents commute to work in Lanark and elsewhere. Forth Parish Church was built in 1875 and a clock in memory of Dr Reid, a general practitioner in Forth from 1900 to 1949, was added in 1952.

About 2 miles (3.2 km.) further along the A706 from Forth is the deserted village of Wilsontown, which was the birthplace of the iron industry in Lanarkshire. The brothers John, Robert and William Wilson established works on the Mouse Water in 1779 using locally found iron ore, coal and limestone. The industry flourished so well that by 1807 the population of the village, in which the Wilsons had built a church, a school and a bakery, exceeded 2000. The ironworks ranked second in Scotland to those at Carron for size. However, because the situation of the village made the transport of iron by horse and cart to the ports of Leith and Bo'ness too costly and because the management of the works was bad, the firm became bankrupt and production ceased in 1812. After rusting away for nine years the works were bought in 1821 by William Dixon of Govan Colliery and Calder Iron works at Whifflet, a man regarded as a pioneer in everything relating to coal and iron. When Dixon died in 1824, his son, William, of 'Dixon's Blazes' in Glasgow, took over the plant, but it functioned only until 1842 when it was closed down and the production transferred to Govan in Glasgow. The remains of the ironworks were removed in 1946. In 1995 a proposal to establish an opencast mine at Wester Mosshat farm near Haywood about 4 miles (6.4 km.) east of Wilsontown was finally given approval. The proposal has engendered much local opposition.

Darmeid Monument, in memory of the Covenanters Donald Cargill, Richard Cameron and James Renwick, is situated at NS 902554 on Auchterhead Muir, where they often preached. It can be reached by taking the B715, which leads from Forth to the A71 (leading to Edinburgh), to a point NS 926559 beyond Climpy and then going along a side road for about a mile and a half (2.4 km.) to a disused mine. The monument, which is in the form of a pillar 10 ft (3 m.) high standing on a flat plinth, is in good condition.

The A721, continuing eastwards from Harelaw, skirts the precincts of Cranley House, the present home of the Monteith family, which has shown much generosity to the parish of Carstairs and also to the town of Lanark through the building of St Mary's Church in 1859. After crossing the Mouse, in the valley of which a challenging 18-hole golf course, known as Kames Country Club, was opened in 1993, the road meets the A70 Ayr to Edinburgh road and runs along it to the far end of Carnwath. The A70, before meeting the A721, has skirted the village of Carstairs, one of the few villages in Scotland to have a village green; this was laid out by Mr Henry Monteith in 1826. Carstairs was erected into a burgh of barony in 1765. On a slight eminence above the village green stands the parish church of which some parts are 400 years old. Some of the contents of the church, which was rebuilt in 1794, when a tower or steeple was added, and extensively altered in 1891, are noteworthy. Among them are an ancient bread paten that has been in continuous use at communion services since early post-Reformation times and two silver communion cups with the stamp of Gilbert Kirkwoode, a silversmith who was admitted to his craft in 1609, on them. In the vestibule there can be seen two pewter patens each with a Celtic cross incised on it and a pewter tankard, all of unknown date but undoubtedly very old. When a new heating system was installed and the floor renewed in 1891, some human remains were found. The bones were collected and re-interred under the pulpit.

The earliest record of a church in Carstairs is dated 1170. The pre-Reformation church of which nothing remains except possibly some stones that were used for the building of the present church, was dedicated to St. Mary and was included in the Diocese of Glasgow. At one time there was a castle in Carstairs belonging to the See of Glasgow which was used as a residence by the bishops until the time of the Reformation. Nothing remains of this castle. It is known that a Bishop Robert Wishart held a court there in 1273 to resolve a dispute between the monks of Kelso and Sir Symon Loccard. The same bishop began sometime later to build a stronger castle, which was not completed by 1292 when Edward I of England, who had been acknowledged as 'sovereign lord' of Scotland in the previous year, sent him a letter discharging him from 'any proceedings against him on account of his having begun the said Castle without our license'.

The village of Carstairs must not be confused with the village of Carstairs Junction about a mile (1.6 km.) to the east, which came into being with the arrival of the railway in 1847. In 1845 the Caledonian Railway Company obtained parliamentary consent to build a railway from Carlisle to join the Wishaw and Coltness railway at Garriongill on the border between the parishes of Carluke and Cambusnethan, with a branch to Edinburgh breaking off at a short distance south of the present Carstairs station. A short but severely curved length of track joins the station to the Edinburgh branch. Carstairs in due course became an important railway centre. Express trains from England divided there, the front portion of the train going to Glasgow (in the early days via Coatbridge) and the rear portion to Edinburgh. There grew up a large and thriving railway community comprising drivers, firemen, guards, signalmen, porters and clerks together with locomotive mechanics, carpenters and plumbers, who laboured in the railway workshops and engine sheds beside the station. Since the electrification of the railway in 1974 and with separate trains running to Edinburgh and Glasgow from England, this activity has more or less ceased. The trains from the south for Edinburgh no longer go through the station, most of those for Glasgow no longer stop, and there are very few local trains to and from Glasgow and Edinburgh. The whole place has an air of desolation and dereliction.

About halfway between Carstairs Village and Carstairs Junction and convenient for both is Monteith Park, a public park extending to more than 23 acres (9.3 ha.) and so named because of the part played by the late Major J. B. L. Monteith in bringing the project to fruition. It contains a football pitch, a putting green, a bowling green and a children's playground as well as facilities for tennis, hockey and cricket. The connection of the Monteith family with Carstairs goes back to 1819 when Mr Henry Monteith, who was an M.P. and twice Lord Provost of Glasgow, bought the barony of Carstairs. He was an extremely wealthy textile merchant concerned with cotton, calico-printing and Turkey-red dyeing. He employed 900 workers at Barrowfield Mill in Glasgow and a comparable number at the purpose-built village of Blantyre. Here housing was provided for the employees together with a school and a church. Conditions must have been above average, for workers came to Blantyre from Owen's mills in New Lanark to better themselves. With factory discipline strictly enforced and the village public house carefully regulated, an industrious and sober population was maintained. In 1821–23 Henry Monteith built the magnificent Tudor Gothic Carstairs House, of which the architect was William Burn of Edinburgh, who a few years later designed Milton Lockhart in Carluke. Situated at NS 942443 on a bank sloping down to the Clyde, it was the home of the Monteiths until early in the present century. It is now a nursing home for the elderly and known as Monteith House. In the grounds of the house there can be seen a mausoleum in the form of a small classical temple standing on a mound, and a disused ice house. Ice houses were used before the days of refrigerators for keeping food cool. They were built mainly

9.1. Carstairs House.

underground and for extra coolness were sometimes built on the bank of a river. Ice was laid on the floor between layers of straw and, when pounded and mixed with salt, would keep for two years. The external appearance of this ice house is that of a circular or oval mound about 10 or 12 ft (3 or 4 m.) across and with a stone entrance. It is thought that the idea of an ice house came from Italy, where peasants stored food in caves using ice gathered from the mountains. An indication of the opulence of some late nineteenth century landowners is provided by the private electric railway, built by Joseph Monteith sometime in the 1880s, which ran for about 1½ miles (2.4 km.) from Carstairs House to the entrance lodge at Carstairs Junction. The electricity was generated at Cleghorn Mill using the water of the Mouse and then conducted over a distance of 4 miles (6.4 km.) by overhead cable.

The road leading on from Carstairs Junction to meet the A70 passes the State (Mental) Hospital, a large complex of buildings on a site of about 200 acres (80 ha.). The institution has had several names over the years but, whatever it may be called, it is essentially a prison for criminal lunatics. On the north side of that stretch of the A70, about 2 miles (3 km.) in length, between its junction with the A721 and the end of the road coming from Carstairs Junction, lots of little hillocks known to geologists as *kames* are to be seen. These deposits of sand and gravel are products of glacial activity during the Ice Age, which ended about 10,000 years ago.

As the A70 progresses eastwards towards Carnwath the first interesting thing to be seen from it is the Carnwath motte standing among trees on Carnwath Golf Course. Situated at NS 975466, it is a most impressive earth work, measuring 29 ft (9 m.) in height and 44 ft (13.5 m.) in diameter. It has no bailey (see p. 25). The motte was probably built about the year 1140 for William de Somerville, an Anglo-Norman who came to Libberton from Yorkshire during the reign of David I. It should really be designated Libberton motte for its site was originally in the parish of Libberton Indeed, the lands of Carnwath, consisting of about 39,000 acres (15,800 ha.), were originally in the Parish of Libberton. When the church in Carnwath was erected in 1167, the Parish of Carnwath, covering about 35,000 acres (14,200 ha.), was created and the remaining 4,000 acres (1,600 ha.) retained by Libberton. The name *Charnwid* appeared at this time and was replaced by *Karnwic* in 1174, by *Carnewith* in 1186 and by *Karnebuth* in 1200: It is derived from the Cumbric words *carn gwydd* meaning 'cairn of (the) wood'. The Somervilles lived first of all at Newbigging but from 1317 until 1602 their seat was Couthally Castle, of which very little now remains, situated north of Carnwath between the B7016 road to Braehead and the railway line to Edinburgh.

The history of the Somervilles and their successors, the Dalzells and Lockharts, is too long to be related in any detail here, but certain things should be said about it. One of the Somervilles fought at the Battle of Largs in 1263. Hugh, the 5th Lord Somerville, was a great favourite of James V, who honoured him by being present at his daughter's wedding at Couthally Castle in 1532. The King renewed his visits on several occasions. The 5th Lord Somerville was taken prisoner at the Battle of Solway Moss in 1542 and died in 1548. His son James, the 6th Lord Somerville, joined Queen Mary at Hamilton with 300 horse after her escape from Lochleven Castle in 1568. He died in 1569 and was succeeded by his son Hugh, who forsook the old religion and attached himself to the Reformers. When Hugh died in 1597 his successor

9.2. Couthally Castle.

was his son Gilbert, the 8th Lord, during whose time the family fortunes declined to such a low ebb that the barony of Carnwath had to be sold. It was bought in 1602 by the Earl of Mar, and resold in 1630 to Robert, Lord Dalzell, who was created Earl of Carnwath in 1639. The Dalzells retained the barony only until the early 1680s, when the 4th Earl sold it to Sir George Lockhart, Lord President of the Court of Session from 1685 until 1689 and second son of Sir James Lockhart of Lee. It was said of Sir George by a rival that 'He might be called a second Cicero. He could arrange his arguments so that they supported each other like the stones of an arch'. Sir George Lockhart was murdered in Edinburgh by John Chiesly of Kersewell after he had acted as an arbitrator in a dispute between Chiesly and his wife, who succeeded in her claim for alimony. Chiesly was so infuriated by his friend's decision that he shot him as he was walking home from church one Sunday. He was immediately arrested, was tried on the Monday and sentenced to have his right hand cut off before being hanged on the Wednesday with the pistol that he had used suspended round his neck.

Sir George Lockhart was succeeded by his eldest son George (1673–1731) who, as an outright Jacobite, played a very significant part in the negotiations leading up to the Union of the English and Scottish Parliaments in 1707. When Queen Anne in 1706 nominated two sets of Commissioners, one Scottish and one English, – each with a pro-Union bias – George Lockhart was the only anti-unionist among the Scottish commissioners. His book, *Memoirs of the Affairs of Scotland from Queen Anne's Accession to the Throne to the Commencement of the Union of the Two Kingdoms of Scotland and England in May, 1707*, published in 1714, gives an account of the events leading up to the Union that goes right to the heart of the matter and, although it has a Jacobite bias, it is accurate as regards facts. Lockhart's character-sketches of the personalities involved, such as Fletcher of Saltoun and the Earl of Seaforth, stand out prominently in the contemporary accounts of the negotiations. The 2nd George Lockhart like his father met with a violent death, being killed in 1731 in a duel whose cause is unknown.

The last George, born in 1700 and son of the 3rd George, who became known as the Hunting George because of his love of sport and to distinguish him from his grandfather, father and son all with the name George, was A.D.C. to Prince Charles. He fought at Culloden in April, 1746 and after a period in hiding joined the Prince to set sail for France in September, 1746. He never returned and for legal reasons was regarded as having died in 1761. He was the George Lockhart whose statue was erected mistakenly on the monument at Glenfinnan. When the 3rd George died in 1765, he was succeeded by his younger son James (1727–1790), who distinguished himself in the service of Maria Theresa and became a count of the Holy Roman Empire. On the death in 1802 of James' son Charles, who was unmarried, the estates of Lee and Carnwath devolved upon his cousin Alexander, son of Charles, youngest son of the 3rd George. Alexander had married Elizabeth Macdonald of Largie (in Kintyre), a distant cousin of Flora Macdonald, and had added her name to his own. The (Macdonald) Lockhart family is still in possession.

St Mary's Aisle, attached to the present Carnwath parish church, is all that remains of a collegiate church built by Thomas de Somerville in 1424. Of special interest is its vaulted roof covered with stone slabs and the fine tracery in the north window. It

9.3. St Mary's Aisle, Carnwath.

contains memorials of Somervilles, Dalzells and Lockharts and is still the property of the Lockhart family. The churchyard in which it stands contains the graves of local Covenanters. The present church was built in 1867 to a design by David Bryce. Its congregation has been formed by successive unions of United Presbyterian, Free and Established churches.

Carnwath was made a burgh of barony in 1451 with the usual privileges but, when this status was confirmed in 1491, a weekly market on Sundays and an additional annual fair were allowed. When, a century later, the General Assembly of the Church of Scotland disciplined the Lord Somerville of the time for holding a market on the Sabbath Day, he 'alleged an ancient custom and privilege granted to him and his predecessors by the kings of Scotland and confirmed by James IV and James V'. However, such was the power and authority of the Church that he agreed 'that no market should be held there any more on that day'. The *Court Book of the Barony of Carnwath, 1523–1542*, edited by W. C. Dickinson and published by the Scottish History Society in 1937, is an invaluable source of information, especially its long introductory chapter.

9.4. The Wee Bush Inn, Carnwath.

The seventeenth century Market Cross, whose column acts as a mileage indicator, stands in front of the modern Town Hall. Many of the houses on the long Main Street are built on the sites of older houses. The Wee Bush Inn, which Robert Burns is known to have visited in 1786, dates from 1750. The inn may possibly have acquired its name from the motto 'Better a Wee Bush than nae Beild' on Burns' coat of arms. The coat of arms was unofficial until 1988, when it was approved, after minor alterations had been made, for the use of the Burns Federation.

An event of some historical interest that is still held annually in Carnwath is the Red Hose Race which, dating back to the year 1508, is thought to be the oldest foot-race in Scotland. It was run on the Feast Day of St John the Baptist. Each year the laird of Carnwath was obliged either to give a pair of red hose as a prize 'to whoever shall run faster (*sic)* from the east end of the town to Calla Cross' or forfeit his lands. The race, now held in August rather than in June, is run in the Sir John Mann Memorial Park.

The B7016 road from Carnwath to Biggar leaves Carnwath about halfway along Main Street and after passing the disused railway line that ran from Carstairs to Dunsyre and Dolphinton from 1867 until 1932 (1950) for passenger (goods) traffic, crosses the Medwin at a place where the river has a sandy bank and where in hot weather children can bathe. The Medwin is formed by the confluence of the North and South Medwins which rise, respectively, on the western and eastern slopes of the Pentlands. The Medwin enters the Clyde after a tortuous course at NS 974443, rather less than half a mile (0.8 km.), as the crow flies, from where the B7016 crosses it.

About a mile (1.6 km.) further on from this point is the hamlet of Libberton, which stands at a height of more than 700 ft (213 m.). The parish church in Libberton was built in 1812 but its interior was extensively and beautifully renovated in 1902 by the widow of Patrick Fraser, M.D., a son of the Rev. John Fraser, the minister of Libberton, who wrote the article on Libberton in Sir John Sinclair of Ulbster's *Statistical Account of Scotland* published in 1792. With several stained-glass windows installed in it as memorials, the church is altogether a fine one. Reference has been made in Chapter 8 to the burial in Biggar churchyard of several ancestors of the statesman W. E. Gladstone, including his great-grandfather John Gladstone (1694–1758), who was the first of them to be buried there. The earlier members of the family, as Gledstanes of that ilk, were buried in Libberton Church. Latterly, they were lairds of Arthurshiel. The family name was changed from Gledstane to Gladstane and finally to Gladstone.

As the B7016 wends its way to Biggar, some fine panoramic views to the north are obtained. At NT 029408 a side road goes off to the right/west to join, after passing Huntfield and Shieldhill, the road from Thankerton to Libberton at Quothquan.

Shieldhill was the home of the Chancellor family, one of the oldest if not the oldest family, in the Biggar district. The Chancellors are thought to have come from France with the Somervilles of Carnwath, whom they regarded as superiors, after the Norman Conquest. The oldest of their charters still extant is dated 1432 and was renewed in 1472. In 1568 William Chancellor fought on the side of Mary, Queen of Scots, that is, on the losing side, at the Battle of Langside and as a result had his mansion house at Quothquan burnt down, just as the Hamiltons had had at Craignethan (see Chapter 6). After this disaster, the Chancellors moved to Shieldhill, where they renovated an old tower and made it habitable. In the early eighteenth century the tower-house was converted into a mansion which, after alterations in the nineteenth century, evolved into the present house, which became a hotel in 1959. During the troubled reigns of Charles I and Charles II Robert Chancellor, distinguished by his loyalty to these two kings, was opposed to, or at least was indifferent to, the Presbyterian form of Church government and in 1639 had an altercation with the Presbytery of Lanark. He had forced open the door of Quothquan Kirk and buried his wife somewhere inside. This deed was abhorrent to the Presbytery, which ordered him to be disciplined by the kirk session of Quothquan Church.

When Robert Chancellor died in 1664 he was succeeded by his son James, whose political and ecclesiastical views were different from those of his father. He was an ardent supporter of the Covenanters and was imprisoned for having given shelter to some of those who had fled after the battle at Bothwell Bridge. James was the Chancellor who violently took possession of the land at Parkholm.

The B7016 between Libberton and Biggar skirts on the right/west the extensive Biggar Common. This was at one time covered with trees, but these were blown down during the terrific storm on the night of 28th December, 1879, when the Tay Bridge collapsed with the loss of 75 lives. Biggar Common has recently been a happy hunting ground for archaeologists.

As the B7016 enters Biggar it passes Loaningdale House which, after being a list D school for young offenders, is now (since 1993) fully operational as a children's holiday and outdoor education centre. The house can accommodate 120 children in bedrooms for from two to eight, while many sporting attractions are offered in its spacious grounds.

10

The Pentland Villages

At the eastern end of Carnwath the A70 turns left/north to continue on its way to Edinburgh along what is known as 'the Lang Whang'; *whang* means a bootlace made of leather. Until it reaches the outskirts of Edinburgh this road is a lonely one and cautious motorists going from, say, Lanark or Carluke to Edinburgh prefer the much less scenic route through Forth and the Calders. They fear having a breakdown, especially after dark, with no nearby house to go to for help, and knowing that a passing motorist fearing a hold-up would be reluctant to stop.

By going northwards along the A70 and branching off towards Calla farm, one can see the remains of a broch at NS 991488. The site of this very dilapidated structure was discovered in 1952 and has not yet been excavated. Standing on a rocky knoll within an oval enclosure of which two long stretches remain, the broch has an inside diameter of 38 ft (11.6 m.) and has walls about 16 ft (5 m.) thick. A little to the north of Calla farm a road going off to the right/east leads to Wester Yardhouse farm not far from which at NT 004507 is the only souterrain – an underground passage built of stone – in Clydesdale. The passage, situated on the crest of a low ridge, is about 39 ft (12 m.) in length and about 5 ft (1.5 m.) in width and in height. The souterrain was excavated in 1923 but its date is unknown. Souterrains are thought to have been used for storage purposes.

Almost on the border of the former Strathclyde and Lothian Regions and approached by a side road leaving the A70 at NT 028552 is the remote village of Tarbrax. Now almost a dormitory village, it was at one time a thriving centre of the shale industry. Shale workings were carried on in Tarbrax from 1864 onwards, but it was only in 1904, when the Caledonian Oil Company took possession of the rebuilt works, that the industry boomed and the village sprang up. At one time the school had fourteen teachers and in 1925, when the mines and works, then owned by the Tarbrax Oil Company, closed down, about 600 workers were employed. The reason for the closure was that unfavourable market conditions had been prevailing for several years; it had become more economical to refine crude oil imported from the Middle East. After the closure of the works more than 200 company-owned houses were demolished and within a few years the remainder were sold off cheaply. There was, however, a renewal of activity in the village during World War II, when American troops were stationed in it. At present only relatively few houses and a distinctive pink-coloured bing remain.

Fully a mile (1.6 km.) from where it parts company with the A70, the A721 reaches the hamlet of Kaimend (so-called because of its position at the eastern edge of a kame), a short distance south of which is Carnwath Mill, immortalised by the song of that name that begins with the words 'I'm no' awa' to bide awa''. The next village on the road is Newbigging, where a side road breaks off to the left/north-east to Dunsyre and Dolphinton, and where the Mercat Cross is noteworthy. The date 1693 and the letters G. L., the initials of George Lockhart, Laird of Carnwath at that time, are incised on the back. According to an oral

10.1. The Mercat Cross, Newbigging.

tradition the cross originally stood at Dolphinton but was moved to Dunsyre when the market was transferred there. At a later date, when the market moved to Skirling, it was arranged for a group of young men to transport the cross to its new resting place but, while doing so, they were caught in a snowstorm at Newbigging and had to leave the cross there temporarily. However, when they returned in due course to take the cross to Skirling, the weavers of Newbigging refused to part with it, and there it has remained.

Dunsyre, standing at an altitude of about 720 to 750 ft (220 to 230 m.) at the foot of the Pentlands and about 5 miles (8 km.) from Newbigging, looks over the valley of the South Medwin to Black Mount, a prominent hill in the area that rises to a height of 1,693 ft (516 m.). The lands of Dunsyre belonged at one time to the Douglases but, about the end of the seventeenth century, they were acquired by Sir George Lockhart, President of the Court of Session, to whose family they still belong. The old castle of Dunsyre, which stood on the banks of the South Medwin, has long since disappeared. The church, around which most of the houses in the village are clustered, stands on a small 'knowe' on which a church of some kind has stood for centuries. The tower of the church dates from about 1820, while the east window and the porch date from late in the nineteenth century. The church bell, dated 1578, was replaced in 1949 by a bell dated 1843 from Blyth Bridge Church, which is now closed. The old bell now rests on a window-ledge in Dunsyre Church. The church also possesses a set of 'jougs', which can be seen in a case on the north wall beside the door of the vestry. After the union of the Dunsyre and Dolphinton congregations in 1941, Dunsyre Church became redundant but, fortunately, is still well cared for and is open for four hours each day.

The Dunsyre area was a great Covenanting district and many conventicles were held on its moors and hillsides. Donald Cargill referred to in Chapter 7, preached his last sermon on Dunsyre Common before being captured at Covington Mill by Irvine of Bonshaw in 1681. Many of the farmers in the neighbourhood of Dunsyre had to shelter among the hills when at times surprise visits from dragoons made living at home dangerous. A notable Covenanter was William Veitch, tenant of the farm of Westhills of Dunsyre, who persuaded Major Learmonth, to be referred to later, to involve himself in the Battle of Rullion Green in 1666. For his part in this battle Veitch was eventually, in 1677, tried in Edinburgh and then imprisoned on the Bass Rock. After his release, he was one of those accused of being involved in the Rye House Plot of 1683, a plan to seize Charles II on a narrow road between high banks near Rye House in Hertfordshire along which he often passed on his way to or from race-meetings at Newmarket, and to place his son, the Duke of Monmouth and Buccleuch, on the throne. The plot failed and Veitch took refuge in Holland. On his return to Scotland in 1685 he was recognised in Edinburgh, arrested and imprisoned in the Tolbooth. After the Settlement of 1690, he became minister of Peebles and then of Dumfries.

The last resting place of John Carphin, a Covenanter who fled wounded from Rullion Green, is marked at Black Law (NT 078522) fully 2 miles north of Dunsyre by a headstone erected about 1841 and inscribed as follows.

SACRED
To the Memory of
A COVENANTER
who fought and was wounded
at Rullion Green
Nov. 28th 1666
and who died at Oaken Bush
the day after the Battle
and was buried here
BY ADAM SANDERSON
OF BLACKHILL

Carphin, dying from his wounds while fleeing over the hills, had reached Blackhill, the home of Adam Sanderson, who offered him hospitality. However, the Covenanter did not accept it, firstly, for fear of reprisals on Sanderson, and secondly, because he might die out of sight of his beloved Ayrshire hills. He continued on, Sanderson accompanying him, until he died at a place called Oaken Bush. Knowing his wish, Sanderson buried him on Black Law from where the Ayrshire hills can be seen through a gap in the hills. Sanderson marked the spot with a boulder on which

10.2. The Covenanter's grave.

he carved a coded inscription that would be incomprehensible to any dragoon who might have come across the stone.

Continuing on from Dunsyre and after crossing the South Medwin, the road meets at a T-junction the road running round the foot of Black Mount, the arm on the right/west leading to Walston and the one on the left/east to Dolphinton. Dolphinton can also be reached directly from Newbigging by continuing along the A721 and, after passing through the agricultural township of Elsrickle, joining at Melbourne Crossing the A702 from Biggar. The only things of interest in Walston are the church and the graveyard surrounding it. The present church dates from the middle of the seventeenth century when a part of it, the Baillie Aisle, was erected at right angles to an older building, running from east to west, on its south side. However, at some time in the eighteenth century the older part of the church was demolished and the aisle extended in a northerly direction, so making the renovated church one of the longest in the district. As a consquence of the union in 1953 of Walston Church with the already united Dunsyre and Dolphinton Churches to form Black Mount Parish Church with the church at Dolphinton becoming the place of worship, Walston Church became redundant and is now in the care of Biggar Museum Trust. Four silver communion cups presented to Walston Church by Christopher Baillie, a merchant in Edinburgh, in 1657 were sold in 1993 for £40,000; two of them can be seen in the Moat Park Heritage Centre in Biggar. The proceeds of the sale were used to buy the redundant school at Dolphinton for use as a hall for the adjacent church. The churchyard at Walston contains two very fine examples of 'portrait' tombstones, one of Robert Wylde, who died in 1705, giving a vivid representation of the costume of the time.

The village of Dolphinton stretches for about a mile (1.6 km.) along the A 702 at a distance from Biggar that may be taken as 7 miles (11 km.) and ends just beyond the eastern boundary of South Lanarkshire District. The name *Dolphinton* is thought to have been derived from *Dolfinnr*, an old Norse personal name, and the Old English word *tun* meaning an enclosure. Although there is no known Viking settlement in Upper Clydesdale, a Norse influence was certainly felt there. Indeed Lowland Scots,

10.3. Tombstone in Walston churchyard.

as spoken by a steadily diminishing number of old people in the district, contains words derived from Old Norse, such as *blate* (bashful), *fell* (a hill), *glegg* (clear-sighted or clever), *toom* (empty), *gar* (to compel), *keekin* (to peep) and *red up* (to make tidy).

The church in Dolphinton, now designated Black Mount Parish Church, was practically rebuilt in 1786 and is surrounded by a graveyard whose circular shape implies that it is very old. Just outside the door of the church is the grave of the Covenanter Major Learmonth of Newholm, without a headstone but surrounded by a stone border with lettering on it, only part of which is now legible. As commander of the horsemen, Learmonth played a leading part in the disastrous battle at Rullion Green in 1666. After his horse had been shot under him he killed one of the four dragoons pursuing him, then mounted the dead man's horse and made good his escape despite the efforts of the other three dragoons. Afterwards every effort was made to catch him. Soldiers often traced him to Newholm but were never able to lay hands on him. His safety was ensured by an underground vault, which could be entered either through a panel on the wall of the hall or from a passage leading from an abrupt bank of the Medwin, where its entrance was covered by a large stone.

10.4. Dolphinton Church.

After taking part in the battle at Bothwell Bridge in 1679, he was betrayed by a maidservant and was imprisoned on the Bass Rock after his death sentence had been commuted. He died at Newholm in 1693 at the age of 88.

Reference has already been made in Chapter 2 to William Leechman (Leishman), D. D., who, born in Dolphinton in 1706, became Professor of Divinity in the University of Glasgow in 1744 and Principal from 1761 until his death in 1785. His classes, along with those of Francis Hutcheson, Professor of Moral Philosophy, were reported to be the best attended of the theological classes in Glasgow at the time. Both men were liberal in their views and they were the first professors to lecture in English rather than in Latin. The famous Alexander ('Jupiter') Carlyle, Minister of Inveresk (Musselburgh), referred to Leechman's lectures as 'memorable'. His preaching was by general consent eloquent. When Leechman was appointed to his chair, Francis Hutcheson predicted that he would 'put a new face on theology in Scotland'. However, this did not happen because the fear of heresy trials and the dread of being branded as an agnostic drove Leechman (and others like him) into evasiveness and silence. A powerful figure in the University, where he was involved in much infighting, Leechman was an academic politician of a high order. He was Moderator of the General Assembly of the Church of Scotland in 1757.

Dolphinton had for a time two railway stations. One was the terminus of a branch line that ran from Carstairs through Bankhead and Dunsyre, while the other was at the end of a branch line that began at Leadburn on the Edinburgh to Peebles railway.

If Dolphinton is reached from Biggar by the A 702, which here follows closely a Roman road, then Candy Mill, where Hugh MacDiarmid lived from 1951 to 1978, is passed about 3 miles (5 km.) from Biggar. Brownsbank, the house occupied by the poet, is actually on the line of the Roman road from which the modern road has deviated at this point. A short distance further on the mansion house of Edmonston, built in 1815 to a design by James Gillespie Graham, who also designed Lee Castle between Lanark and Carluke, is seen on the left. In its grounds there stand the ruined remains of the High House of Edmonston, a tower-house dating from late fifteenth century.

11
Biggar to Daer

At a distance of 3 miles (5 km.) in a southerly direction along the A702 from Biggar is the small village of Coulter. The name, pronounced 'Cootir', which appears in various forms in the old charters and as Culter in several place-names of the present day, has a Brythonic ring about it and may well come from the Cumbric word *culdir* meaning a narrow stretch of land, which indeed the parish of Coulter is. The first known owner of the lands of Coulter was Alexander de Cutir whose twelfth or thirteenth century home may have been the motte at Wolfclyde referred to in Chapter 7. The village, a most attractive one, is surrounded by several large mansion houses which, unlike so many others in the Clyde Valley, are still occupied. The oldest of them is Culter House at NT 024343, which dates from 1668. It is reached by a long avenue of trees from an entrance lodge on the main road. Then, Coulter Mains (or Maynes) near the Clyde at NT 015346 was built in 1838 for the famous antiquarian Adam Sim (1805–1868). Sim's vast collection of all sorts of things from relics dug up by the plough to torcs made of gold from the Leadhills/Wanlockhead district rivalled that of Sir Walter Scott at Abbotsford. His friends marvelled at how he was able to amass such a large collection and one of them, the Rev. James Proudfoot, was moved to write in one of his lighter moments:

> How he got them all collected
> It is safer not to say;
> Some of them, it is suggested,
> Have come in a doubtful way.

Much of Sim's collection was inherited by his niece, Jane White of Netherurd, who, in 1889, presented it to the National Museum of Antiquities of Scotland. An oil painting of Adam Sim and another including Jane White can be seen in the Moat Park Heritage Centre in Biggar. It was Adam Sim who encouraged

William Hunter to write the book *Biggar and the House of Flem-ing*, Vere Irving and Murray to write their monumental *The Upperward of Lanarkshire* in three volumes, and J. B. Greenshields to write *Annals of the Parish of Lesmahagow.*

Cornhill House, beautifully situated with a fine square tower on the right bank of the Clyde at NT 018352, was built in 1868 and Culter Allers at NT 026340 in 1880, the former for long used as a home for the elderly but now converted into a hotel.

In the village of Coulter itself the old corn mill, converted into a restaurant in 1990, and the Library, across the road from it and dating from the middle of the nineteenth century, are note-worthy.

Culter Church, standing at NT 028342 in a circular and there-fore very old churchyard, was either founded or re-established by the monks of Kelso in the twelfth century. When very sub-stantial alterations were made to the building in 1810, the chancel on the east side was blocked off from the rest of the church and then used as a mausoleum. Adam Sim is buried there. The interior of the church is beautiful and the silver communion cups, which date from 1618, are among the oldest in use in the Church of Scotland. In the north-eastern part of the graveyard there can be seen the tombstone of Anthony Murray, minister of Coulter and a well-known Covenanter. He was one of those ministers 'outed' from their parishes when episcopacy was forced on the Church by Charles II in 1662. He is reputed to have gone to Kilbucho where, being a medical doctor as well as a minister, he ministered to the people in two capacities. He was reinstated to Coulter parish some time later.

At NT 028354 on the A702 between Biggar and Coulter stands Culter Free Church, which was built after the Disruption of 1843, when more than a third of the ministers and congregations of the Church of Scotland seceded from that Church and constituted themselves as the Free Church of Scotland. The Culter congre-gation with its ever-declining membership was served for many years by a visiting minister from Edinburgh, and latterly by a Divinity student from the Free Church College in Edinburgh. In 1993, the sesquicentenary of the Disruption, the church was closed down. It has since been sold minus the pews downstairs.

Culter Fell, rising to a height of 2454 ft (748 m.), is the highest

of the Culter hills, a group forming the highest part of a considerable tract of hill country lying between the Clyde and
the upper reaches of the Tweed. A straightforward ascent of
Culter Fell can be made by taking the minor road from Coulter
village to Birthwood farm, then going a short distance along the
road leading to Culter reservoir and finally following, on either
side, the Kings Beck Burn from where it joins Culter Water. For
the keen hill walker other hills of interest in the group are
Chapelgill Hill with a height of 2282 ft (696 m.) at NT 068304,
Hillshaw Head with a height of 2139 ft (652 m.) at NT 048246,
Hudderstone Law with a height of 2055 ft (626 m.) at NT 022272
and Gathersnow Hill with a height of 2257 ft (688 m.) at NT
059257. The summits of Culter Fell and several other hills of the
group lie on the former county boundary between Lanarkshire
and Peeblesshire.

At a distance of 3 miles (5 km.) from Coulter in a southerly
direction along the A 702 is the village of Lamington, a very fine
example of a model Victorian village with its rustic cottages and
gardens in a beautiful rural setting with meadow land through
which the Clyde winds its way to the west. The name Lamington
is derived from the Flemish immigrant Lambin to whom Malcolm
IV (1153–1165) granted a portion of the royal lands of Clydesdale.
Then, in 1368, David II granted a charter to William Baillie, who
had married the heiress of Lamington, in these terms translated
from the Latin: 'David by the grace of God, King of the Scots,
know all that I have given, conceded and by this charter confirm,
to our beloved and faithful servant, Sir William Baillie, the whole
barony of Lambinestun'. The lands of Lamington were held for
centuries by the Baillies, whose family history up to 1862 is given
in the classic *Biggar and the House of Fleming* by William Hunter,
published in that year.

In 1837 Alexander Dundas Ross Wishart Baillie-Cochrane inherited the estate through his mother, who was the wife of
Admiral Sir Thomas Cochrane. The new laird was born in 1816
and was educated at Eton and Trinity College, Cambridge, where
he graduated B.A. in 1837. He was a member of the Young
England party, a group of very distinguished and very idealistic
young men, who emphasised to Disraeli that the Tory government should be a more caring one. Convinced that workers on

the land should be handled in a parental way, Mr. Baillie-Cochrane certainly looked after his own estate workers very well. He moved in influential circles and he might well have attained high office in the State as did some less able contemporaries. Possessed of considerable literary gifts, he wrote novels and poetry as well as a book on Italy. It has been said that his novel *Ernest Vane* might have become of some importance had not Lord Lytton and Disraeli described the society of the time with greater skill. He served as an M.P. for various constituencies over a period of nearly 40 years – for a time he was Queen Victoria's M.P. on the Isle of Wight – and in 1880 was raised to the peerage with the title Lord Lamington. At this time he changed his name from Baillie-Cochrane to Cochrane-Baillie. When he inherited the Lamington estate it was in an extremely rundown condition but, with patience, perseverance and the expenditure of a vast amount of money, he had transformed it into a beautiful estate by the 1850s. Land was drained, new farmhouses were built, comfortable cottages were provided for the estate workers and a substantial mansion in Tudor style with gardens and waterfalls was built for himself. The motto above the door of the house is interesting: *Pax intrantibus, salus exeuntibus, benedictio habitantibus*, i.e. peace to those coming in, safety to those going out and a blessing to those living in it. An Episcopalian chapel, Holy Trinity, with fine stained-glass windows, was built in 1857. It was greatly enriched by gifts from titled relatives and friends of the laird and his wife. The laird got little encouragement from his own bishop for this project, but it was warmly welcomed by the Church of Scotland Presbytery of Biggar (long since incorporated in the Presbytery of Lanark). Lord Lamington died in 1890 and was buried in a mausoleum adjoining the chapel.

The 2nd Lord Lamington, Charles Wallace Alexander Napier Cochrane-Baillie, born in 1860, was educated at Eton and Christ Church, Oxford and in 1895 married Mary Hozier, a daughter of the 1st Lord Newlands of Mauldslie, Carluke and therefore a full cousin of Clementine Hozier, wife of Sir Winston Churchill. Lord Lamington was Governor of Queensland from 1895 until 1901 and of Bombay from 1903 until 1907. He died in 1940.

The 3rd Lord Lamington, Victor Alexander Brisbane William Cochrane-Baillie, born in 1896, was badly handicapped by wounds sustained in World War I. He took a great interest in the village of Lamington and especially in its children. During World War II he allowed Lamington House to be used as a home for physically disadvantaged children from Edinburgh. He died in 1951 leaving no male issue and so the title became extinct. His widow, however, survived him for many years. Most of Lamington House was demolished in 1953. Both the motto stone and the heraldic stone are now in Holy Trinity Chapel.

At NS 992309 on the hillside due east of Lamington village there is a motte which, presumably, was the home of Lambin, the original owner of the lands of Lamington. Lamington Tower, of which little now remains, is situated near the Clyde at NS 980320 and is dated 1589. Tradition has it that the rest of the building was blown up at a later date by the factor of the Lamington estate to provide stones for a new building. It is possible that there was an earlier building on the site, in which case it could have been the home of Hugh Braidfute, the father of Marion whom Wallace married in Lanark in 1296; it is more likely that his home would have been the motte already referred to. According to Blind Harry, Marion Braidfute had a daughter by Wallace, and it is supposed that either this lady or her daughter

11.1. Lamington Tower.

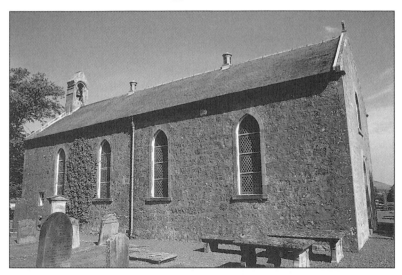

11.2. Lamington Church.

and heiress married the William Baillie to whom David II granted the charter in 1368.

The original parish church in Lamington, which was dedicated to St Ninian, was largely rebuilt in 1721 and successively restored in 1828 and in 1870 when the outside stairs were removed. Fortunately, the twelfth-century Norman doorway on the north wall of the church has been retained. The present church bell, presented by the 2nd Lord Lamington in 1929 as a thank-offering for his wife's recovery from an illness, replaced a bell cast in 1647 by James Montieth, who also made the bell in Quothquan Kirk, presented by one of the Baillies in 1650. It is noteworthy that 200 Jacobite soldiers were imprisoned in the church in 1715 and that, when Robert Burns visited the church in February, 1789, he was very unimpressed and scribbled down these words (which were not published until 1824):

> As cauld a wind as ever blew,
> A cauld Kirk and in't but few,
> As cauld a minister's ever spak,
> Ye's a' be het or I come back.
> [You'll all be hot ere I come back]

The minister at the time was the Rev. Thomas Mitchell. The church, no longer used as a place of worship, is now under the care of Biggar Museum Trust, as is the Episcopal chapel of Holy Trinity. The former is the workshop and studio of Mr C. McCartney, an artist whose work is represented by a stained glass window installed in Biggar Kirk in 1991, while it is hoped that the latter may become a centre for the history of Lamington and the Baillie family.

About a mile (1.6 km.) south-west of Lamington the B 7055, leading to the A70 near Rigside, branches off from the A 702 and, after crossing the Clyde and the A73, enters the hamlet of Wiston. The bridge across the Clyde was built in 1835 or 1836, at which time a long stretch of the Lamington side of the river was embanked at a cost of £2,000.

Wiston was founded with the name Wicestun by Wice (or Wicius) – a name not uncommon in Flanders – who gave it to the Abbey of Kelso some time between 1160 and 1164. Wiston church, now a dwelling house, dates from 1886. Its congregation united with that of Roberton in 1938 and then in 1971 this united church became united in a triple union with Crawfordjohn and Abington Church and with Lamington and Wandel Church to form Duneaton Parish Church, Abington Church being used as the place of worship. The two principal residences in the district are Hardington House and Wiston Lodge. Hardington House, built in 1720, was owned at one time by Lord Braxfield (see Chapter 2), who added a spacious wing to each end of it. After having been owned by several of Braxfield's descendants, it had a succession of owners unrelated to each other; it is presently occupied by Mr Robin McCosh. Wiston Lodge, a nineteenth-century house set in a peaceful rural environment, was built by Mr James Ferguson, who had started life as a miner at Auchenheath. Mr R. D. Macgregor, who took possession during World War I, was a generous benefactor of Wiston. He built the village hall and gave an endowment to the church. Belonging to the evangelical wing of the Church, he often gave hospitality to Christian workers in his home and arranged for religious services to be held in the hall that he had built. Since he left no male heir when he died, his house might well have been demolished had it not been that, on the outbreak of World War II, Lanarkshire

County Council requisitioned it as a school for evacuated children. After the house was released, it was bought in 1946 by the YMCA as a conference and holiday centre and is still in use in that capacity. It is open to people of all creeds and colours, and of all faiths or none.

Greenhill farmhouse, the seventeenth century laird's residence that was transported stone by stone to Burnbraes, Biggar, and re-erected there as a Covenanters' Museum, stood on the north side of the B 7055 at NS 936327, rather more than 1¼ miles (2 km.) from Wiston village.

About 2.5 miles (4 km.) south-west of Lamington there stand on a rocky promontory the remains, almost level with the ground, of the fortalice known as the Bower of Wandel. Being surrounded by the Clyde on three sides, it must have been in a strong position in feudal times. It is likely that it was the tower-house of the Jardine family, who owned land here for generations from the twelfth century onwards. George Jardine (1742–1827), Professor of Logic in the University of Glasgow from 1774 until 1827, was a native of Wandel. He greatly improved the teaching of Logic in the University and commanded the respect of the students even in his old age. (In 1768 a student, David Woodburn, had asserted that 'more good was to be got by attending the theatre, than the drowsy shops of Logic and Metaphysics'. He was solemnly rebuked for making this shocking statement, after a nine days' trial in the Rector's Court.) Jardine was one of the founders of Glasgow Royal Infirmary and later was its Secretary. His portrait, belonging to the University of Glasgow, hangs in the present Board Room of the Infirmary. James V is reputed to have used the Bower of Wandel as a hunting lodge.

On the A73 on the opposite side of the Clyde from the Bower of Wandel and about 2.5 miles (4 km.) to the south of Wiston stands the hamlet of Roberton on the burn of the same name and with some of its houses perched on the steep slopes above the stream. At one time it was a popular holiday resort although, unlike Symington and Abington on either side of it, it lacked a railway station. The hamlet owes its name to Robert, the brother of Lambin already referred to. There is a reference in an early charter to a chapel at Roberton. The church, situated in a circular graveyard, was built in 1891 and united with the church in

Wiston in 1938. The building is now private property. The corn mill in Roberton with its lade dates from the end of the eighteenth century. The bridge spanning the burn at Roberton is thought by some to date from 1661–1663 but by others to date from 1769.

Two Roman remains at Wandel have been discovered by aerial photography. At NS 944268 there is a fortlet, trapezoidal in plan, occupying the summit of a small hill. Because of cultivation of the land, nothing of the fortlet can be seen on the surface; it was only by probing and a limited amount of excavation that any information was gleaned. Of the temporary camp, which is due south of the fortlet at NS 944266, only a part of the rampart is visible.

At a short distance south-west of Wandel the A702 crosses the Clyde and, after being met by the A73, crosses the Duneaton Water, a substantial tributary of the Clyde, rising on the slopes of Cairntable on the boundary between Lanarkshire and Ayrshire. Rather less than a mile (1.6 km.) further on, Abington motte with its bailey is clearly seen between the road and the Clyde at NS 932249. Built by John, stepson of Baldwin, possibly the Fleming, the motte is defended on the south-east by the river, down to which there is a steep drop of about 33 ft (10 m.) and on the south-west by a burn running into the Clyde. The oval-shaped mound is 6.6 ft (2 m.) in height and measures 66 ft by 39 ft (20 m. by 12 m.) on the top. The bailey, which lies mainly to the north of the mound and within an earthen rampart, measures 263 ft by 190 ft (80 m. by 58 m.). The monument on the top of the mound commemorates Matthew McKendrick (1848–1926), who was postmaster at Abington and who did much to improve angling on the Clyde.

At Nether Abington the A702 merges at a roundabout with the B7078 and the recently constructed M74, which have come over the moor from Douglas. At about 3 miles (4.8 km.) back along the B7078, the B740 breaks off to pass through the hamlet of Crawfordjohn and ultimately to meet the A76 near Sanquhar. Crawfordjohn, lying in the luscious valley of the Duneaton Water about 2 miles (3.2 km.) along the B740, was at one time a well-populated rural community. The earliest notice of it appears in the charter already referred to by which Wice (or Wicius), Lord of Wiston, granted to the monks of Kelso, some time between 1160 and 1164, the lands of Wiston, which included Roberton and Crawfordjohn. The charter refers to Crawfordjohn as the *villa* of John, the stepson of Baldwin. It is often assumed, though it can be argued that it is wrong to do so, that Baldwin was the famous Baldwin of Biggar, the first Sheriff of Lanarkshire. Crawfordjohn was erected into a burgh of barony by a charter granted by Charles II to Anne, Duchess of Hamilton, in 1668. The Duchess in due course conveyed the lands to her son, the Earl of Selkirk, from one of whose successors, the 4th Earl, they were purchased by Sir George Colebrooke at a date no later than 1793, when he is known to have exercised his right of patronage of Crawfordjohn Church. During the nineteenth century, the Colebrooke family were very distinguished in public life as bankers, politicians, Indian administrators and Scottish lairds. One of them, Henry Thomas Colebrooke (1765–1837), during his 32 years' stay in India,

11.3. Henry T. Colebrooke.

became very interested in the language and culture of that country and, as a consequence of his study of Sanskrit, realised the connection between the Indian and European languages. Max Müller, the leading authority in his day on comparative philology, paid him this tribute:

> His most lasting fame will not only be that of the able administrator, the thoughtful financier and politician, but also that of the founder of Sanskrit scholarship in Europe. In the latter character, Colebrooke has secured his place in the history of the world.

Sir Thomas Edward Colebrooke, Henry's son, who was born in 1813, was a fine classical scholar, a close friend of W. E. Gladstone, and played a prominent part in the deliberations leading to the passing of the great Education Act of 1872. His son, Sir Edward Arthur Colebrooke, was raised to the peerage in 1906, became a Privy Councillor and, as Lord Colebrooke, was Lord-in-Waiting to King Edward VII from 1906 until 1911. He entertained the Prince of Wales, later King George V, at Glengonnar House in 1904 and Edward himself in 1906. According to oral tradition the King's visit, which lasted for five days, was extraordinarily costly. The extravagances that the King expected his hosts to provide on such visits were almost unbelievable. The first royal visit to Crawfordjohn was by James V in 1541 when he came on a hunting expedition and at the same time investigated the gold-bearing potential of the district.

In due course, the Colebrookes sold their land of about 27,000 acres (11,000 ha.) to the Douglas Homes one of whom, Lord Home of the Hirsel, owned a house in the district until his death in 1995. Another family who left their mark on the district were the Mitchells of tobacco fame, one of whom founded the Mitchell Library in Glasgow. In 1921 Stephen Mitchell, M.P. bought Gilkerscleugh House, a beautiful mansion which was, unfortunately, burnt down and then demolished in the 1950s. The stones were used as bottoming for the A 74 (now B7078).

Crawfordjohn Kirk, standing on the site of a medieval church and built in 1817, is now a heritage centre displaying amongst other things copies of local records, a plan of the kirkyard as it was in 1889, school logbooks and photographs, and various

11.4. Crawfordjohn Kirk.

artefacts. The church is now included in the ecclesiastical parish of Glencaple, with Abington Church as the place of worship.

The mill in Crawfordjohn, no longer in use, was driven by the Duneaton Water. Crawfordjohn was famous at one time for the manufacture of curling stones from the igneous rock essexite, a variety of alkali gabbro, found at Craighead. Ailsa Craig was its only rival in this respect.

Some time after the Revolution Settlement of 1689–1690, Crawfordjohn became the headquarters of the Cameronians, the religious sect formed under the leadership of Richard Cameron and Donald Cargill that now objected to the Settlement and wished to see again the ecclesiastical polity that had prevailed between 1638 and 1649. Unfortunately for the movement, its only ministers, three in number, joined the Church of Scotland in 1690, so that from that time until 1706, when the Rev. John Macmillan, the deposed minister of Balmaghie in Kirkcudbrightshire, was appointed minister at Crawfordjohn by the Cameronian "Societies", there was no preacher available to dispense the sacraments. Many children were never baptised. Working single-handed for 37 years from his headquarters in Crawfordjohn, Macmillan visited the Cameronian dispersion in Lanarkshire, Fife, the Lothians, Perth, Ayr and elsewhere, not only preaching but clearing up the arrears of baptisms that had accumulated. The zenith of Macmillan's career was reached in 1712 when he presided over a conventicle, held on Auchensaugh Moor near Crawfordjohn (but actually in the parish of Douglas), at which the Covenants were renewed. The proceedings lasted from a Thursday until the following Monday with a Communion service on the Sunday at which it is said that more than a thousand people participated in relays. At the 'fencing of the tables' Macmillan not only forbade the unworthy to come forward – a standard practice then and for long afterwards – but also took the opportunity to excommunicate Queen Anne, her Parliament and all her adherents. With the changed climate of public opinion prevailing by this time, his utterances were simply ignored. After his long and faithful ministry Macmillan went to live in Dalserf where he died in 1753 at the age of 84 and, as mentioned in Chapter 6, was buried in the churchyard there. When the Cameronians acquired a second minister, Thomas Nairn, in 1743, the Reformed Presbyterian Church of Scotland was founded. In due course it expanded and set up sister churches in Ireland, North America, Australia and Japan. The church united with the Free Church in 1876 except for a small minority whose successors still carry on; in 1998 this minority had only five congregations in Scotland with 275 members in all.

The Crawfordjohn district is very interesting archaeologically. During the construction of the M74 to the north of the A74 (now B7078) a circle of 23 stones was discovered at Wildshaw in 1990. The stones belong to either the late Neolithic Age (4000–2000 B.C.) or the early Bronze Age (2500–600 B.C.). Then, at Snar and at Glendorch, the ruins of bastle houses (see Chapter 4) dating from the late sixteenth century have been found. Mention must also be made of an Iron Age (600 B.C. to A.D. 400) fort at Black Hill (NS 908239). The nearly circular region bounded by the rampart, which is 23.9 ft (7.3 m.) thick at the base and stands 5.9 ft (1.8 m.) in height above the ditch, whose greatest depth is 3.28 ft (1 m.), measures about 200 ft (say, 60 m.) in diameter. Within there is a nearly circular but not concentric region about 121 ft (37 m.) in diameter bounded by a stone wall now in a ruinous state. Other remains of minor importance include a barrow and two cairns on the flanks of Black Hill.

As regards education in Crawfordjohn, the account written for the New (i.e. Second) Statistical Account of Scotland in the middle of the nineteenth century is interesting in that it shows the emphasis placed on the Classics in Scottish education at that time. The dominie, who taught English, Writing, Arithmetic, Geography, Latin, Greek and French, had an average of about 80 pupils, or scholars as they were called at that time and for long afterwards. In 1836 he had three advanced pupils, two of them aged 14 and one aged 11. These children, continuously drilled in Latin grammar, had read three books of Livy and almost the whole of Horace. They were also given instruction in Latin verse composition. In addition, they had read two of the Gospels in the original Greek and were about to begin the study of French. They must have been both able and industrious! The same remark applies to the boys whom Dorothy Wordsworth met in the Mennock Pass (see Chapter 12).

As the M74 approaches Abington, a small estate village set up by Sir Thomas Colebrooke, which it bypasses, Arbory Hill, 1407 ft (429 m.) high is prominent on the other/east side of the Clyde. On the summit at NS 944238 there are the very well preserved

11.5. Abington from the north.

remains of an Iron Age (600 B.C. to A.D. 400.) hill-fort. With the ground falling off steeply on three sides, the fort was readily accessible only from the east. Defended by both inner and outer ramparts, each with a ditch, the interior of the fort measures 269 ft by 226 ft (82 m. by 69 m.). Within the inner rampart there are the ruins of a stone wall enclosing a nearby circular area of about 141 ft (43 m.) in diameter. The wall, within which there are traces of three wooden houses, is thought to be of a later date than the ramparts. The fort has five entrances.

Glengonnar House, formerly the home of the Colebrookes, at the southern end of Abington, is no longer in existence. Nearby, on the site of Abington House, burnt down in 1898, is Glengonnar Centre, an outdoor education centre for young male offenders.

A road leaving the M74 at NS 941205 and rejoining it at NS 959200 after a distance of about 2 miles (3 km.) serves the long straggling village of Crawford. The village, standing at an altitude of about 900 ft (270 m.) and therefore a very cold place in winter, is of nineteenth-century origin. Having until 1965 a railway station on the main line from Glasgow and Edinburgh to the South, and being therefore readily accessible from these two cities, it became a popular holiday resort. Good angling on the Clyde was and still is one of its attractions.

Crawford Church was built in 1874 when the congregation, feeling that its church was too close to the railway, moved away from the centre of the village. The new church got a new bell, and the old bell, thought to date from about 1570, is now the property of the Crawfordjohn Heritage Venture Trust. Crawford Church was united with Duneaton Parish Church to form Glencaple Parish Church, the church in Abington being the place of worship. The Glencaple and Lowther Churches have now been linked and are served by one minister, who preaches in both Abington and Leadhills.

Across the Clyde from Crawford are the ruins, now in a dangerous condition, of Castle Crawford or Tower Lindsay, for generations the ancestral home of the Lindsay family. David Lindsay was created Earl of Crawford in 1398 and was given a charter by Robert III elevating Crawford, which had been erected into a burgh of barony by Robert II in 1370, into a regality. A few significant events in the history of Crawford are the following.

The castle came into the possession of Archibald, Earl of Angus ('Bell the Cat'), in 1488; it eventually passed from the Angus branch to the Hamilton branch of the Douglas family with whom it remained until the time of Duchess Anne, who passed it on to her son, the Earl of Selkirk. Then, about the end of the eighteenth century, it was sold to Sir George Colebrooke. It has now been deserted for about two centuries. The 20 ft (6 m.) high mound was probably a twelfth century motte.

James V is reputed to have given a dinner party at Crawford Castle at which the guests, when they sat down, found a covered plate in front of each of them. When they lifted off the covers, after Grace had been said, they were surprised to find their plates heaped with silver from the mines in the Leadhills area.

A little to the west of the castle are the remains of a Roman fort, which was located and partially excavated in 1938, but whose existence had been surmised by General Roy in the eighteenth century. From further excavations made between 1961 and 1966 it has been concluded that the fort had three periods of occupation. The fort, which was built in the Flavian period about A.D. 80 or 81 and early in the campaign of Agricola, was a small one and could not accommodate a whole regiment. It was

11.6. Castle Crawford.

demolished in A.D. 86 or 87 after Agricola, despite his successes and, in particular, his victory over the Picts at Mons Graupius in A.D. 84, was ordered to withdraw and return to Rome. His son-in-law and biographer Tacitus wrote bitterly of this in his oft-quoted remark that *perdomita Britannia et statim omissa*, i.e. Britain was subdued and immediately given up. Subsequently, the Romans adopted a defensive rather than an offensive strategy in Scotland.

In due course native pressure began to increase and reached its peak at the beginning of the reign of Antoninus Pius in 138 A.D. Lollius Urbicus was appointed Governor of Britain with the special task of expelling the invading tribes and of creating a new frontier. The wall now known as Antonine's wall was built from the Forth to the Clyde about A.D. 142 and, as forts and roads were still required to maintain the security of the hinterland, the large fort at Castledykes and the small fort at Crawford were reoccupied. The occupation of Antonine's wall and of these two forts lasted until A.D. 154 or 155, when the troops were moved away to help deal with the Brigantes, the tribe occupying the territory south of Hadrian's wall, which had been built from the Solway to the Tyne in A.D. 121. After the Brigantes had been pacified and Hadrian's wall made secure, the Antonine wall was reoccupied about A.D. 158. However, in A.D. 163 Hadrian's wall was regarrisoned and the Antonine wall with its associated forts was eventually abandoned. The third occupation of the Crawford fort thus came to an end.

The fort, being situated at the junction of the road from Annandale and the road coming up through Durisdeer from Nithsdale, had extensive views along the valley of the Clyde to the south-east and to the west. It guarded the bridge or ford by which the latter road crossed the Clyde. The view to the north was not so good. The road going in that direction climbed up the south-eastern face of Castle Hill in a zig-zag manner skilfully engineered to ensure that the gradient was nowhere greater than 1 in 6, and reached a height of 351 ft (107 m.) above the floor of the valley before descending the north side of Castle Hill to reach level ground at NS 937246 near Cold Chapel. The reason for this tortuous upland diversion from a route simply following the Clyde is that at about a mile (1.6 km.) or so onwards from the fort the road would have had to traverse a narrow strip of level ground with a steep rocky scarp on one side and a steep drop to the river on the other, a situation suitable for an ambush or a blockade.

A minor road going in an easterly direction from the fort and Crawford Castle and passing the farm of Midlock, well known for long as a home of pedigree Blackface sheep, leads to the Camps reservoir. This was built by the Lanarkshire County Council to provide water for industrial Lanarkshire. It took fourteen years (1916–1930) to complete and at one time up to about 200 German prisoners of War were engaged on the work. The grave of one of these prisoners, marked by a German Military Cross, can be seen in the old graveyard at Kirkton about halfway between Abington and Crawford. In 1992 some archaeologists excavated part of a Bronze Age site normally submerged by the reservoir and found the remains of a cemetery. Cremation was evidently the practice.

About 2.5 miles (4 km.) southwards from Crawford along the M74 the A 702 leaves this road to pass through the hamlet of Elvanfoot before going down the Dalveen Pass to reach Carron-bridge in Nithsdale. At Elvanfoot, and near where the Elvan joins the Clyde, the B7040 breaks off from the A702 to reach Leadhills 5 miles (8 km.) away. The church at Elvanfoot, now a dwelling house, contained a stained-glass window, now the property of Lowther Kirk Session, in memory of Wilson Barret, the celebrated actor, who lived for a time at Watermeetings House near where the Daer and the Potrail Waters meet at NS 954137. Watermeetings is reached by a road leaving the A702 at NS 950133 about 3 miles (5 km.) south of Elvanfoot and leading to the Daer reservoir.

The construction of the Daer reservoir, which provides a copious supply of water for central Lanarkshire, must rank as one of the greatest achievements of the Lanarkshire County Council. Work having started in 1948, the reservoir was opened officially on 18th October, 1956 by Queen Elizabeth II, who was presented with a brooch made of gold from Leadhills as a memento of the occasion. With a capacity of 5,600 million gallons, the reservoir has a daily output of around 28 million gallons. The water is not only particularly clean but is also low in aluminium content. The treatment works have now been upgraded at a cost of £4 million. The reservoir embankment, being about half a mile (800 m.) in length and 130 ft (40 m.) in height, was at the time of its construction the largest earth dam in Britain. Four shepherds' houses lie beneath the surface of the reservoir, which is surrounded by hills rising in the south-west to more than 2,000 ft (610 m.). Trout fishing from boats but not from the bank is allowed on the reservoir. Anglers must bring their own engines and have permits, which are obtainable from Kilbride Angling Club.

The Daer Water, which flows through the reservoir, rises on Queensberry Hill, the highest hill 2286 ft (697 m.) in the neighbourhood, now regarded as the source of the Clyde.

For several years local archaeologists have been working on a seventeenth century bastle house discovered near Glenochar Farm about three miles (5 km.) southwards along the A702 from Elvanfoot. The site, which is of particular interest because the layout of the 'fermtoun', i.e. the group of farm-steadings containing the bastle house, can be seen, can be reached by crossing a stile on the west side of the main road and walking along a footpath marked by white posts.

About 3 miles (5 km.) south-east of Elvanfoot the M74 and the railway reach Beattock Summit at altitudes of 1015 ft (310 m.) on the railway and 1029 ft (314 m.) on the road. To the east of the road and the railway there stood a Roman temporary camp at NS 994159. Conveniently close to the Roman road from Annandale to Clydesdale, the camp was almost exactly rectangular and measured 1443 ft (440 m.) by 951 ft (290 m.). Most of the northern half of the rampart and its south-eastern corner are still visible.

12

Leadhills and Wanlockhead

The village of Leadhills stands about 7 miles (11 km.) along the B797, which follows the course of the Glengonnar Water, south from Abington and about 5 miles (8 km.) along the B 7040, which follows the course of the Elvan Water, from Elvanfoot. Wanlockhead, which is in Dumfries and Galloway Region rather than in South Lanarkshire Region, is about 1½ miles (2½ km.) further along the B797 from Leadhills and, standing at a height of about 1400 ft (427 m.) above sea-level, is the highest village in Scotland, a distinction mistakenly awarded in some books to Tomintoul in Banffshire. The figure of 1531 ft (467 m.), which is sometimes given as the altitude of Wanlockhead, is the altitude reached by the B797 road a short distance north of the village. The villages owe their existence to the deposits of minerals, mainly lead, in the surrounding Lowther Hills. Of these, Lowther Hill 2379 ft (725 m.) and Green Lowther 2402 ft (732 m.) are conspicuous because of the radar station with its enormous white dome on the top of the former and the telephone and radio repeater station and television booster on the top of the latter. The two summits, which are about 1 mile (1.6 km.) apart, may be reached by a road open to walkers, but not to cars, that runs from a point at the north-east end of Wanlockhead right to the top of Lowther Hill and then on to Green Lowther. Extremely high winds are experienced on the tops with gusts of over 90 m. p. h. (145 k. p. h.) recorded in most months of the year, April, July and August being the exceptions. The view from the Lowthers is magnificent and includes the Solway Firth, the hills of the Lake District, Ailsa Craig, the Arran peaks, the Paps of Jura and the Grampians. Lowther Hill was at one time used as a place of burial of suicide victims who, because of their sin of having taken their own lives, could not be buried in the hallowed ground of a churchyard. Bodies were carted from near and far to be buried on the border of Lanarkshire and Dumfriesshire.

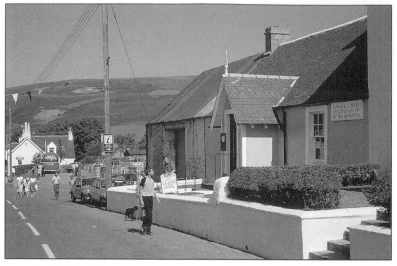

12.1. Leadhills village.

The Southern Upland Way from Portpatrick to Cockburnspath passes through Wanlockhead before heading south-east towards Beattock.

Lead in the form of galena (lead sulphide) has been mined at Crawford Muir, the ancient title of a tract of land that includes Abington, Crawford, Leadhills and Wanlockhead, for hundreds of years. As far back as 1239 a charter was granted to the monks of Newbattle Abbey to work a mine by the Shortcleugh Water, which flows a mile or two to the east of Leadhills. Then, in 1590, Thomas Foulis, an Edinburgh banker and goldsmith, obtained a royal charter to work mines at Leadhills. These were taken over in 1641 by Sir James Hope, a son-in-law of Foulis, and in 1649 his title to them was confirmed by an Act of Parliament. The mines then began to prosper and entrepreneurs became interested in them. Thus, in 1729 the north-eastern part of the mining grounds was leased to the Scots Mining Company, whose capital came from an association of London merchants, which ran the mines for the next 132 years. When, in 1735, the mines ceased to be profitable, the company appointed as manager James Stirling, a mathematician of repute whose name can be found in any size-able book on the history of mathematics. He was outstandingly successful in his business work and the innovations that he introduced at Leadhills have shown him to have been a social reformer of no mean accomplishment. Having found the miners in a poor state of health when he arrived – working conditions in the mines were terrible – he reduced the working shift from 12 to 6 hours. He also introduced the idea of group bargaining whereby a group of miners would undertake to do a certain amount of work for a fixed sum; they were therefore paid for what they did rather than for the time spent in doing it. By the terms of the lease given by the Earl of Hopetoun the company had the right to ground for houses and 'yards' for their men. Stirling interpreted the word 'yard' liberally and handed over to any miner who wanted it as much ground as he and his family could cultivate. Tenure was guaranteed, as also was the right of sale to any other employee of the company. The cottages and gardens dotted over the hillside in Leadhills are a present-day reminder of this aspect of Stirling's work. The miners made regular contributions to a health insurance and pension scheme.

In 1741 the Allan Ramsay Library, named after one of the two most distinguished natives of Leadhills, was set up by James Stirling and the miners themselves. It is often stated that the library was founded jointly by Ramsay and Stirling but it is doubtful if Ramsay, who left Leadhills in 1700 to live in Edinburgh, ever had much to do with it. The library is said to be the oldest in Scotland founded by public subscription, but this claim is disputed by some Orcadians, who maintain that Kirkwall Library was founded by James Baikie in 1683. Membership of the Allan Ramsay Library was not automatic, every person nominated being subjected to a secret ballot by the members who put either white or black balls into a box. There was an entrance fee of three shillings and a weekly subscription of fourpence. All books had to be returned at meetings held once a month and fines were imposed on borrowers who did not comply. During the nineteenth century the membership fluctuated between 60 and 100, and the stock of books increased from about 1000 to about 4000. In the early days the popular demand was for religious and historical works but in later years this was replaced by a demand for English literature and novels in particular. When Dorothy Wordsworth visited Leadhills in 1803, she was surprised to find that there was a library in the village and that it contained the works of Shakespeare. It is now a reference library combined with a museum rather than a lending library. An item of special interest in the museum is a bracelet made of gold from Leadhills, which was given in 1887 by James Hozier, later the second Lord Newlands (see Chapter 6), to his wife, who was Lady Mary Cecil, daughter of the third Marquis of Exeter. After becoming M.P. for South Lanark in 1886, Lord Newlands was anxious to give his wife something made of gold from his own constituency. Sometimes loaned for display in the museum is the Islay Goblet, made of silver and presented in recognition of the advice given to the miners on Islay by John Taylor, the leading man of his time in Leadhills. According to his tombstone in Leadhills grave-yard, he died in 1770 at the age of 137, but oral tradition puts his age at death as 133.

Stirling carried on as mine manager until his death at the age of 78 in 1770. During his term of office disputes were rare, rules and compulsory subscriptions were not found irksome, and the men were healthy, happy and contented. He greatly influenced David Dale, who started spinning in New Lanark in 1786. When Stirling went to Leadhills in 1735, he was given a salary of £210 per annum – a parish schoolmaster's salary at that time was about £11 per annum – and a house designed by William Adam (1689–1748) (father of the famous Robert (1728–1792), who had designed Hopetoun House in West Lothian) together with a well-stocked wine-cellar.

In 1751, during Stirling's time, the Scots Mining Company extended its field of operations and, continuing to prosper, did so again in 1805. However, things went wrong later and in 1830 the company was unable to pay a dividend. By this time, too, another company, the Leadhills Mining Company, had been formed and was operating in the south-eastern part of the mining grounds. A dispute arose over the right to draw water from the Shortcleugh Water and litigation that started in 1840 went on for 20 years with a devastating effect on the economy of the village. Eventually, in 1861, the Scots Mining Company gave up the lease of its mines, after which the Leadhills Mining Company reigned supreme and took over all the mines in the Leadhills area. The company prospered but eventually economic forces

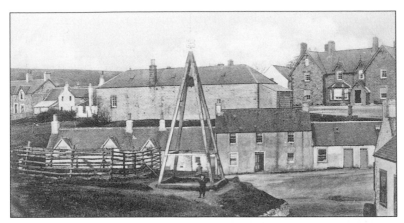

12.2. The Curfew Bell, Leadhills.

outwith its control led to the closure of the mines in 1928. The Curfew Bell, rung to mark the times of shift changes in the mines, still stands in the village and is now used for summoning hill-rescue parties and for ringing in the New Year. It dates from 1770.

The mining operations in Leadhills and Wanlockhead were completely separate, the former village being on the Hopetoun estate and the latter on the Buccleuch estate. Lead ore (galena) was certainly mined in the Wanlockhead district as early as the late seventeenth century, when lead was being increasingly used as a building material and in the making of glass and pottery. Various companies, such as the Quaker Lead Company, and private individuals carried on operations in the early eighteenth century before a company, founded in 1756 by Ronald Crawford, a Glasgow merchant, with his brother and a David Telfer, worked the mines until 1842. By this time the Marquis of Bute had become a major shareholder and the name of the company had been changed to the Wanlockhead Lead Mining Company. Unfortunately, the company got into difficulties after 1832, when a change of Government policy regarding foreign imports led to the price of lead falling by a factor of three. Within a few years about 200 miners with their families left Wanlockhead. However, in 1842, the Duke of Buccleuch took over the mines and with sound management ran them economically until the end of the century. When the Disruption took place in 1843, some of the miners displeased the Duke by seceding from the Church of Scotland and joining the newly formed Free Church; they were dismissed and emigrated to become coal miners in Pennsylvania. In 1906 the Wanlockhead Lead Mining Company took over again and carried out an extensive modernisation of the plant both above and below the ground. Lead and zinc were mined from a depth of about 500 ft (152 m.) below sea level. Unfortunately, because of the cost of pumping up water from such a depth and because of the economic conditions prevailing after World War I, the business was unable to remain competitive and the mines had to be closed down in the 1930s. In 1957 an attempt was made to revive the industry by reopening one of the mines. However, because of the falling price of lead, the mine functioned for only about two years. There is no doubt that large amounts of lead and zinc ores remain untapped in the hills, but whether or not they will ever be mined is an open question.

An indication of what conditions were like in a Wanlockhead lead mine in 1792 is given by Maria Riddell in a letter to her mother in which she describes the visit to a mine by a party including the poet Robert Burns. Maria Riddell with her husband and two relatives together with Burns made a journey to Edinburgh with the object of introducing Maria, who had written a book on the West Indies, to William Smellie, the publisher of the Edinburgh edition of Burns' poems. Maria insisted that they make a detour to Wanlockhead to see the lead mines there. They left Friar's Carse, the home of the Riddells near Dumfries, very early on a cold January morning, had breakfast at Sanquhar and then took a post-chaise to Wanlockhead. Maria wrote that 'the beauties of the majestic scenery, joined to the interesting remarks and fascinating conversation of our friend Burns, not only beguiled the tediousness of the road, but likewise made us forget its danger'. She described the mine as 'a dark and narrow cavern carved out of the solid rock'. Walking along the tunnel, each with a lighted taper, almost doubled up and often wading in muddy water, they were soaked by water dripping from the roof. Maria relates that 'after we had proceeded about a mile in the cavern, the damp and confined air affected our fellow-adventurer Burns so much, that we resolved to turn back after I had satisfied my curiosity by going down one of the shafts. This you will say was a crazy scheme – assailing the Gnomes in their subterranean abodes! Indeed there has never been before but one instance of a female hazarding herself thither'. Burns' views of the expedition do not seem to have been recorded.

Crawford Muir, which embraces Leadhills and Wanlockhead, has also been famous at different times for the gold deposited there. In 1502, during the reign of James IV, a substantial nugget weighing 2 lb 3 oz. (990 gm) was found at Crawford, and in 1511 James financed Sir James Pettigrew to prospect for gold in the area. James, it should be said, was very extravagant and maintained a brilliant court. However, just as his goldmines were becoming profitable, James was killed at Flodden in 1513. Thereafter, the mines were administered by regents – James V was only two years of age when his father died – who directed that the whole output of gold should be sent to the Scottish Mint in Edinburgh for the manufacture of coins. An Act of Parliament of 1524 forbade the export of gold from Scotland. Nevertheless, leases were granted in 1526 to Dutch and German prospectors who, by means of large bribes, were able to circumvent the Act and export great quantities of ore for refining abroad. Likewise, in 1535, miners from Lorraine were allowed to work the gold deposits. In 1542, the year in which he died, James V directed that regalia be made for himself and his queen, using only 'the King's own gold'. According to the Chamberlain Rolls, 3lb 10oz (1644 gm) of gold was used for the King's crown, 35 oz (992 gm) for the Queen's crown and 19.5 oz. (556 gm) for a belt for the Queen. Then, in 1567, licences to search for gold were granted to a syndicate led by Cornelius de Voss, a Dutch artist and lapidary and Nicholas Hilliard, a goldsmith in London, who was regarded as the 'principal drawer of small portraits, and embosser of our medals of gold'. A hundred workers, both men and women, recruited by the company to work for fourpence (4d.) per day, produced in 38 days about 8lb (3.63 kg.) of gold valued at £450; the profit was substantial. However, because of the bullion laws, which would not allow the gold to go to London, and the size of any bribe required for their circumvention, the syndicate gave up its licences.

The most famous of all those who searched for gold on

Crawford Muir was Mr. (later Sir) Bevis Bulmer, a mining engineer who obtained a grant to work the mines from 1578 until 1592. Recommended by Queen Elizabeth, he was allowed by James VI 'to adventure and search for gold and silver mines' in Leadhills. Initially his work was very successful, for within three years his workforce of 300, operating only in the summer months, had produced gold to the value of £100,000. Bulmer is said to have inscribed over the doorway of his house in Glengonnar, long since demolished,

> In Wanlock, Elvan and Glengonnar
> I won my riches and my honour.

Some of the nuggets dug out by Bulmer weighed up to 6 oz. (170 gm). Bulmer, descended from a famous Yorkshire family, later returned to England. He presented Queen Elizabeth with a gold porringer and in due course was knighted by James VI and I with whom he had had long discussions about mines and mining. Despite his successes, Bulmer died in poverty with debts amounting to £340. He squandered a lot himself; he gave generously in the hope of being praised and honoured, and he was plagued with hangers-on.

An eminent contemporary of Bulmer was George Bowes who was commissioned by Queen Elizabeth 'to dig and delve as he would'. At Wanlockhead he discovered 'a small vaine of gold, which had much small gold upon it' and, after working it for some time, he sealed up the shaft and got his men to swear that they would keep its location a secret and 'never disclose same unto the King of Scotland, nor his Counsell'. After successfully working another vein, he returned to England with gold worth £140, whereupon the Queen, encouraged by his success, commanded him to continue his work in the following summer. Unfortunately, on visiting a mine in Cumberland, he fell down a shaft and was killed. It is not surprising that during the reigns of James IV, James V and James VI the Leadhills and Wanlockhead district became known as 'God's treasure-house in Scotland'.

After this time the mining of gold on Crawford Muir became spasmodic and was replaced by the mining of lead. Searching for gold became a recreation and was, of course, used by the lead miners as a supplement to their wages. Gold could always be found if required for any special purpose. Thus, Charles I had his coronation medals made of gold from Crawford Muir, the bracelet for Lady Newlands referred to above was made of gold from Leadhills, as was the brooch presented to the present Queen when she opened the Daer reservoir in 1956. Also, in recent times local women have had wedding rings made from Wanlockhead gold. The last occasion, when a substantial nugget of gold was found was in 1940 when John Blackwood, a retired miner, found a lump of gold-bearing quartz weighing 500.2 gm in the shingle beside the Windgate Burn, which runs down from the Green Lowther. The lump, more than half of which is pure gold, was the largest nugget found in Scotland for more than 200 years. A final remark: gold can be found in veins but it can also be obtained from alluvial deposits in streams. Heavy rainfalls liberate gold from the ground and wash it into the streams where it is carried downstream until it is caught in a crevice or brought to rest behind a rock. This gold is recovered by the ancient method of panning. Goldpanning championships are held in the area each year.

For the benefit of readers interested in mineralogy there follows a list of the minerals found in the Leadhills/Wanlockhead area. Specimens of the minerals can be found on the old tips such as the one at the disused Glencrieff mine, which can be reached by going from Wanlockhead down the valley of the Wanlock Water for about half a mile and then taking a track that goes off to the left/west and crosses the stream. The principal minerals are galena or lead sulphide (PbS), which has a metallic grey colour with cubic cleavage, zinc blende or zinc sulphide (ZnS), which is brownish or black in colour, iron pyrites or iron sulphide (FeS_2) which occurs in the form of brass-yellow cubic crystals, and copper pyrites, a sulphide of both iron and copper ($CuFeS_2$), which has a deeper colour than iron pyrites and may or may not be crystalline. The commonly occurring minerals of no metallurgical value are quartz or silicon dioxide (SiO_2), calcite or calcium carbonate ($CaCO_3$) and dolomite, a calcium and magnesium carbonate ($CaMg(CO_3)_2$). Pure quartz is colourless or white and occurs in the form of hexagonal crystals. Calcite is colourless to white and, unlike quartz, can be scratched with a knife; it fizzes when a drop of acid falls on it. Dolomite can be distinguished from calcite by its yellowish-brown colour and its failure to fizz in acid.

For a long period of time much of the lead produced at Leadhills and Wanlockhead was conveyed to Leith by horse and cart, the journey taking two days with an overnight stop at Biggar. Coal for the smelters was carried on the return journey. However, the transport situation improved greatly in the middle of the nineteenth century when the Caledonian Railway Company constructed the line from Glasgow to Carlisle with a station at Elvanfoot, and the Glasgow and South-Western Railway Company constructed the one from Kilmarnock to Dumfries. The two villages now being little more than 7 miles (11 km.) from a railway either to the east or to the west, it was natural to consider laying a branch line from one or other of the main lines to serve them. The major difficulty was that the branch line would have to climb through something like 700 ft (213 m.) and yet comply with all the Board of Trade regulations concerning gradients and curvatures. However, after the passing of the Light Railways Act in 1896 with its less stringent conditions, it was possible to proceed. The construction of a railway from Elvanfoot station at an altitude of 813 ft (248 m.) above sea level to a station at Leadhills at an altitude of 1405 ft (428 m.) was embarked upon in November, 1899 and opened in October, 1901, the engineer being Charles Forman, who designed the West Highland Railway, and the contractor being Robert MacAlpine, who built that same railway. The line was extended to Wanlockhead a year later, having climbed to a height of 1498 ft (457 m.) before descending to the station at Wanlockhead at an altitude of 1413 ft (431 m.). A noteworthy feature of the line was a handsome viaduct with eight arches over the Risping Cleuch. Like the Glenfinnan viaduct on the Mallaig extension of the West Highland Railway, it was built of concrete, MacAlpine's predilection for this material having earned him the nickname 'Concrete Bob'. There being no intermediate station on the line between Elvanfoot and Leadhills, passengers could be picked up or set down anywhere on the line. Also, since the line passed through the unfenced land of four large sheep farms, cow-catchers had to be fixed to both the front and the rear of the locomotive. The time taken for the 7 miles 24 chains (11.68 km.) from Elvanfoot to Wanlockhead was 40 minutes. Apart from its use for freight traffic, the line provided a useful means of public transport to Glasgow or Edinburgh. Leaving Wanlockhead at 7.15, the train connected at Elvanfoot with the famous Tinto Express which for many years left Carlisle at 6.00, reached Carstairs, where passengers could change for Edinburgh, at 8.30 and arrived in Glasgow at 9.25. On the return journey the train left Glasgow at 16.45 and enabled passengers for Wanlockhead to arrive there at 18.55. The demise of the lead-mining industry led to the closure of the branch line, which was never profitable, in January 1939. The elegant viaduct was reluctantly demolished because of its unsafe condition in December 1991.

Since 1988 the Leadhills and Wanlockhead Railway Society, founded in 1983, has operated a 2 ft narrow-gauge tourist railway, built on part of the old standard gauge track between Leadhills and Wanlockhead. At present a train, hauled by a steam locomotive, runs between Leadhills and Glengonnar summit, where the line reaches an altitude of 1498 ft. It is hoped that before long the track will be extended to near where the road to Lowther Hill leaves the B 797.

The miners in Wanlockhead, being keen seekers after knowledge like those in Leadhills, set up a subscription library in 1756. The 5th Duke of Buccleuch gave them strong support by presenting a large number of books to the library. From 1783 miners from Leadhills could join if they wished. Borrowers were provided with a 'bag sufficient to keep out the rain, without which no book will be given'. As in the case of the Leadhills library a meeting was held once a month for the exchange of books. The stock of the library grew steadily and by the mid nineteenth century amounted to about 2000 volumes on subjects ranging from natural science to religion and English literature. The library closed in 1948 when the mobile library service began, but since 1974 both the books and the building have been under the care of the Wanlockhead Museum Trust which was founded in that year by a group of local residents and local authority representatives. After a major refurbishment the library was reopened as a museum in April 1996.

At this time the village schoolmaster (or dominie, in Scotland) was often a man of sound learning and well versed in the Classics,

12.3. Allan Ramsay, senior, drawn by his son Allan.

who could prepare able boys for direct entrance to the University. Thus, Dorothy Wordsworth recorded in her *Recollections of a tour made in Scotland* that, when she visited these parts with her brother William and the poet Coleridge in 1803, they met a group of barefoot boys in the Mennock Pass, who told them that they lived in Wanlockhead and went to the school there, where they read Virgil in Latin and Homer in Greek. Dorothy was also impressed with the good manners of the people. Relating how a group of men cleared a blocked road for the party, she recorded that 'they were decently dressed and their manners decent: there was no hooting or impudent laughter'.

Something must now be said about Allan Ramsay and William Symington, the two most distinguished natives of the Leadhills area.

Allan Ramsay (1686–1758), though born in Leadhills, the son of a manager of the lead mines, is associated mainly with Edinburgh, which was the centre of his commercial and intellectual life, and the Pentland Hills on the border between Midlothian and Peebleshire. He went to Edinburgh some time around 1700 to become an apprentice to a wigmaker and eventually established himself in business, becoming a burgess in 1710. He was very upset over the loss of the Scottish Parliament in 1707 and, regretting the decline of the capital city, was determined to add what lustre he could to it by making himself famous in the field of literature, which was his first love. The popularity of some poems that he wrote encouraged him to produce a volume of verse in 1721. Indeed, his success was so great that he abandoned wigmaking and became a full-time writer and (pioneer) bookseller. In 1724 he published a two-volume anthology of early Scottish poetry, such as that by Dunbar and Henryson, entitled *The Evergreen*, and in 1728 another collection of his own verse. He also edited a collection of Scottish songs and ballads, some old, some new, some adapted and some by himself, known as *The Teatable Miscellany*, which appeared in four volumes between the years 1724 and 1732. This collection sold extremely well and was reprinted 24 times within the next 80 years. Ramsay's best-known work, however, is *The Gentle Shepherd*, a pastoral comedy in five acts, which appeared in 1725 and was enlarged to become a ballad opera in 1728. The work, remarkable for its appreciation of rural scenery, customs and characters, became very popular and was performed all over the country by both amateurs and professionals. It has been performed at least once at the Edinburgh Festival. By his realism, wit, human sympathy and gift for lyric Ramsay foreshadowed Robert Burns. Having become both famous and wealthy, he moved to new premises near the Mercat Cross and St. Giles' in Edinburgh and in 1725 set up there the first circulating library in Scotland from which a book could be borrowed for twopence a night. By opening his library, Ramsay fell foul of the orthodox Calvinists, who accused him of corrupting the city. Thus, Robert Woodrow says in his *Analecta*: 'Profaneness is come to a great hight, all the villainous profane and obscene books and playes printed in London by Curle and others, are gote doune from London by Allan Ramsay, and lent out, for an easy price, to young boyes, servant weemen of the better sort, and gentlemen, and vice and obscenity dreadfully propagated'. Ramsay also annoyed the orthodox by his encouragement of theatrical performances, tickets for which were available in his shop. He himself opened a theatre in Carrubber's Close in Edinburgh, but the hostility of the Church, which made use of an Act of Parliament of 1737 prohibiting theatrical performances outside London unless the sovereign was present, led to its closure within six months. It was six years after Ramsay's death in 1758 before a license for a theatre was obtained in Edinburgh.

When he retired early from business in 1740, Ramsay built an octagonally shaped house on the north slope of Castle Hill, Edinburgh, which to his intense irritation was nicknamed 'the goosepie' because of its shape; in the 18th century pie dishes containing goose meat were octagonal in shape. This house formed the nucleus of the prestigious property now known collectively as Ramsay Garden. When the Jacobites occupied Edinburgh in 1745 they seized 'the goosepie' and used it as a site from which to fire on the sentries at the Castle. Ramsay at this time sought safety at Penicuik.

Ramsay died on 17th January 1758 and was buried in Greyfriars Churchyard in Edinburgh. A statue to his memory was erected in Princes Street, Edinburgh in 1865. An obelisk had previously been erected by his friend Sir John Clerk on his Penicuik estate. A well-known chalk drawing of Ramsay was made by his son Allan (1713–1784), who became a portrait painter of real distinction and was court painter to George III.

William Symington was born in Leadhills in 1763 but was brought up in Wanlockhead, where his brother George was a

12.4. The
Symington
Monument,
Leadhills.

mining engineer. He was the first person to use successfully a
steam engine to propel a boat, an achievement for which he has
not been given due recognition. As a young man he made a
model of a steam engine that could run on roads, and then in
1788 he was commissioned by Patrick Miller of the Dalswinton
estate near Dumfries to build a boat with paddles operated by
steam. Miller (1731–1815), a prominent businessman with diverse
interests and at one time Deputy-Governor of the Bank of Scotland, had carried out experiments on paddle boats and in 1787
had sailed a boat with manually operated paddles to Sweden. It
is interesting to note that the King of Sweden presented him
with a gold box containing a packet of turnip seeds which were

the progenitors of the swedes that became a popular agricultural product in the late eighteenth century. Symington, helped by James Taylor, son of John Taylor of Leadhills, referred to above for his longevity, designed a steam engine suitable for the boat, which made its maiden voyage on Dalswinton Loch on 14th October, 1788. The poet Robert Burns, living nearby at that time, is known to have been present on that day.

Symington's next endeavour was to design, at the request of Lord Dundas, Governor of the Forth and Clyde Canal Company, a steam engine for a tugboat to operate on the canal. Dundas felt strongly that there should be a more expeditious and more economical way of hauling boats along the canal than simply by horse-power. Symington's engine was sufficiently powerful to enable a boat, the *Charlotte Dundas*, to tow two barges weighing altogether 140 tons at 3 miles per hour against a strong breeze. Unfortunately, the owners of the canal asserted that the boat could generate waves strong enough to wash away the banks of the canal, and so they decided to prohibit any further experiment. The *Charlotte Dundas*, the first successful steamboat, was then laid up (in 1802) in a creek at Bainsford and allowed to fall to pieces. (The famous *Comet* of Henry Bell appeared on the Clyde in 1812.) Symington suffered another setback when an order from the Duke of Bridgewater for eight boats to operate on his mine-canals near Manchester was cancelled on the Duke's untimely death. Lord Dundas had indicated to the Duke how well pleased he had been with the performance of the *Charlotte Dundas*.

Symington, by now an embittered man, turned his attention to steam pumping engines, but here again he was frustrated by a patent of James Watt, which ensured that the Birmingham firm of Boulton & Watt had a monopoly of the building of steam engines. Symington died in 1831 and a granite obelisk to his memory stands beside Leadhills cemetery overlooking the house in which he is thought to have been born.

Nobody passing through Wanlockhead should fail to visit the Museum of Lead Mining, the creation of the Wanlockhead Museum Trust founded in 1974. The present Visitor Centre, opened in 1992 at a cost of £30,000 and financed by a variety of agencies and authorities, has been constructed with both traditional and modern materials to produce a building in keeping with the

12.5. The
Museum of
Lead Mining,
Wanlockhead.

character of the village. It contains, of course, display cabinets containing samples of the minerals found in the area, some of which are very fine specimens on loan from the Hunterian Museum in the University of Glasgow and elsewhere. Fibreglass castings have been made of the rock wall of a mine and there are life-size figures of the miners. Working models of the famous Wanlockhead beam engine and the pumping engine from the Glencrieff Mine are also on show. The Visitor Centre includes a shop selling souvenirs and a restaurant capable of serving 60 people at very solidly built tables and chairs specially made by the sculptor Neil Ferguson.

The Museum Trust has also restored the library already referred to and rebound the books where necessary. The church, abandoned as a place of worship in favour of Leadhills Church in 1986, the two congregations having united in 1952, is likewise in the care of the Trust. The church in Leadhills, now known as Lowther Parish Church, is linked to Glencaple Parish Church, referred to in Chapter 11. The building originally belonged to the Free Church.

One of the most important accomplishments of the Trust was the reopening of the entrance to the Lochnell Mine. Here, visiting parties are conducted along a horizontal distance of about 200 yards (183 m.) and, as the first 25 yards (23 m.) or so of the narrow passage are low in height, visitors have to crouch there and wear crash helmets. The passageway, which is also damp, is illuminated electrically, although in the early days of the mine only candles were available. Another noteworthy accomplishment of the Trust has been the restoration of Straitsteps cottages. Here visitors can see what a miner's home was like in 1740 and how much improved it was by 1890. The famous beam engine stands nearby. In 1993 the Museum was joint winner of the Gulbenkian Award for the most improved rural gallery in Britain.

It need hardly be said that, although the district around them has great scenic attraction, Leadhills and Wanlockhead, standing at such high altitudes, are very cold places in which to live, especially in winter. Retired people much prefer to live in places standing at about half their altitudes such as Biggar and its neighbouring villages.

13

Douglas

After crossing Hyndford Bridge and turning to the right/south, the A70 is met on the left/east at NS 909406 and at NS 902387 by side roads leading to Carmichael and at NS 895379 by a road on the right/west that leads to Sandilands, crosses the track of the railway line from Lanark to Muirkirk, closed in 1964, then crosses the Douglas Water and eventually reaches Kirkfieldbank. Further on at NS 885354, where there once stood Muirfoot toll-house, the A70 is met by the B7055 from Wiston. From the highest point on this moorland road at an altitude of 1125 ft (343 m.) a magnificent view of the hills to the south and east is obtained; when the heather is in bloom the scene is delightful. The side road going north from Muirfoot toll leads to Douglas Water, a village that grew up when the coalfields in the valley of the Douglas Water were opened up in the early years of the present century. Following the demise of the coal industry in the 1960s – only the pit bings remain – the miners' houses in the village were demolished, leaving the place more or less derelict. A short distance along the A70 from Muirfoot toll is the village of Rigside which, like Douglas Water, was originally a mining village.

About 10½ miles (17 km.) from Hyndford Bridge the A70 reaches Douglas, a small town with a population of 1615 at the 1991 census, situated in the lovely woodland valley of the Douglas Water, which rises on the slopes of Cairntable and flows for 19 miles before entering the Clyde about a mile (1.6 km.) upstream from Bonnington Falls. The Douglas family, with which the town is strongly associated, has played a very prominent part in Scottish history.

The family tree of the Douglases, who were probably of Norman or Flemish origin, may be regarded as starting with Sir William, le Hardi ('the Tough'), lord of Douglas, who died in 1298. One of his sons, 'the Good' Sir James, known to the English as 'the Black' Douglas, became, after helping Robert the Bruce to defeat John of Lorne in the Pass of Brander in 1308, one of Bruce's two principal lieutenants in the war with England.

It has recently come to light that the well-known story of Bruce and the spider as told by Sir Walter Scott in his *Tales of a Grandfather*, published in 1820, is a greatly distorted version of an incident involving 'the Good' Sir James, told in a history of the Douglases written by Hume of Godscroft about the beginning of the seventeenth century. The traditional story is that Bruce, while hiding in a cave in Rathlin Island, off the coast of Northern Ireland, was persuaded to persevere in his efforts to ensure the freedom of Scotland by watching a spider fail six times to climb a web and then succeed on the seventh attempt. The story told by Hume of Godscroft is as follows. Bruce, while sheltering somewhere in the Hebrides in 1307, sought the advice of his companions about his future plans. 'The Good' Sir James spoke out and said, 'I spied a spider clymbing by his web to the height of an trie and at 12 several times I perceived his web broke, and the spider fel to the ground. But the 13 tyme he attempted and clambe up the tree'. Sir James then implored Bruce to take his cue from the spider and to 'poush forward your Majestie's fortune once more'.

Another story handed down about Sir James tells of the episode known as 'The Douglas Larder'. On Palm Sunday, 1307 Sir James recaptured his castle, at that time occupied by a garrison of English troops, by first of all entering the church while the soldiers were at worship and either slaughtering them or taking them prisoner. The castle, being undefended, was then easily taken. After James and his men had eaten the dinner prepared for the English soldiers, James, realising that he could not retain the castle, killed the prisoners and piled up their bodies along with the garrison's provisions, such as food, wine and cattle, within the castle to which he then set fire. Because of Sir James' threat to avenge any future attempt to capture the castle, the fortress became known as Castle Dangerous. It provided the setting of Sir Walter Scott's novel of the same name.

Sir James Douglas was killed by the Moors in Spain in 1330 while on his way to the Holy Land with Bruce's heart. A heart was added thereafter to the Douglas coat of arms. The grant of lands to Sir James by Bruce in gratitude for his help initiated the rise of the Douglas family to a dynasty of great power. The earldom of Douglas was created in 1358. William, the first earl, married a sister of the Earl of Mar and, since the latter died without issue, his title passed to the Douglas family about 1374. The rise to power of the Douglases was facilitated by a number of marriages, some of them royal. James, the 2nd Earl, who married Isobel Stewart, daughter of Robert II, succeeded to the earldom in 1384 but was killed at Otterburn in 1388. The 3rd Earl, known as Archibald 'the Grim', was a son of 'the Good' Sir James, and was married to the widow of the Earl of Bothwell. After receiving a gift from the King (Robert II) of all the land between the Nith and the Cree in Galloway, he bought the remainder of Galloway and became lord of Douglas, Bothwell and Galloway. Deeply religious, his acts of generosity included the rebuilding of St Bride's Church in Douglas and the restoration of Sweetheart Abbey south of Dumfries. He died on Christmas Eve, 1400.

By this time the Douglas family possessed land stretching from Roxburghshire through the southern counties of Scotland to Ayrshire as well as land in Banffshire, Moray and Ross. Archibald, the 4th Earl, who married Margaret Stewart, daughter of Robert III, was Lieutenant-General of the French Army and Duke of Touraine when he was killed in battle in 1424 and buried in the cathedral at Tours.

When James II was crowned King at Holyrood on 25th March, 1437, he was only six years of age and the Regent appointed to act for him was Archibald, 5th Earl of Douglas, an extremely powerful nobleman and next in line to the throne. When Archibald suddenly died in June, 1439, William, the elder of his two sons and only about sixteen years of age, succeeded him as the 6th Earl, while Sir William Crichton, who had been Master of the Household to James I and was Keeper of Edinburgh Castle, succeeded as Regent after a power struggle with Sir Alexander Livingston, Keeper of Stirling Castle. Crichton, being afraid of the immense power of the Douglases and regarding the young earl as a potential source of trouble, invited him with his younger brother and his family counsellor, Sir Malcolm Fleming of Biggar and Cumbernauld, to dine with the young king in Edinburgh Castle on 25th November, 1440. Despite having being warned that there was possible danger in store, they all accepted the invitation. When the dinner was over, Crichton placed a black bull's head, a symbol auguring death, on the table and then, after a fabricated trial in which he accused the young earl of intended treason, beheaded him on the castle hill together with his brother and Fleming. William was succeeded by his great-uncle James as 7th Earl, whose excessive corpulence earned him the nickname of 'the Gross' and who died in 1443, being succeeded by his son William as 8th Earl. In 1449 James II at the age of nineteen took control of his kingdom and ruled until 1460. He tried hard to suppress the great power of the Douglases but all his attempts at reconciliation with the 8th Earl, who seemed to go out of his way to provoke him, failed. Accordingly, James invited the earl to Stirling Castle where, at dinner on 22nd February, 1452, the King himself stabbed him to death. Then, in 1455, he overthrew the 9th Earl, after which event the Douglas estates were forfeited to the Crown and Douglas Castle levelled to the ground.

After the fall of the Black Douglases, the Red Douglases replaced them as the chief menace to the Crown. The Red Douglases were descended from George Douglas (a Black Douglas), an illegitimate son of William, 1st Earl of Douglas, who married Mary, a daughter of Robert III, who was created Earl of Angus in 1397. They became powerful and important when, in 1455, George, 4th Earl of Angus, was granted the lands of Douglasdale. Archibald, the 5th Earl of Angus, is well known in historical story books because of the nickname 'Bell-the-Cat' that he acquired in the following way. A number of Scottish nobles including Archibald, from whom James III had alienated himself and who hated the King's favourites, hanged these courtiers over Lauder Bridge in July, 1482. When there was difficulty in deciding who was to initiate the proceedings, one of the nobles recalled the story of the mice, who wanted to hang a bell round the neck of the cat that was preying upon them but had difficulty in deciding which one should bell the cat. Archibald immediately volunteered to do the needful and so acquired his nickname 'Bell the Cat'. Gavin Douglas (c. 1475–1522), 3rd son of 'Bell the Cat', became Bishop of Dunkeld and is known to any serious student of Scottish literature as the translator of Virgil's Aeneid into Scots. The translation shows the Lowland vernacular at its best, rough

and guttural for rustic themes but resplendent for noble ones.
A further royal connection of the Douglases was made in 1514
when Archibald Douglas, 6th Earl of Angus, married Margaret
Tudor, the widow of James IV. Their daughter Margaret married
the 4th Earl of Lennox and was the mother of Lord Darnley,
who married Mary, Queen of Scots.

Substantial volumes could be written on the history of the
Douglases, but enough has been said here to indicate their prominent place in Scottish history. Lucy Elizabeth Montagu, who
married the 11th Earl of Home, succeeded to the estates in 1859
on the death of her mother Jane Margaret Douglas. Her great-
grandson, Lord Home of the Hirsel, Prime Minister (as Sir Alec
Douglas-Home) from 1963 until 1964, was the feudal baron of
Douglas until his death at the age of 92 on 9th October, 1995.
The first and last Duke of Douglas, who died without issue in
1761, commissioned Robert Adam, the famous architect, to design
a castle for him similar to but larger than Inveraray Castle, the
home of the Duke of Argyll, to replace a former castle that had
been built in 1457 and burnt down in 1758. Unfortunately, only
one wing had been built when the Duke died. Eventually, underground mining operations damaged the foundations of the castle
to such an extent that it had to be demolished in 1938. Some
Jacobite soldiers returning from Derby in December 1745 carried
from the old castle, in which they were quartered, the state sword
of 'the Good' Sir James. However, it was later recovered, though
not without difficulty, by the Duke of Douglas. Only a solitary
tower of the old castle escaped destruction by the fire and now
remains. It is often mistakenly referred to as Castle Dangerous.

St Bride's Parish Church, Douglas, founded in the 12th century
and rebuilt at the end of the 14th century, is of great historical
interest. The octagonal tower, which was built in 1618, contains
a clock believed to have been presented to the church in 1565 by
Mary, Queen of Scots. If this is correct, then it is the oldest
working clock in Scotland. It is at present in perfect condition,
new hands having been fitted in 1993. In keeping with the Douglas
motto *Never Behind*, it chimes three minutes before each hour.
The church was abandoned as a place of worship in 1782 and
stood exposed to the weather and to vandals until 1880, when
the 12th Earl of Home restored the chancel. 'The Good' Sir James

13.1. St Bride's Church, Douglas.

is buried in the chancel and a casket thought to contain his heart
can be seen under glass in the floor of the church. Sir Walter
Scott said of his tomb 'that the monument in its original state
must not have been inferior to the best of the same period in
Westminster Abbey'. Another casket contains the heart of Archibald ('Bell-the-Cat'), 5th Earl of Angus, who died in 1513 a few
months after the Battle of Flodden at which his two eldest sons
were killed. A beautiful effigy of Lady Lucy Elizabeth, Countess
of Home and the last of the Douglases, made of alabaster and
resting on a black marble base, lies in the centre of the chancel.
The church also possesses two very fine stained-glass windows
given by the Archbishop of Canterbury to the Earl of Home
when the restoration was made in 1880. Two old Cameronian
regimental flags hang in the church and there are memorial
tablets on the walls to the men of the Lanarkshire Yeomanry
who fell in the two World Wars.

When St Bride's Church was abandoned, it was not only
ruinous but, with only the chancel and part of the nave fit for
use, its accommodation was inadequate. The heritors, therefore,
at a meeting in 1779 were faced with two alternatives, either to
carry out an extensive restoration or to build a new church. After

consulting Archibald Douglas, the principal heritor, they adopted the latter alternative. Accordingly, the foundation stone of the present parish church was laid on 29th March, 1781 and the building opened for use on 3rd February, 1782. The cost of erection was £500. Some improvements were made to the building in 1824 and the interior was completely altered in 1869. In Douglas there were congregations of the United Presbyterian Church and the Free Church, dating from 1817 and 1845 respectively, which united in 1904 to form Douglas United Free Church, the building used being that of the former Free Church. When this Church joined the Church of Scotland at the 1929 Union, it took the name New St Bride's, while the Parish Church adopted the name Old St Bride's. When both churches became vacant in 1963, it was felt that one church was all that was needed and that the two congregations should unite. This was agreed to unanimously and, on the basis of an architect's report, it was decided that the building of Old St Bride's should be the one to be used. The united congregation was then renamed as St Bride's Parish Church, Douglas. The former New St Bride's building was demolished in 1969.

Not far from St Bride's and overlooking the Douglas Water there stands on a freestone base 12 ft high a very fine bronze statue, executed by Thomas Brock, of the Earl of Angus, the first colonel-in-chief of the Angus Regiment, raised on 14th May, 1689 and later known as the Cameronian Regiment. The statue, which was erected at the bicentenary of the raising of the regiment, shows an outstretched hand of the earl pointing to the field where the regiment was raised. It was the earl, aged only 19 at the time, and William Cleland, who had fought in the battle of Drumclog, who raised the regiment and named it after Richard Cameron, the Lion of the Covenant, who had been killed at Airds Moss near Muirkirk on 22nd July, 1680. A service is held annually on Cameronian Sunday,the Sunday nearest 14th May, with sentries posted as in Covenanting times, and a wreath is laid at the base of the statue. Traditionally the service was held in the open, but it is now held in the church. The regiment, each man of which carried a Bible in his kitbag, was disbanded on 14th May, 1968 at a dignified and moving ceremony held on a site near the old castle and now marked by a monument.

13.2. The Angus Monument.

Across the Main street from St Bride's Church stands the oldest
building in Douglas. Dating from 1621, it was originally the
Tolbooth, the upper storey being the courtroom of the local
barony court and the lower storey the prison. Douglas was erected
into a burgh of barony in 1458 by a charter still in existence but,
as the Red Douglases took over from the Black Douglases in
1455, it may well be that this charter simply confirmed an earlier
one. For a long time the old building was the Sun Inn. Its modern
restoration as a dwelling-house has preserved its architectural
characteristics. When a party of government troops was conve-
ying the head and hands of Richard Cameron, already referred
to, from Airds Moss to Edinburgh for display as a warning to
Covenanters, they spent a night in the Sun Inn and rested the
remains in the courtroom.

At the top of Bell's Wynd and opposite the main gate into the
old St Bride's Church is the Douglas Heritage Museum. Thought
to have been originally a dower house, the building was converted
into a school and schoolhouse by the Douglas family in 1706. It
then became a Poor-house in which vagrants were given accommodation for the night, their breakfast in the morning and a
penny to help them on their way. The building was next used

13.3. The Sun Inn, Douglas.

as a dwelling-house and then as a workshop until 1961, when it became St Sophia's Chapel, replacing the private Episcopal chapel for the castle which was demolished soon after the demolition of the castle. Finally, in August, 1993, the building became the Douglas Heritage Museum. Many of the features of the chapel still remain, for example the font and six stained-glass windows. The museum contains local memorabilia, many relating to the no longer existing mining industry in the Douglas area.

In a small public garden on Main Street in Douglas there is a memorial cairn to James Gavin, a tailor to trade and a persecuted Covenanter who, in 1684, having had his ears cut off with his own scissors, was banished to Barbados. The story is told that, fearing arrest, he hid in a cave somewhere to the west of Douglas but was arrested when his little dog, who was keeping him company, barked just as Claverhouse and some soldiers, coming over the moor from Sanquhar, were passing by. After the troubles were over, he returned to Douglas in 1688 and rebuilt his house, on the lintel above the door of which he carved his initials and the symbols of his trade. When the house was eventually demolished, the lintel was retained as part of the memorial erected to him behind the site of the house.

Another building in Douglas worth noting is the Lady Home Cottage Hospital, situated on the A70 as it enters Douglas and built in 1889. It is one of the many examples of the beneficence of the Home family to the people of the district.

In the nineteenth century the Parish of Douglas was largely an agricultural and, to a lesser extent, a weaving community. Thus, Weavers' Yards is a lane connecting houses, where the gardens of the Douglas weavers used to be. However, the discovery of large seams of coal about the end of the nineteenth century transformed the Douglas district into an important and prosperous mining area. Douglas West, about a mile (1.6 km.) west of Douglas, was built as a mining village early in the present century and a new road to it from Douglas was paid for by public subscription. Unfortunately, the coal industry gradually declined until in 1967 the last pit in the district was closed. There is, however, the possibility that opencast coalmining may be started up in the Glespin area. Douglas West, like Douglas Water, is now derelict. There are some modern industries in the Douglas area, which has been found to suffer very little from electrical interference and to be pollution-free. Douglas, too, is only 2 miles (3.2 km.) from the M74 motorway.

14

Lesmahagow

About 2½ miles (4 km.) from its junction with the A72 at NS 841443, a point between Kirkfieldbank and Hazelbank known locally as 'the Check', the B7086 reaches the village of Auchenheath. Auchenheath was one of the places where the famous Lesmahagow 'cannel' or 'licht' coal was mined as early as 1793, when the (first) Statistical Account of Scotland was published. Cannel coal was so-called because it released its gas so quickly when heated that a piece of it thrown on to a household fire would illuminate the room like a candle. The coal, obviously ideal for the production of gas, became famous all over the world. When street-lighting by gas was introduced in Glasgow in 1818, it was cannel coal which was used for the production of the gas. It is interesting to note that, when cannel coal was transported to Edinburgh along the 'Lang Whang' in the 1830s, the toll payable at the first tollbar in the County of Edinburgh was double that payable for ordinary coal. In due course, the demand for cannel coal died out, not because of any shortage but because technological advance had led to cheap extraction of gas from more ordinary coal. Auchenheath House at NS 806438, formerly known as Auchenheath Cottage, was in the mid-nineteenth century the home of James Ferguson of the mining company of that name. Ferguson was generous in his support of many good causes and for over a period of 40 years was held in the highest regard by his workmen and their families. He died in 1872. Auchenheath House is now a private residence, but the Auchenheath Christian Fellowship enjoys the privilege of holding its meetings in it.

After descending from Auchenheath and crossing the Nethan, the B7086 climbs up into the village (or small town) of Kirkmuirhill and on to underpass the M74. Kirkmuirhill came into existence in the days of the Glasgow to Carlisle stagecoach. Horses were changed there and stables, an inn and dwelling houses were built. The village grew up from these small beginnings, but it changed its character when coalmining began in the district. There are few engineering firms in Upper Clydesdale, but Atlas Hydraulics Loaders Ltd at Kirkmuirhill with about 100 employees produces lorry-mounted cranes and offshore equipment.

In 1868 a United Presbyterian church was opened in Kirkmuirhill. After becoming a United Free church in 1900, it became a Church of Scotland one in 1929. The congregation, which at present belongs to the evangelical wing of the Church, had in 1996 the highest general income per head in the Presbytery of Lanark. The figure of £188 was approached only by Abbeygreen Church, Lesmahagow with £183, the larger churches in the Presbytery having figures in the range £40 to £80.

North of Kirkmuirhill and merging into it to form a small town with a population of 3800 in 1991 is the village of Blackwood; the two components of the town still retain their individual names. Blackwood, which is shown on Blaeu's atlas, published in 1654, was a fruit-growing area which blossomed with the coming of the railway. The railway has long since gone, and the residents of Blackwood, who cannot find employment nearby, commute to work further afield.

About 1½ miles (2.5km.) in a southerly direction after it leaves Blackwood/Kirkmuirhill the B7078, which has passed through the town as Carlisle Road, reaches Lesmahagow. This village with a population of 3266 in 1991 stands at an altitude of around 620 ft (190 m.) on the river Nethan and at a short distance from the M74. The meaning of the name *Lesmahagow* is puzzling. Considering the name *Lesmahagu* in an important charter of 1144, some scholars take the *les* part as coming from the Latin word *ecclesia* (church) while others think that it is derived from the Cumbric word *lios* (enclosure or garden). (It should be remembered that Cumbric (early Welsh) was the language spoken in Strathclyde at this time and, indeed, until the reign of Alexander III (1249–1286), by which time it had been displaced by the early form of English spoken by the Angles in the south-east of Scotland.) Again, some scholars identify Mahagu with the saint with the name Sanctus Machutus in the early (Latin) charters while others regard Mahagu and Machutus as being independent names and argue that the name *Lesmahagow* comes from Lios Mo-Fhegu (my Fechin's enclosure). Machutus was a British saint to whom a church in the Deanery of Abergavenny in Monmouthshire, called Lann Mocha in Welsh, was dedicated. In Brittany the saint was known as St Malo or, in the common speech of the district, St Mahou. His day in the calendar is 15th November.

For the early history, mainly ecclesiastical, of Lesmahagow the primary source is the Liber de Calchou (Book of Kelso), written in difficult non-classical Latin and reprinted in two volumes by the Bannatyne Club in 1846. In 1113 the Earl of Tweeddale, later David I, established a monastery at Selkirk by bringing 13 monks over from the Abbey of Tiron in the diocese of Chartres in Northern France. Soon after his succession to the throne in 1124 and, acting on the advice of his teacher and mentor, John, Bishop of Glasgow, David in 1128 moved the monks to Kelso, near to his sheriff, his castle and the burgh of Roxburgh, and granted them a new charter. Selkirk was regarded as an unsuitable place for an abbey. Thus was founded the important (Tironensian) abbey of Kelso. The Tironensians were Benedictines who, although they regarded the Rule of the Order as basic, modified it to make life simpler and to put a new emphasis on craft work.

In 1144 David I, again on the advice of John, Bishop of Glasgow, 'for the soul's weal of himself, his ancestors and successors gave to the Abbey of Kelso and to the abbot and monks serving the Lord there, the church of Lesmahag and the whole land of Lesmahagu ..., in free and perpetual alms, to be held for prayers for the weal of souls; ... that the Abbot and monks of Kelso might ordain a prior and as many monks of their own order and dress as the place would honestly support and for the reception of poor travellers, also that it should be a place of refuge or sanctuary for those who in danger of life or limb should flee to the said cell or come within the four crosses standing around it; of reverence to God and St Machutus, the King granted his firm peace'. In those days every properly constituted church and its churchyard was by statute a place of sanctuary, but certain churches had a larger area of sanctuary attached to them, the limits being marked by crosses. Consequently, at the King's desire and with the approval of John, Bishop Glasgow, a prior and monks belonging to the Tironensian order were brought to Lesmahagow and a priory established there as a daughter-house of the Abbey of Kelso. It was never completely independent, the prior being always subservient to the Abbot of Kelso. In the opinion of J. B. Greenshields (an advocate by profession), the author of *Annals of the Parish of Lesmahagow* (1864), the extent of the sanctuary, in which persons other than murderers could take refuge, was more or less the modern parish. Crossford, otherwise Nethanfoot, may have been where one of the crosses stood.

In the thirteenth century various lands or churches were added to the Priory of Lesmahagow. Then, in 1321, at the request of Robert the Bruce, the Bishop of Glasgow and his Chapter conveyed to the Abbey of Kelso the church and teinds of Eglismalesock (or Eglismalescok) at Mauldslie in Carluke as a recompense for the sufferings of its monks, who were known for their hospitality during the Wars of Independence. Bruce, also, in 1316 granted to the monks of Lesmahagow ten merks sterling annually from the revenue of his mills at Mauldslie, to buy eight lights, of a pound of wax each, to burn at the tomb of St Machutus on Sundays and on festival days. If, as some believe, the saint was buried in France, the tomb must have been simply an altar.

In *c.* 1335, John of Eltham, Earl of Cornwall and brother of Edward III of England, set fire to the Priory of Lesmahagow when, after the death of Bruce in 1329, another attempt was made by the Balliols to regain the Scottish Crown. The monks at Lesmahagow had always been loyal to Bruce. After the burning of the Priory, the Lesmahagow Missal, which had been specially written for the Priory in 1240, was removed to England for safe keeping. It was indeed fortunate that this was done, for otherwise the missal would have been unlikely to have survived the Reformation in 1560. It is the second oldest surviving Scottish missal and is now kept in the National Library of Scotland in Edinburgh.

After the Reformation the nave of the Priory became the Parish Church. The building was either replaced or added to, for it is known that it had an aisle built in 1595 for the Weirs of Blackwood and one built in 1725 for the Weirs of Stonebyres. By the end of the eighteenth century the heritors decided that the church should be replaced and, as a result, the foundation stone of the present Old Parish Church was laid in 1803 (with full masonic honours, as seemed to have been customary at that time). The church,

14.1. Old Lesmahagow Church.

which cost £2,500 to build, seated 1600. It had two ministers, a second charge having been erected by Anne, Duchess of Hamilton, in 1644; it was 1648 before the first incumbent was appointed. The first and second charges were united in 1934. It was to the same Anne that Charles II granted a Charter in 1661, which was confirmed by Parliament in 1669, erecting Lesmahagow into a burgh of barony with the privileges of weekly markets and annual fairs. Excavations made in 1978–1979 on the south side of the church have revealed the foundations of the cloister and refectory of the Priory. In the graveyard to the north of the church several Covenanters are buried or commemorated.

In the Lesmahagow district there were many Covenanters whose resistance was so great that soldiers were quartered there to restrain them. Some of them took part in the battles at Rullion Green in 1666, at Drumclog on 1st June, 1679 and at Bothwell Bridge on 22nd June, 1679. One of those killed at Drumclog was Thomas Weir of Waterside. Fighting on horseback and his reins having broken, he was carried by his horse right into the midst of the enemy. He was buried in Lesmahagow Churchyard.

Robert Lockhart of Birkhill and his brother Walter of Kirkton, Carluke, fought at Drumclog. Robert died when his horse was shot from under him at Bothwell Bridge. After their defeat at this battle, some of the Covenanters suggested that as a devotional exercise they should sing a psalm. Walter Lockhart disagreed as the enemy were in close pursuit and quickly climbed a tree. The others were captured. However, worn out by fatigue and privations, Lockhart was found lying dead in a moss. He was buried secretly by night in Carluke Churchyard. Also, after the battle at Bothwell Bridge, George and Robert Weir were taken prisoner and after trial banished to Barbados. The vessel transporting them there was wrecked off the Orkneys with the loss of over two hundred passengers, including the Weirs.

During the 'Killing Times' of the 1680s many in Lesmahagow suffered badly. John Smith and John Wilson were shot in 1683 by Colonel Buchan and the laird of Lee. A little later John Brown was shot at Blackwood and buried after dark in the field where he fell.

Another martyr was David Steel, tenant of the farm of Nether Skellyhill at NS 789374, who, after fighting at Bothwell Bridge, attended open-air meetings instead of services held by the curate of Lesmahagow. He was so pursued by the troops that he was forced to live in a turf hut near the source of the Nethan four miles from his home. On 12th December, 1686, he was at home with his family when a party of troops led by a Lieutenant Chrichton suddenly arrived. Steel escaped by a window, and ran towards the Logan Water, after crossing which he made for the Nethan. Before reaching this river, he became exhausted and was overtaken by Chrichton, who called on him to surrender, promising him quarter and a fair trial in Edinburgh. On these conditions he surrendered and was taken back to Skellyhill, where Chrichton treacherously ordered his dragoons to open fire on him. They refused to do this, but the Highland infantry obeyed and opened fire. Steel was buried in Lesmahagow Churchyard. He was an ancestor of Sir David Steel, Presiding Officer of the Scottish Parliament. Thomas Steel, a brother of the farmer David and an elder in the Kirk, was fined £300 for adhering to Presbyterian principles.

Another Covenanter, Archibald Stewart of Underbank, is commemorated in Lesmahagow Churchyard by a large red granite stone. Stewart and a friend John Steel, both known Covenanters,

14.2. Lesmahagow churchyard.

were attacked near the top of Kirkfieldbank Brae while on their way to Lanark to ask one of the persecuted ministers, reputed to be hiding there, to come and baptise a recently born child of Steel's. (A variant version of this story is that they were trying to find a doctor.) John Steel, although left for dead from a blow administered by the miller of Mousemill, managed to escape and survived the 'Killing Times'. Stewart, however, was captured and hanged in Glasgow in 1684 at the age of about 19.

In Lesmahagow Churchyard there is also a monument to the Linning family, in particular to Thomas Linning, who was minister of Lesmahagow from sometime between 1688 and 1691 – the precise date is uncertain as Presbytery records do not seem to have been kept at the time of the Glorious Revolution – until his death in 1733. He was educated as a Cameronian and studied for some time in Holland. After returning home he, along with William Boyd and Alexander Shields, renewed the Covenants and dispensed the Sacrament to a vast concourse of people at Boreland Hill (NS 835404) in March, 1689. Thomas Linning's son Thomas, a divinity student, along with Richard Meikle and several other Lesmahagow men, apprehended Donald Macdonald of Kinlochmoidart, Secretary to the Young Pretender, at Broken

Cross Muir south-west of Lesmahagow while he was on his way to
England in 1745. Macdonald was taken to Edinburgh and imprisoned. Linning became minister of the first charge in
Lesmahagow in 1761. Tradition has it that in revenge some Highlanders on their way home from Derby burned down Meikle's
house.

A congregation of the Relief Church was founded in Lesmahagow and a church built on New Trows Road in 1837. Its first

14.3. A. D. Lindsay (Lord Lindsay of Birker).

minister, the Rev. Alexander Lindsay, who was ordained in 1838, had very distinguished offspring. His son, T. M. Lindsay (1841–1914), was appointed to the Chair of Church History in the Free Church College in Glasgow in 1872 and served as Principal of the (by now United Free Church) College from 1902 until his death. He was liberal in his views. His *A History of the Reformation* in 2 volumes (1906–1908) is a very substantial Scottish account of the Reformation with a particular interest in its social and domestic aspects. He also wrote important articles for the ninth edition of the *Encyclopaedia Britannica* (1875–1888) and chapters in the Cambridge Modern and Medieval Histories. A. D. Lindsay (1879–1952), son of T. M. Lindsay, was appointed Professor of Moral Philosophy in the University of Glasgow in 1922, became Master of Balliol College, Oxford, in 1924, was raised to the peerage as Lord Lindsay of Birker in 1945 and became the first Principal of the University College of North Staffordshire (later the University of Keele), when it was founded in 1949. He wrote many books, one of which was a widely used translation of the *Republic* of Plato. The most noteworthy minister of the Relief Church was the Rev. Robert Cordiner, who was elected in 1846, the year before the Relief Church joined with the United Secession Church to form the United Presbyterian Church. Mr Cordiner, who exercised a long and faithful ministry, was remembered and spoken highly of for many years after his death in 1897. When the United Presbyterian Church united with the Free Church to form the United Free Church in 1900, Lesmahagow United Presbyterian Church became known as the Cordiner United Free Church. A congregation of the Free Church which had been founded in the town in 1844 after the Disruption of 1843 became known as Abbeygreen United Free Church. Both churches became Church of Scotland congregations when the United Free Church united with the Church of Scotland in 1929; then in 1941 they united under the name of Abbeygreen Church of Scotland, the Cordiner building being closed as a place of worship.

A Secession (Old Light Burgher) congregation was founded in Lesmahagow in 1816, but most of its members joined the Free Church at the Disruption in 1843. The minority formed a congregation of the Reformed Presbyterian Church in 1844 and built a church in 1847. However, the congregation did not thrive and by 1868 was deeply in debt. it was then dissolved and the church and manse were handed over to the minister, the Rev. John MacMeeken, as payment for arrears of stipend. The church was bought by Mr Hope Vere of Blackwood, who presented it to the town. As the Jubilee Hall, it stands at the top of Jubilee Brae.

The Hope Vere family in Blackwood was for long prominent in the affairs of the Lesmahagow district. The earliest mention of a Weir in the area is found in the Liber de Calchou (Book of Kelso) and dated 1276. In 1572 James Weir of Blackwood, a follower of Mary, Queen of Scots, was accused of complicity in the murder of Damley, but no trial seems to have followed. In 1733 Catherine Weir, heiress of Blackwood, married the second son of the 2nd Earl of Hopetoun. Their son, William Hope, who inherited the estates of Blackwood and Craigiehall, adopted the name Vere. Colonel Hope Vere, who died in 1933, was the last of the Hope Veres in Blackwood. Blackwood House no longer exists. The Veres of Stonebyres and those of Blackwood had a common ancestor in Rotaldus Weir, whom the Abbot of Kelso appointed as baron bailie of Lesmahagow in 1398. In 1650 Sir William Weir of Stonebyres received a testimonial from the Presbytery of Lanark for 'his constancy and faithfulness in the Covenant during the time of unlawful engagement'. The family name was changed to Vere early in the eighteenth century.

One of the oldest buildings in Lesmahagow is the Craignethan Hotel, which stands on the north side of Church Square beside the Old Parish Church. Known at one time as the Commercial Hotel, it bears the inscription 16JH33.

South of the Old Parish Church and the Priory and on the left bank of the Nethan is situated the Public Park, known sometimes as the McKirdy Park, since it was gifted to the town in 1901 by Mr McKirdy of Birkwood. In the late 1880s the same benefactor offered £100 towards the cost of a new water supply for Abbeygreen provided that an ornamental fountain was erected at a suitable place in the village. It was indeed erected at the junction of New Trows Road with Abbeygreen but, with ever increasing traffic as the years went by and buses using the junction as a turning-point, it had to be demolished in the mid-1920s. The road junction is still known as 'The Fountain'. Birkwood House at NS 809392 was the home of the McKirdy family until

1920. Since 1923, when it was bought by Lanark County Council for £10,000, it has been used as a residence for the mentally handicapped. The estate of Birkwood belonged originally to the Weirs of Blackwood.

At the northern end of the main street, i.e. Abbeygreen followed by Nethan View, can be seen the site, renovated in 1987 by the Lesmahagow Civic Society, of the tollhouse and nearby the bridge across the Nethan built by Telford when he was constructing the Carlisle to Glasgow turnpike road in the 1830s.

At the southern end of Nethan View there begins Station Road, which led to the railway station of bygone days and which was originally part of the old turnpike road from the north. The station was closed in 1964 and the nearby viaduct demolished in 1983. The area is now covered by new houses and by an extension to Lesmahagow High School.

A visitor to the area around Lesmahagow, including Auchenheath, Blackwood and Coalburn, cannot but notice the proliferation of disused railway lines. These came and went with the rise and fall of the coal industry. In 1856 a branch line 18 miles in length and financed by a group of business men was opened from Motherwell to pass through Ferniegair, Larkhall, Auchenheath and Brocketsbrae and end at Bankend beyond Coalburn. Its purpose was to convey the 63 million tons of coal, estimated to lie in its neighbourhood, to a railhead whence it could be either distributed to feed the steelworks, factories and houses of central Lanarkshire or sent further afield. For the first 7 miles the line ran over continuous seams of coal up to 30ft thick. It then ran for 3 miles over the Auchenheath cannel coal already referred to and finally it entered the Douglas coalfield which at that time was unexploited. It is noteworthy that no consideration was given to passenger traffic at this time; this came 10 years later. As the demand for coal continued, many more railway lines were laid down until the development culminated with the opening in 1904–1905 of a number of lines in the Larkhall, Stonehouse and Lesmahagow districts. Until this time the village of Lesmahagow was served from Brocketsbrae but now, the difficulties of making cuttings, a tunnel and a viaduct having been overcome, it had a station of its own. After peaking during World War I, the coal industry went into a decline, which brought with it the decline of these railways. The original line from Ferniegair to Brocketsbrae was closed to passenger traffic in 1951 while the line from Hamilton to Larkhall, Stonehouse, Blackwood, Lesmahagow and Coalburn was closed to passengers in 1965. Auchlochan colliery at Coalburn was the last pit in the district to close. When the last train left it on 12th July, 1968, 112 years of railway transport came to an end. Although deep coal-mining has disappeared from Clydesdale, opencast mining started in the late 1980s at Dalquhandy, Coalburn. Covering an area of more than 64 acres (26 ha.), it is the largest concern of its kind in Europe and has a life expectancy of 20 years. The coal is transported by road to a rail link at Ravenstruther near Carstairs.

The Lesmahagow area is famous for its Silurian rocks and fossils. The oldest complete fish in the world came from the *Jamoytius Horizon*, a Site of Special Scientific Interest which lies along both banks of the Logan Water around NS 737346 and south-south-west of Logan House at NS 739353. Of three expo-sures on the north side of the river the central one is a 30 ft (9 m.) cliff face capped by thick greywackes.

John Wilson, whose poem *The Clyde* has been quoted from in Chapter 3, was born the son of a small farmer in Lesmahagow in 1720. Unfortunately, he had to leave school at the age of 13 because, after the death of his father, his mother was unable to pay the necessary fees. He had, however, advanced to such an extent that he was able to undertake some private teaching, which maintained him until he reached manhood. In 1746 he was appointed parochial schoolmaster of Lesmahagow and held this post until 1764 when he moved to Rutherglen, where he was employed privately by some gentlemen to teach Classics to their sons. In 1764 he published *The Clyde*. Then, in 1767, he was offered the mastership of the Grammar School of Greenock but on condition that he would abandon 'the profane and unprofit-able art of poem-making'; the puritanical Covenanting spirit evidently still survived. With a wife and family to maintain, he felt obliged to accept the offer. He burned the manuscripts of some unfinished poems, but a few fragments and an improved version of *The Clyde* were found among his papers after his death in 1789. The bailies in Greenock, who framed the conditions of his appointment, either ignored or were unaware of the ruling of the General Assembly of the Church of Scotland made in 1645 that 'for the remedy of the great decay of poesy, no schoolmaster be permitted to teach a grammar school in burghs or any considerable parish but such as, after examination, shall be found skilful in Latin, not only in prose but in verse'. The final version of *The Clyde* was published in 1803 by a John Leyden.

Another native of Lesmahagow worthy of note is Alexander Muir, son of John Muir, the dominie of Skellyhill School, who was born at Yonderton near the present Yonderton Farm at NS 790367 on 5th April, 1830. When Alexander was three years old the family emigrated to the town of York, which in 1834 reverted to its Indian name of Toronto, in Canada, where his father continued teaching. Alexander attended Queen's University in Kingston from where he graduated in 1851. In 1867 he composed both the words and the tune of *The Maple Leaf Forever*, a patriotic song frequently sung instead of an official national anthem until *Oh! Canada* was recognised as such. After his death in 1906 a memorial fund was set up, which led eventually to the creation of a Memorial Garden in the Alexander Muir Park in Toronto. In Newmarket, north of Toronto, there was at one time a school named the Alexander Muir Public School. The building has since been demolished and in its place stands the Alexander Muir Retirement Home. A plaque to Muir's memory can be seen on what remains of the walls of Skellyhill School.

Finally, yet another son of Lesmahagow of whom mention should be made is Sir Alexander K. Cairncross, one of the leading economists of his time and Chancellor of the University of Glasgow from 1972 until 1995. The important positions that he held and the advisory bodies on which he served are too numerous to list here; suffice it to say that he was at different times Director of Programmes at the Ministry of Aircraft Production (that was), Professor of Applied Economics in the University of Glasgow, Economic Adviser to H.M. Government and Master of St. Peter's College, Oxford, from which appointment he retired in 1978. He was the author of many books, a Fellow of the British Academy and was the holder of nine honorary doctorates. He died on 21 October 1998.

Further Reading

Andrew, K. M. & Thrippleton, A. A. *The Southern Uplands* (Scottish Mountaineering Club Guide, Edinburgh, 1972)

Beveridge, A. *Clydesdale* (Carluke, c. 1881)

Bonnar, J. *Biographical Sketch of George Meikle Kemp* (Edinburgh, 1892)

Burleigh, J. H. S. *A Church History of Scotland* (London, 1968)

Callender, R. M. *Gold in Britain* (Beaconsfield, 1990)

Cameron, C. W. *Scottish Witches* (Jarrold Colour Publications, no date)

Clelland, W. *Lesmahagow* (Greenock, 1990)

Cowan, I. B. *The Scottish Covenanters 1660–88* (London, 1976)

Davidson, H. *Lanark* (Privately printed, 1910)

Dickinson, W. C., revised by Duncan, A. A. M. *Scotland from the Earliest Times to 1603* (3rd edition, Oxford, 1977)

Donnachie, I. & Hewitt, G. *Historic New Lanark* (Edinburgh, 1993)

Fraser, A. *Mary, Queen of Scots* (London, 1st edition, 1969)

Glaister, J. *Life of William Smellie* (Glasgow, 1894)

Glen, D. *Splendid Lanarkshire* (Kirkcaldy, 1997)

Greenshields, J. B. *Annals of the Parish of Lesmahagow* (Edinburgh, 1864)

Hodgson, J. & Waters, J. *Kirkmuirhill. A church and its parish 1863–1993* (Kirkmuirhill, 1994)

Hunter, W. *Biggar and the House of Fleming* (Biggar, 1862)

Hutchison, J. D. & MacFeat, G. *Douglasdale. Its history and traditions* (Glasgow, 1940)

Ireland, A. *The Leadhills and Wanlockhead Light Railway* (Kelso, 1990)

Liddell, K. *Bygone Clyde Valley – The Orchard Country* (Ochiltree, no date)

Lockhart, S. Macdonald *Seven Centuries. The History of the Lockharts of Lee and Carnwath* (Privately printed, 1976)

McDiarmid, M. P. *Harry's Wallace* (2 volumes, Edinburgh, 1968)

Macivor, I. *Craignethan Castle* (HMSO, Edinburgh, 1978)

MacKay, J. *A Biography of Robert Burns* (Edinburgh, 1992)

McLaren, D. J. *David Dale of New Lanark* (Milngavie, 1990)

McLellan, R. *Linmill Stories* (Edinburgh, 1990)

Macleod, I. & Gilroy, M. *Discovering the River Clyde* (Edinburgh, 1996)

Methven, J. F. *An Appreciation of the Life and Work of George Meikle Kemp, Joiner and Architect* (Glasgow, 1988)

Miller, W. J. *The Clyde from its Source to the Sea* (London, 1888)

Osborne, B. D. *Braxfield, The Hanging Judge* (Glendaruel, 1997)

Paul, G. *Another Look at Carnwath* (Privately printed, 1989)

Porteous, J. M. *God's Treasure-house in Scotland* (Edinburgh, 1876)

Price, R. *Scotland's Golf Courses* (Aberdeen, 1989)

Rankin, D. R. *Notices Historical, Statistical & Biographical Relating to the Parish of Carluke from 1288 till 1874* (Privately printed, 1874)

Richens, R. (editor) *Your Loving Father, Gavin Scott. Letters from a Lanarkshire Farmer* 1911–1917 (5 booklets) (Privately published 1981 onwards)

Reid, T. *Crawfordjohn* (Edinburgh, 1928)

Robertson, A. D. *Lanark: The Burgh and its Councils 1469–1880* (Lanark, 1974)

Robertson, A. D. & Harvey, T. *Lanark Grammar School 1183–1983* (Strathclyde Regional Council, 1983)

Robertson, U. A. *Dining from Doocots* (*Scots Magazine*, November 1990, 151–157)

Stevenson, J. R. *Exploring Scotland's Heritage: The Clyde Estuary and Central Region* (H.M.S.O., Edinburgh, 1985)

Stott, L. *Waterfalls of Scotland* (Aberdeen, 1987)

Thomson, G. (editor) *The Third Statistical Account of Scotland. Vol. 8 Lanarkshire* (Glasgow, 1960); *Ancient Monuments of Clydesdale* (Clydesdale District Council, 1989); *Clydesdale Built: Buildings & Structures in Clydesdale District* (Clydesdale District Council, 1994); *Historic Buildings of Clydesdale* (Clydesdale District Council, 1987); *Lanarkshire: An Inventory of the Prehistoric and Roman Monuments* (The Royal Commission on the Ancient and Historical Monuments of Scotland, 1978)

Index